Law and Society
Recent Scholarship

Edited by Melvin I. Urofsky

A Series from LFB Scholarly

The Detention of Unlawful Enemy Combatants during the War on Terror

Colleen E. Hardy

LFB Scholarly Publishing LLC
El Paso 2009

Library of Congress Cataloging-in-Publication Data

Hardy, Colleen E., 1979-
The detention of unlawful enemy combatants during the war on terror / Colleen E. Hardy.
p. cm. -- (Law and society)
Includes bibliographical references and index.
ISBN 978-1-59332-325-7 (alk. paper)
1. Terrorism--United States--Prevention. 2. Detention of persons--United States. 3. National security--Law and legislation--United States. 4. War on Terrorism, 2001---Law and legislation--United States. 5. Civil rights--United States. 6. Combatants and noncombatants (International law) I. Title.
KF9430.H37 2008
345.73'02--dc22

2008047873

ISBN 978-1-59332-325-7

Printed on acid-free 250-year-life paper.

Manufactured in the United States of America.

TABLE OF CONTENTS

LIST OF TABLES

ACKNOWLEDGEMENTS

This book is dedicated to my loving family, my parents, Michael and Shanon Hardy, my sister Devon Hardy, my grandparents Ruth and Jim Donegan and in loving memory of Jean and Robert Hardy and Skylar Cloonan. I am extremely grateful for all your support and unwavering encouragement.

I would also like to thank Dr. Peter Leitner, Professor Ronald Rotunda, Professor Joseph Zengerle, and Dr. Kenneth Alibek. This book would not have been possible with their support and encouragement.

CHAPTER ONE

Introduction

> *On the morning of September the 11th, 2001, our nation awoke to a nightmare attack. Nineteen men, armed with box cutters, took control of airplanes and turned them into missiles. They used them to kill nearly 3,000 innocent people. We watched the Twin Towers collapse before our eyes -- and it became instantly clear that we'd entered a new world, and a dangerous new war.*
>
> President George W. Bush, September 06, 2006 [1]

The tragic events that occurred on the morning of September 11, 2001, ignited several changes in the United States. A key impact of the attacks was the psychological and emotional change on Americans' perceptions of security. One poll found that 70% of respondents had cried or experienced episodes of depression since the attacks. [2] Another poll surveyed a group of individuals to assess how people were personally affected by the attacks. Results from this poll found that 16% of the respondents were directly affected, 17% indirectly affected and a majority (67%) expressed that they were "touched as Americans."[3] Clearly, the country had experienced an emotional change; Americans realized that the United States is not immune from attacks from terrorists from other countries. A new enemy named al Qaeda[4] had a face; nineteen faces to be exact.

---

[1] President Bush. "President Discusses Creation of Military Commissions to Try Suspected Terrorists." The East Room, Washington, D.C. 06 Sept. 2006. 21 Oct. 2006 http://www.whitehouse.gov/news/releases/2006/09/20060906-3.html.

[2]Gallup_Poll,_http:/brain.gallup.com/search/results.aspx?SearchTypeAll=terrorist%20attacks&SearchConType=1&Place=H.

[3] Real Clear Politics, Poll Averages, NBC News/WSJ, http://online.wsj.com/public/resources/documents/poll-01-22-07.pdf.

[4] The Taliban is implied in the discussion as part of the opposition in the War on Terror because they created safe havens for al Qaeda members. Note: The author acknowledges that the organization al Qaeda has multiple spellings (due

Major changes were felt in other facets of life as well, new and increased security initiatives (i.e., at airports, ports, subway stations) designed to help deter future acts of terrorism in the US homeland, led to altered travel restrictions and concerns about border protection. Long lines at airports, inspection of bags on subways, and new screening devices at ports were just a few of the new measures initiated for protection of the United States citizens. Security measures were also heightened in homes, offices, and schools when in September and October 2001, a white substance was found in letters mailed to congressional members and members of the news media. This white substance, identified as Anthrax, was a new bioterror threat, causing Americans to be fearful when opening their personal mail. Direct or indirect changes impacted almost everyone.

The new security practices intended for the country's increased protection, awareness of bioterror threats, knowledge of a terrorist organization focused on harming Americans, and the devastating emotional effect of the terrorist attacks on September 11, 2001 on the American public, also resulted in new legislation.[5] According to one commentator, terrorism impacts the law in numerous ways. For example, the law prohibits terrorist acts (murder and kidnapping e.g.,), but more importantly the law "limits and regulates governmental responses to terrorism. The law for example, specifies requirements for fair trials, it constrains methods of investigation, and it may prohibit certain forms of military actions against suspected terrorists."[6] One purpose of the new laws was to help law enforcement officials apprehend and interrogate suspected terrorists. The existing national security laws on September 11, 2001 were deemed not robust or definitive enough to handle these threats and the new enemy, a non-nation state enemy motivated by a religious-based ideology. Therefore, new laws were enacted to prosecute those associated with and participating in terrorist activity. This legislation was adopted to assist

---

to English translation difficulties). The author has selected the spelling "al Qaeda" which will be used throughout the dissertation. However, if the author is citing a source, the spelling appearing in the quotation will be used.

[5] *See also* Gregory E. Maggs, *Terrorism and the Law*, (Thomson West 2005) "In addition, as the United States and other nations confront the threat of terrorism, new statues, cases, and policies seem to emerge almost daily."

[6] *Id.* at 3.

the nation with the War on Terror and the prevention of future acts of terrorism.

The War on Terror, like most wars in the United States' past, has provoked discussion on new legal and political questions which are being examined by all branches of the United States government: judicial, legislative and executive. Although the United States has fought unconventional foes before, such as the Barbary Pirates and Chinese "boxers" in the Boxer Rebellion, the new enemy the United States is facing is based on a non-nation state enemy embracing a religious-based ideology.

Historically, enemy combatants referred to members of the armed forces of the state with which another state is at war. However, this new non-nation state enemy, involved in bioterror and other attacks, was accused of not following historical doctrines or principles of war.[7] Thus new interpretations of laws and policies were enacted, attempting to address the unique situation. Additionally, new emergency legislation was created such as the USA PATRIOT Act,[8] passed by Congress, to expand investigatory and surveillance powers to the federal government.[9] It was hoped that these laws would be sufficient to protect American citizens and any future attacks on the United States, which was now a compelling possibility.

The Imperial Japanese Navy attacked Pearl Harbor on December 7, 1941.[10] This was the first major attack on American soil since the War of 1812. The sixty years after Pearl Harbor, the United States remained immune from wide-scale attacks on its soil. The United States immunity against foreign attacks ceased to exist on Tuesday, September 11, 2001 at 8:46 a.m. At that time, American Airlines Flight 11 crashed into the North Tower of the World Trade Center.

---

[7] John Yoo, *War by Other Means*, (2005).

[8] Uniting and Strengthening American by Providing Appropriate Tools Required to Intercept and Obscure Terrorism Act of 2001 [hereinafter USA PATRIOT Act], Pub. I. 107-56, 115 Stat. 272 (codified in sections of 8, 15, 18, 22, 31, 42, 49 & 50 U.S.C.)

[9] Rosa E. Brooks, *War Everywhere: Rights, National Security Law, and the Law of Armed Conflict in the Age of Terror,* 153 U. Pa. L. Rev. 677, 696 (2004).

[10] Pearl Harbor, wikipedia
available at: http://en.wikipedia.org/wiki/Attack_on_Pearl_Harbor

Americans were suddenly faced with the harsh reality that they were no longer untouchable.

Flight 11 and three other American commercial airplanes were hijacked by members of an Islamic terrorist organization known as al Qaeda.[11] The second plane, United Airlines Flight 175, crashed into the South Tower of the World Trade Center at 9:02 a.m. Another plane, American Airlines Flight 77, crashed into the Pentagon at 9:37 a.m. The final hijacked plane crashed in Shanksville, Pennsylvania at 10:03 a.m. Almost three thousand (2,973) people were killed as a result of these attacks, over 500 more people than lives lost due to the attacks on Pearl Harbor.[12] The hijackers meticulously planned every detail of their attack to kill as many Americans as possible.[13]

Al Qaeda members specifically chose cross-country flight destinations, to ensure optimum fuel capacity, resulting in larger explosions. Additionally, the attacks on September 11, 2001 were uniquely planned because the hijackers intentionally targeted innocent civilians rather than directing their attack against a military target. It was their intent to kill and injure as many innocent civilians as possible rather than striking a military target. Not only did the terrorists target innocent civilians, they targeted buildings with monumental emotional and economical significance to the United States.

The World Trade Center was built in 1966 by architect Minoru Yamasaki.[14] The magnificent buildings symbolized both the financial might and industrial strength of the United States' economy and the American way of life and freedoms. Yamasaki stated, "I feel this way about it. World trade means world peace…The World Trade Center is a living symbol of man's dedication to world peace…beyond the compelling need to make this a monument to world peace, the World

---

[11] Brooks, *supra* note 9, at 710. (The nineteen hijackers claimed nationality from several different countries including Saudi Arabia, United Arab Emirates, Lebanon and Egypt.)

[12] Spartacus Educational, Pearl Harbor, available at: http://www.spartacus.schoolnet.co.uk/2WWpearl.htm.

[13] Joseph Bialke, *al Qaeda and Taliban: Unlawful enemy Detainees, Unlawful Belligerents, in the International Law of Armed Conflict,* 55 A.P.F.L. Rev. 1 at 37 (2004).

[14] Great Building, The World Trade Center, Available at: http://www.greatbuildings.com/buildings/World_Trade_Center.html viewed 10/21/06.

Trade Center should, because of its importance, become a representation of man's belief in humanity, his need for individual dignity, his beliefs in the cooperation of men, and through cooperation, his ability to find greatness."[15]

The Pentagon also represents the United States and is more than a symbol of defense; it encompasses the core of United States defense: protection, security and resistance. It was built in 1941 and according to the Department of Defense; the Pentagon is one of the world's largest buildings and houses over 23,000 employees[16].

According to the 9/11 Commission Report, the fourth plane was heading towards the United State's Capitol.[17] The United States Capitol is the heart of the legislative capabilities and power of America. The United States Capitol was built in 1793, however the building has been expanded throughout the years. The United States Capitol houses members of Congress and priceless historical artifacts. All of these buildings encompass American's rights to freedom, which is at the root of the terrorists' disagreement with United States values and principles.

After the terrorists' attacks, US citizens responded not only with a monumental sense of loss but also with overwhelming pride and nationalism. Citizen's collective response was the determination to honor the victims and assure that their deaths were not in vain. US citizens also became aware of the threats that extremists posed. The government reacted with determination to protect its citizens from future attacks on American soil.

One of the first pieces of legislation enacted after the September 11 attacks was the Uniting and Strengthening America by Providing Appropriate Tools Required to Intercept and Obstruct Terrorism (USA PATRIOT) Act. [18] The USA PATRIOT Act enabled law enforcement and the intelligence community to aggressively, yet constitutionally, apprehend and interrogate individuals suspected of terrorist activity. It

---

[15] Great Building, The World Trade Center, available at: http://www.greatbuildings.com/buildings/World_Trade_Center.html viewed 10/21/06

[16] The Pentagon: Facts & Figures: Overview, available at: http://pentagon.afis.osd.mil/facts.cfm viewed on 10/21/06

[17] Final Report of the National Commission on Terrorist Attacks Upon the United States, Official Government Edition, available at http://www.9-11commission.gov/report/911Report.pdf.

[18] USA PATRIOT Act, *supra* note 8.

also emphasized the need for greater cooperation between different intelligence and law enforcement agencies. In addition, the USA PATRIOT Act clarified the legal parameters surrounding new technology that assisted law enforcement survey and apprehend possible suspects. Finally, the Act created harsher penalties for those committing terrorist acts.

Concerns have been raised about components of the USA PATRIOT Act and about other decisions occurring immediately after September 11, 2001. One concern is the detention of US citizens who may have been involved in terrorist activity. One such person is Jose Padilla, a US citizen, who was apprehended by federal agents on May 8, 2002 at Chicago O'Hare Airport. Padilla had just arrived from Pakistan and was detained after he stepped off the plane. Padilla was suspected of planning a terrorist attack in Chicago. Authorities believed he planned to detonate a dirty bomb in a high rise building. On June 9, 2002 President Bush declared Padilla an unlawful enemy combatant and ordered him to be detained in a military brig in South Carolina. The next day, Attorney General John Ashcroft stated, "We have captured a known terrorist who was exploring a plan to build and explode a radiological device or 'dirty bomb' in the United States."[19] Padilla was detained at a South Carolina military brig for almost three years. He was indicted in Miami, Florida in November, 2005. He was released in January, 2006 from the military brig and sent to Miami to stand trial. Padilla, and two co-defendants, were found guilty of terrorism conspiracy and providing material support to terrorists in August, 2007. Padilla was sentenced to 17 years in prison in January, 2008.[20]

Padilla's case sparked several legal debates. One important issue in Padilla's case focused on the President's authority to detain a United States citizen as an enemy combatant without charge. In addition, other questions raised from Padilla's case include 1) the definition of enemy combatant, 2) the right of an enemy combatant to meet with an attorney, and 3) an enemy combatant's right to view the government's evidence, both classified and unclassified used to designate them as an

---

[19] Seamas McGraw, Crime Library, *Jose Padilla*, available at: http://www.crimelibrary.com/terrorists_spies/terrorists/jose_padilla/2.html.

[20] Curt Anderson, *Former 'Dirty Bomb' Suspect Sentenced*, Foxnews, January 23, 2008, available at: http://www.foxnews.com

enemy combatant. Many of these issues have subsequently been addressed in the judicial system, including Supreme Court decisions.[21]

Jose Padilla is not the only US citizen to be designated and detained as an unlawful enemy combatant. Many al Qaeda and Taliban members have been captured in Iraq and Afghanistan, including those who claim United States citizenry. Some of the captured al Qaeda and Taliban members are detained in Department of Defense custody, while others are in Department of Justice custody and placed through the criminal justice system. Several hundred enemy aliens apprehended on the battlefields in Iraq and Afghanistan were sent to Guantanamo Bay, a military base in Cuba, or to prisons in Afghanistan and Iraq. Individuals sent to Guantanamo Bay were designated as unlawful enemy combatants and as such are not entitled to prisoner of war privileges.

In November, 2001, President George W. Bush authorized Guantanamo Bay detainees to be prosecuted through Military Commissions.[22] A previous mandate of the military commissions granted 'some' rights to the detainee, including the right to counsel and the right of the accused to be present during parts of the trial. However, it did not include the right to see all evidence brought against him. An appeal brought by Salim Ahmed Hamdan, a detainee at Guantanamo Bay, who was charged with several war crimes, focused on two questions: whether President Bush had the authority to convene military commissions and whether Guantanamo Bay detainees have the right to challenge their detention in US federal court. On June 2, 2006, the Supreme Court of the United States ruled that the President does not have the authority to convene military commissions unless Congress authorized it by statute.[23]

After the Supreme Court rejected the government's claim that the President had such authority, Congress passed the Military

---

[21] See *Hamdi v Rumsfeld*, 337 F. 3d 335, 341 N. 1 (4th Cir. 2003) vacated and remanded by 124 S. Ct. 2633 (2004): *Rumsfeld v Padilla*, 124 S. Ct. 2711 (2004).

[22] 66 Fed. Reg. 57, 833 (Nov. 16, 2001).

[23] *Hamdan v Rumsfeld*, 548 U.S. 557,126 S.Ct. 2749, 165 L. Ed. 2d 723 (2006).

Commission Act of 2006.[24] President Bush signed the Military Commission Act of 2006 into law on October 17, 2006.[25]

George Bernard Shaw once said, "We are made wise not by the recollection of our past, but by the responsibility for our future."[26] It is always critical to consider our history to understand present actions and beliefs. This book examines the historical aspects of enemy combatants and discusses how those lessons learned can successfully be applied to today's War on Terror and continued justice and protection for all American citizens. The focus of the analysis represents three major components of the United States' detainment of unlawful combatants.

The first focus centers on the legal aspects surrounding the classification of lawful and unlawful combatants. By analyzing judicial decisions, international treaties and relevant legislation, the author provides a thorough legal examination of the US' historical, current and future use of unlawful combatants. Secondly, this book includes a thorough investigation of policies relating to lawful and unlawful combatants. Anytime in history there is a controversial issue, many scholars, academics, and politicians advocate their opinion to the issue. The author discusses several political, legal and academic views concerning lawful and unlawful combatants. Finally, this book extensively discusses terrorism and military and legal responses to fighting terrorism.

These three aspects of understanding provide important knowledge to the continuing debate on the War on Terror legislation and policies. Current literature does not include a thorough examination of the historical practices of the United States during times of conflict with non-nation states. Although many US citizens believe this is the first time that the United States is facing a non-nation state enemy, this is not the case. The United States has a long history of encounters and conflicts with non-nation states. For example, in the early 1800s, Thomas Jefferson waged war against the Barbary Pirates. This book will expand the discussion on the United States' history regarding

---

[24] Military Commission Act of 2006, Pub. L. 109-366 [hereinafter MCA].

[25] The Whitehouse, President Bush Signs Military Commission Act of 2006, Oct._17,_2006,_available_at:
http://www.whitehouse.gov/news/releases/2006/10/20061017-1.html

[26] History Quotes, George Bernard Shaw, available at:
http://www.wisdomquotes.com/003165.html (Oct. 22, 2006).

unlawful combatants and an extensive discussion on the current, policies concerning the detention and prosecution of unlawful enemy combatants. The historical references provide a framework to the establishments of international treaties concerning the detention and treatment of enemy combatants in previous conflicts. Additionally, most literature on enemy combatants focuses exclusively on Guantanamo Bay detainees, while this book also encompasses US citizens detained as unlawful combatants. By examining both US citizens and non-United States citizens detained as unlawful combatants, it contributes to the general overall knowledge of the United States legal practices during times of conflict.

The War on Terror and subsequent actions, politically, legislatively, and militarily, has sparked passionate debate concerning the legal rights of unlawful enemy combatants. It is believed that this book can add information and knowledge to the discussion and assist in future legal cases.

CHAPTER TWO

Unlawful Enemy Combatants in US Conflicts

> "The requirement of distinction between combatants and civilians lies at the root of the laws of international armed conflict."[27]

The American Ex-Prisoners of Wars Organization is a national organization for American citizens who were captured by the enemy. Membership is comprised of former prisoners of war from any war, and former civilian internees (i.e., Japanese citizens interned during World War II) and their families. Each and every member is entitled to all privileges of membership.[28] According to the organization's webpage, after family members learned of the cruel treatment to their captured loved ones in Japanese prison camps in the Pacific during World War II, they launched a campaign directed at Congress to assist these prisoners of war. The organization's motto is "We exist to help those that cannot help themselves."[29]

Today, although the American Ex-Prisoners of War Organization is still active, domestic and international laws have also been created to prevent the repeat of such atrocities to prisoners of war. These doctrines range from United States domestic law, such as the USA PATRIOT Act, to the Geneva Conventions, all with detailed rights and responsibilities afforded to the aforementioned combatants. Despite these laws and their interpretations, much debate has arisen as to the specifics to which these rights should be accorded. This discussion is particularly relevant to the accused individuals involved in the present

---

[27] Yoram Dinstein, *The Conduct of Hostilities under the Law of International Armed Conflict*, 82 (2004).

[28] American Ex-Prisoners of War Organization, available at: http://www.axpow.org/.

[29] *Id.*

War on Terror; specifically those persons detained at Guantanamo Bay Naval Base and US citizens designated and detained as unlawful combatants.

Presently, individuals detained at the US Naval Base, Guantanamo Bay, Cuba, are designated and detained as unlawful enemy combatants.[30] These individuals have been declared as the "most dangerous" of captured combatants.[31] Unlawful combatants are not afforded certain protections under the Geneva Conventions, including rights and benefits associated with the status of prisoners of war. Several critics have emerged to question the designation from the US government of these individuals as unlawful enemy combatants, and policies associated with this designation. They argue that those held at the Guantanamo Naval Base should be either entitled to the protections under the Geneva Conventions, or should be placed through the criminal justice system.[32]

Before discussing the distinction between lawful and unlawful combatants, a framework must be established that examines the law of armed conflict traditionally referred to as *jus in bello* ("law in war" or rules about methods of war and protection of those not engaged in conflict) contrasted with *jus ad bellum* ("law to war" or rules about recourse to war or when it is proper to resort to armed conflict).[33] The

---

[30] See News Release, U.S. Department of Defense, DoD Announces Draft Detainee Review Policy (Mar. 3, 2004) ("The law of war permits the detention of enemy combatants for the duration of the conflict. It permits this detention 'without the use of a review process.'") Available at http://www.dod.gov/release/2004/nr20040303-0403.html.

[31] See Deputy Secretary of Defense Paul Wolfowitz, "Prepared Statement for the House & Senate Services Committee: Building a Military for the 21st Century (Oct. 3-4, 2001); available at: http://www.defenselink.mil/speeches/speech.aspx?SpeechID=446; See also Brief *Rumsfeld v. Hamdan*, available at: http://wwww.aclj.org/media/pdf/041208_Rumsfeld_v._Hamdan_Amicus_Brief.pdf

[32] See Amnesty International, *United States of America – Rubber stamping violations in the 'war on terror.' Congress fails human rights.* (29 September 2006) Also available at: http://web.amnesty.org/library/Index/ENGAMR511552006?open&of=ENG-2AM

[33] Nathaniel Berman, "*Privileging Conflict? Contemporary Conflict & the Legal Construction of War*," 43 Columbia J. of Transnational Law, 1 (2004) (rethinking the role of international law in relation to war). Emphasis added.

United Nations Charter is widely acknowledged as the regulating entity in regard to recourse to war or *jus ad bellum.*[34]

SECTION ONE: Is the United States involved in an international armed conflict?

An important question that has been argued since September 11, 2001 is whether the War on Terror is an accurate description of the current US conflict. Since its inception, the United States has been involved in six declared wars (Civil War, War of 1812, Mexican-American War, Spanish-American War, and World Wars I and II). Additionally, the United States has engaged in multiple military conflicts that[35] while not formally declared wars, were explicitly authorized by Congress,[36] (i.e., Barbary Pirates, Viet-Nam, and Gulf War).

The process for declaring war and the use of armed forces for the United States is precisely outlined in the US Constitution. The Constitution states, "Congress shall have the power to…declare war."[37] However, Congress has not officially declared war since World War II but has subsequently authorized the President to determine the appropriate actions for armed forces in armed conflicts or allocated funds for the war.[38] One example of this change in procedural authority is the Korean War. President Harry S. Truman did not apply for declaration of war or authorization from Congress but did request,

---

[34] Curtis A. Bradley & Jack L. Goldsmith, "*Congressional authorization and the war on terrorism*" 118.7 Harv. L. Rev. 2047-2133 (2005). (The designation of armed conflicts versus term "war" will be addressed later in this chapter.)

[35] Ellen C. Collier, "*Instances of Use of United States Forces Aborad*, 1798-1993." Washington, DC: Congressional Research Services Library of Congress, Oct. 7, 1993: http://www.history.navy.mil/wars/foabroad.htm. (there are over 234 instances in which the US used its armed forces abroad in conflicts, other than normal peacetime. The majority of the armed force actions were brief Marine or Navy actions prior to WWII to protect US citizens or promote US interests, or actions against pirates or bandits.)

[37] U.S. Cont. art. I § 8.

[38] Barry Goldwater, "*War Without Declaration: A Chronological List of 199 U.S. Military Hostilities Abroad Without a Declaration of War*, 1798-1972," *Congressional Record*, V. 119, July 20, 1973, pp. S14174-14183; Francis Wormuth & Edwin Firmage, "*To Chain the Dog of War – The War Power of Congress in History and Law*," University of Illinois Press (1989).

and receive, funding for the war from Congress.[39] Congress additionally renewed selective service laws to allow for the military draft. The President's request was approved in support of the United States assistance to the Republic of Korea (based on a UN Security Resolution[40]), which had been invaded by northern force. These previously accepted policies regarding Presidential Authority and the use of armed forces, and the designation of armed conflict, are being debated in US political and legal communities in regards to the current War on Terror.

The examination concerning the validity of using the term War on Terror is not only an important issue addressed in the United States but it is also being debated in international policy areas. This is a complex matter, because prior to September 11, 2001, it was perceived that a clear distinction existed between war and peace.[41] To solidify the characteristic differences between war and peace, the international community has resolved to create treaties and protocols to address international armed conflicts, and subsequently also noninternational conflicts.

One of the first treaties impacting the interests of the United States was the Treaty of Paris that was signed between the United States and Great Britain (Sept. 3, 1783) which granted American independence.[42] A second relevant international conference concerning international armed conflicts was The Conference of Paris (1856) that sought to create naval warfare rules and increase international cooperation. Similarly, the United States developed its own warfare rules and

---

[39] Bradley & Goldsmith, *supra* note 34, at 2130 (the authors note that there is still debate on whether Truman had authority to involve the United States in the Korean War).

[40] UN SC Res. 82, 83, S/1501,1511, (June 25, 1950) (Resolutions resolved that North Korea's invasion of the Republic of Korea constituted a breach of the peace and when hostilities did not cease, recommended that members of the United Nations furnish such assistance to the Republic of Korea as may be necessary to repel the armed attack and to restore international peace and security in the area.)

[41] Brooks, *supra* note 9, at 677 (noting that boundaries are no longer clear; previous conflicts different nation-states formally declared war on numerous other nation-states; hostilities were widespread and ongoing; and millions upon millions of regular, uniformed soldiers were directly involved in the fighting.)

[42] Great Britain also signed treaties with France and Spain and the Netherlands at this time.

regulations with a set of guidelines created in 1863 with the Lieber Code also known as General Order No. 100.[43] However, in 1864, perhaps the most influential and important principle for international relations and armed conflicts was constructed, the Geneva Convention for the Amelioration of the Condition of the Wounded in Armies in the Field (1st Geneva Convention.)[44] The primary purpose of this doctrine was to speak to the matter of the sick and wounded in armed conflicts.

Responding to further international armed conflicts, peace conferences were held at The Hague (First International Peace Conference, 1899; 1907) which led to various Hague Conventions[45] that addressed elements of laws and customs of war, such as characteristics of belligerents and the rights and privileges of prisoners of war. The Hague Conventions or Regulations were deemed necessary for as the founders determined "Seeing that, while seeking means to preserve peace and prevent armed conflicts between nations, it is likewise necessary to bear in mind the case where the appeal to arms has been brought about by events which their care was unable to avert."[46] It was hoped that through these regulations international crises might be averted. However, history attests to the fact that international disputes continued.

Recognizing the inevitability of armed conflicts among nation-states, the League of Nations was established in 1919, during World War I, under the Treaty of Versailles; the organization's mission was to

---

[43] General Order No. 100 of April 24, 1863. Available at: http://www.yale.edu/lawweb/avalohn/lieber.htm (included rules relating to the treatment of civilians.) (Dec. 26, 2006).

[44] Convention for the Amelioration of a Condition of the Wounded and Sick in Armed Forces in the Field, Geneva, 22 August 1864. Available at: http://www.spj.org/gc-history.asp (ten European states ratified the 1st Geneva Convention – the basis of International Humanitarian Law (IHL).

Av Hague Convention (No. IV), 18 October 1907, Respecting the Laws and Customs of War on Land, with Annex of Regulations, Annex art. 1, 36 Stat. 22777, T. S. No. 539 (Jan. 26, 1910) (hereinafter "Hague Conventions" or "Hague Regulations").

[45] Hague Convention (No. IV), 18 October 1907, Respecting the Laws and Customs of War on Land, with Annex of Regulations, Annex art. 1, 36 Stat. 22777, T. S. No. 539 (Jan. 26, 1910) (hereinafter "Hague Conventions" or "Hague Regulations"). Available at: http://www.spj.org/gc-history.asp (ten European states ratified the 1st Geneva Convention) .

[46] *Id.* See, http://net.lib.byu.edu/~rdh7/wwi/hague/hague5.html.

promote international cooperation and to achieve peace and security.[47] The League of Nations was a forerunner to the current international organization, The United Nations. The United Nations charter was established in 1945 with the aspiration to strengthen the prevention of waging aggressive war. Article 2 of the U. N. Charter declares that "All members shall settle their international disputes by peaceful means…and reframe in their international relations from the threat or use of force against the territorial integrity or political independence of any state."[48] The U. N. charter was signed by representatives of 50 countries on June 26, 1945 and was officially recognized on October 24, 1945. Throughout its history, the United Nations has continued to expand on codifying treaties and outlining rules of law, particularly with the passage of the four Geneva Conventions and three Additional Protocols to the Geneva Convention.

The intent of the evolution of national and international doctrines on armed conflicts is to differentiate between war and peace particulars (*jus ad bellum and jus in bello*). Nevertheless, boundaries between armed conflicts and its participants have clearly been blurred with recent skirmishes and wars. Because of the ambiguity of the classification, many critics and legal scholars have discussed whether or not the terrorist attacks on September 11, 2001 initiated an armed conflict or whether they were criminal acts. Some argue that the hijackers used the planes as missiles and thus initiated an international armed conflict. Others argue that the hijacker's use of the plane was not an act of war, but should be considered as criminal acts. They argue that if al Qaeda actually fired missiles into the World Trade Center buildings and the Pentagon, then an international armed conflict would be evident.

The question of whether the United States is involved in an armed conflict is a critical issue because of the importance of the answer. As Derek Jinks stated, "Indeed at stake is the proper distinction of transnational antiterrorism law and policy; and, more specifically,

---

[47] Philip J. Strollo, "*League of Nations Timeline: The World at War.*"(President Wilson proposed '14 Points' intended to serve as basis for world peace. Point 14"A general association of nations should be formed on the basis of covenants designed to create mutual guarantees of the political independence and territorial integrity of States, large and small equally." There were 43 original members of the League of Nations at its charter meeting, Jan. 10, 1920.)

[48] UN Charter, art. 2, paras. 3-4.

whether and to what extent the rule of law might guide the collective response to what Harold Koh has called 'the globalization of terror.'"[49]

If the United States is engaged in an international armed conflict, different sets of laws and policies would be utilized to fight al Qaeda and Taliban members. However, if the United States is not involved in an international armed conflict, then the United States must fight al Qaeda and Taliban members with the criminal justice system and the tools that encompass them. "In war, nations use special powers to prevent future attacks on their citizens and territory, not to punish past conduct. Law enforcement tries to solve crimes that have occurred in the past."[50] Those who believe we are not engaged in an armed conflict argue that we cannot detain unlawful combatants, but that those individuals must be placed through the criminal justice system.

The determination of the country's war time status also impacts how and if enemy combatants are detained and designated (lawful or unlawful combatants). If the United States was not involved in an armed conflict, all those captured in Iraq and Afghanistan would have to be brought to the United States and charged with crimes and placed through the criminal justice system. Additionally, as one commentary noted, combatant status, including prisoner of war status is only pertinent within the context of an international armed conflict, as opposed to an internal or non-international armed conflict.[51] Therefore, it has been argued, because Congress authorized the use of force, the laws of armed conflict apply and our armed forces may capture and detain both lawful and unlawful combatants.

---

[49] Derek Jinks, *September 11 and the Laws of War*, 28 Yale J. Int'l L. 1 at 2 (2003), quoting: Harold Hongju Koh, T*he Spirit of the Laws*, 43 Harv. Int'l L.J. 23, 26 (2002).

[50] Yoo, *supra* note 7, at 8.

[51] Terry Gill & Elies van Sliedregt, *Guantanamo Bay: A Reflection on the Legal Status and Rights of 'Unlawful Enemy Combatants,'* http://www.utrechlawreview.org/ Volume 1, Issue 1 (September 2005). *See also*: Nathan A. Canestaro, *"Small Wars" and the Law: Options for Prosecuting the Insurgents in Iraq*, 43 Colum. J. Transnat'l L. 73 (2004) at 100. "Typically, the distinction between lawful and unlawful combatants I only a factor in international conflict, as state parties seldom recognize the legitimacy of non-state adversaries in internal conflict, regarding them as criminals and treating them as such."

On September 18, 2001 Congress enacted Public Law 107-40, Authorization for Use of Military Force (AUMF);[52] the "central statutory related to the war on terrorism."[53] The AUMF authorized military force against individuals responsible for the terrorist's attacks against the United States.[54] The AUMF recognized that it was both necessary and appropriate for the United States to defend itself and protect citizens abroad and at home.[55] Furthermore, the AUMF empowered the President's authority not just to those involved with the 9/11 attacks, but also with those "nations, organizations, or persons he determines planned, authorized, committed, or aided the terrorist attacks that occurred on September 11, 2001, or harbored such organizations or persons, in order to prevent any future acts of international terrorism against the United States by such nations, organizations or persons."[56] Therefore, Congress authorized the President to use force, not only against those involved in the horrific 9/11 attacks, but also those involved in future terrorist attacks against the United States.[57]

International response to the attacks was also immediate. On September 12, 2001, the United Nations Security Council passed a resolution[58] that "recognized the inherent right of individual and collective self-defense" (a right that under the Charter is only applicable in response to an "armed attack.")[59] The United Nations

---

[52] Authorization for Use of Military Force, Pub. L. No. 107-40, 115 Stat. 224 (2001). Available at: http://www.access.gpo.gov/nara/publaw/107publ.html ([hereinafter AUMF]

[53] Bradley & Goldsmith, *supra* note 34, at 2047.

[54] AUMF, *supra* note 59 (constituted a *de jure* authorization of war and ratified the President's actions.) For a comprehensive explanation and understanding of the AUMF and powers of Congress, see Bradley & Goldsmith, *supra* note 34.

[55] *Id.*

[56] *Id.* Sec. 2(a).

[57]See *Mitchell v. Laird*, 488 F.2d 611, 615 (D.C. Cir. 1973) (holding how Congress gives its consent to engage in war to be a "discretionary matter for Congress to decide in which from…it will give it consult.) See also Authorization for Use of Military Force Against Iraq Resolution of 2002, Pub. L. No. 107-243, 116 Stat. 1498 (2002).

[58] S.C. Res. 1368, U.N. SCOR, 56th Sess., 4370th mtg., U.N. Doc. S/Res/4370 (2001).

[59] Berman, *supra* note 33, at 32. *See also*, Dinstein, *supra* note 27, at 183 ("…Article 51 permits self-defense solely when an 'armed attack' occurs'…").

Security Council also adopted Resolution 1373 on September 28, 2001.[60] "It not only condemned terrorism as a threat to international peace and security, but implicitly recognized that al Qaeda's use of commercial aircraft as weapons constituted an 'armed attack' within the meaning of Article 51 of the UN Charter."[61] Equally emphatic of supporting the United States, the North Atlantic Treaty (NATO) alliance enlisted Article 5 which states, "that an armed attack on one or more of (The Allies) in European N. America shall be considered an attack against them all."[62] Additionally, Article IV of the ANZUZ Pact (between the United States and Australia) was invoked. Article IV declares "Each party recognizes that an armed attack on any to the Parties would be danger to its own peace and safety and declares that it would act to meet the common danger."[63] These international declarations were aligned closely with US proclamations.

On November 13, 2001, President Bush issued an executive order on the "Detention, Treatment, and Trial of Certain Non-Citizens in the War Against Terrorism."[64] This executive order stated, "International terrorists, including members of al Qaida, have carried out attacks on United States diplomatic and military personnel and facilities abroad and on citizens and property within the United States on a scale that has created a state of armed conflict that requires the use of the United

---

[60] Fred L. Borch & Paul S. Wilson, Preface from International Law Studies, Vol. 79 at 1 2003. Article 51: Nothing in the present Charter shall impair the inherent right of individual or collective self-defense if an armed attack occurs against a Member of the United Nations, until the Security Council has taken measures necessary to maintain international peace and security. Measures taken by Members in the exercise of this right of self-defense shall be immediately reported to the Security Council and shall not in any way affect the authority and responsibility of the Security Council under the present Charter to take at any time such action as it deems necessary in order to maintain or restore international peace and security.

[61] *Id. See also* Yoram Dinstein, *War Aggression and Self-Defence*, 183 (2005) ("...Article 51 permits self-defense solely when an 'armed attack' occurs'...").

[62] North Atlantic Treaty, Apr 4, 1947, art 5, 63 Stat. 241, 34 U.N.T.S.243.

[63] Security Treaty Between Australia, New Zealand, and United States of America, Sept. 1, 1951, 131, U.N.T.S., 83, 86.

[64] 66 Fed. Reg. 57,833 (Nov. 16, 2001), available at http://www.whitehouse.gov/news/releases/2001/11/20011113-27.html (hereinafter Bush Order).

States Armed Forces."[65] "The ability of the United States to protect the United States and its citizens, and to help its allies and other cooperating nations protect their nations and their citizens, from such further terrorist attacks depends in significant part upon using the United States Armed Forces to identify terrorists and those who support them, to disrupt their activities, and to eliminate their ability to conduct or support such attacks."[66] "As part of the administration's overall response to the crisis, it authorizes the trial of non-citizens 'for violations of the laws of war and other applicable laws by military tribunals.'"[67] Concerns were raised in the academic literature concerning the possible unlimited Executive Powers pertaining to the war against terrorists. Numerous captured individuals filed petitions in US federal district court challenging their detention and the appropriateness of US decisions concerning the War on Terror. A few of these cases proceeded to the United States Supreme Court.

A brief account of the United States Supreme Court's ruling in two vital cases reveals that the Supreme Court affirmed the President's policy response to the September 11 attacks. In *Hamdi v. Rumsfeld*, the Court examined whether the President had the authority to designate an American citizen as an unlawful combatant.[68] Justice Sandra Day O'Connor wrote in the *Hamdi* decision:

> "There can be no doubt that individuals who fought against the United States in Afghanistan as part of the Taliban, an organization known to have supported the al Qaeda terrorist network responsible for [the September 11] attacks, are individuals Congress sought to target in passing the [Authorization for Use of Military Force]. We conclude that detention of individuals falling into that limited category we are considering, for the duration of the particular conflict in

---

[65] *Id.* Section 1(a) The Bush Order provides in part, that individuals subject to the order include: (1) current or past members of al Qaeda; (2) individuals who "engaged in, aided or abetted, or conspired to commit, acts of international terrorism, or acts in preparation therefore" that adversely affected wide United States interests; and (3) individuals who "knowingly harbored one or more individuals."

[66] *Id.* Section 1(d).

[67] Jinks, *supra* note 49, at 3, as cited in: H. Lauterpacht, *The Problem of the Revision of the Law of War*, 29 Brit. Y.B. Int'l L. 360, 262 (1952).

[68] *Hamdi v. Rumsfeld*, 542 U.S. 507 (2004).

> which they were captured, is so fundamental and accepted an incident to war as to be an exercise of the 'necessary and appropriate force' Congress has authorized the President to use.'"[69]

The Court also addressed the legality of the war in *Hamdan v. Rumsfeld* and declared that the United States was engaged in a legally recognizable armed conflict to which the laws of war apply.[70] One scholar noted that after an examination of Supreme Court decisions concerning the War on Terror "analysis shows that none of the courts under consideration squarely rejected the government's claim that the conflict with Al-Qaeda can be viewed as a war to which at least some aspects of the international and domestic laws of war should attach."[71] A culmination of these edicts sparked intense debate as to the decision to declare the War on Terror as an international armed conflict. The Bush Administration has defenders who agree with their designation and conversely, critics who disagree with the Administration's response. Before a thorough examination of the validity of these arguments, it is important to define what constitutes an international armed conflict or universally agreed principles of armed conflicts.

Agreeing on the elements can be a difficult process, in as much as some in the discourse consider the word "war" to be obsolete and believe the term "armed conflict" to be more accurate.[72] Nonetheless, abiding by rules of *war or armed conflicts*[73] has been an expectation of soldiers throughout the modern history of warfare. What, then, are these principles of combat and how can they be applied to the current War on Terror?

As proposed by Canestaro, "international armed conflicts or the laws of war are based on two foundations: customary international law

---

[69] *Id.*

[70] *Hamdan v Rumsfeld*, 548 U.S. 557,126 S.Ct. 2749, 165 L. Ed. 2d 723 (2006). See David Rivkin & Lee Casey, Jr., "*The Gitmo Decision*," July 11, 2006, The Washington Times Op-ed.

[71] Berman, *supra* note 33, at 70.

[72] Berman, *supra* note 33, at 16; *see also* Bradley & Goldsmith, *supra* note 34, at 2054; Dinstein, *supra* note 27, at xii ("There is a tendency today to avoid the use of the term 'war', regarding it as arcane and largely superseded by the phrase 'international armed conflict.'")

[73] *Emphasis added.*

and treaty law."[74] Customary law develops from consistent state practice and "on *opinio juris* (the state's belief that it is acting under a legal obligation)."[75] Treaty law, on the other hand, develops from a series of internationally accepted conventions and agreements. Furthermore, the content of the law can be separated into two segments. The first segment regulates the "means and methods" of warfare by prohibiting certain actions or wartime strategies. The second segment consists of humanitarian portions of the law. The humanitarian laws create minimum standards of humane treatment for non-combatants, including prisoners of war and the sick and wounded. "Although both affect wartime conduct in different ways, together they serve to limit unnecessary suffering during wartime."[76]

It is significant to note that the drafters of the international treaties, did not concede that non-state actors could be significant resistance groups and consequentially conflicts between an occupying power and non-state groups historically have not been questions of international law. As a consequence, prior to 1949, the laws of war were framed on the assumption that in order for an armed conflict to amount to a war, it must be conducted between states and such internal conflicts, such as civil wars, were only matters for domestic law enforcement.[77] Non-state actors were rarely recognized as belligerents and therefore not accorded the privileges and rights of international law. International law usually applied when the conflict entailed characteristics of an inter-state war.[78] As internal conflicts developed with significant capabilities of non-state groups, debates grew whether internal conflicts should be regulated by the laws of war.

The attempt for international humanitarian law to regulate internal conflicts with a state and non-state actor has been more successful. "The principle embodiment of the humanitarian law regulating internal conflict is Common Article 3 to the four Geneva Conventions of

---

74 Nathan A. Canestaro, *Small Wars and the Law: Options for Prosecuting the Insurgents in Iraq,* 43 Colum. J. Transnat'l L. 73, 87-88 (2004).
75 *Id.*
76 *Id.* at 88.
77 Mark A. Drumbl, *Victimhood in Our Neighborhood: Terrorist Crime, Taliban Guilt, and the Asymmetries of the International Legal Order*, 81 N.C.L. REV. 1 at 30 (2002).
78 *Id.* as cited in: Lindsay Moir, *The law of Internal Conflict,* 5 (Cambridge Studies in International and Comparative Law 2002).

1949."[79] Common Article 3 is only applicable in the case of "armed conflict not of an international character" occurring within the territory of a party to the treaty.[80] Furthermore, Common Article 3 requires basic humanitarian standards to all parties involved, regardless of the level or intensity of the conflict.[81] The language in subsection 2 states, "the application of the preceding provisions shall not affect the legal status of the Parties to the conflict."[82] One commentator stated, "Although the treaty applies to all parties to the conflict—regardless of whether they are a state actor or a non-state insurgent group—its application to a non-state belligerent does not imply recognition or legitimacy."[83]

The language in Common Article 3 produced uncertainties in its application: the Convention does not specify what constitutes an "armed conflict not of international character." "Even in the context of international warfare there is no accepted definition of 'armed conflict' but when used in reference to internal violence, the term could arguably include any type of organized violence, including protests, riots or other forms of armed civil unrest."[84] In July, 2006 the United States Supreme Court[85] held that the current conflict with al Qaeda was governed by Common Article 3, prior to that it had not been applied before and consequentially, it was viewed as an unsuccessful attempt to regulate internal conflict. Accordingly, some international bodies have attempted to eliminate the distinction between international and non-international armed conflicts so that the laws of war will apply to internal violence.[86]

The most recent examples to employ treaty laws to conflicts between state and non-state actors are the 1977 Protocols Additional to

---

[79] Jinks, *supra* note 49, at 11-12.

[80] Geneva Convention (I) for the Amelioration of the Condition of the Wounded and Sick in Armed Forces in the Field, August 12, 1949, 6 U.S.T. 3115, T.I.A.S. 3362, 75 U.N.T.S. art.3 (1) (hereinafter GWS).

[81] *Id.* Citing Major Alex G. Peterson, *Order out of Chaos: Domestic Enforcement of the Law of Internal Armed Conflict*, 171 MIL. L. REV. 1 at 18 (2002). Jinks *supra* note 49, at 48; Moir *supra* note 78, at 31.

[82] *Id* citing Geneva Convention I (GWS), *supra* note 80, art. 3(1).

[83] Canestaro *supra* note 74, at 94.

[84] *Id.*

[85] *Hamdan v. Rumsfeld,* 548 U.S.557,126 S.Ct. 2749, 165 L. Ed. 2d 723 (2006).

[86] Canestaro, *supra* note 74, at 97.

the Geneva Convention (Protocols I and II).[87] The United States did not ratify these treaties because US officials asserted the Protocols were too lenient with regards to non-state belligerents and the use of guerrilla warfare.[88] Therefore, it follows then that if a state has not ratified a treaty which applies international law to internal conflicts, such conflicts with non-state belligerents are regulated by domestic law.[89] Thus, "the need to categorize [violence] as either armed attacks or criminal attacks is an awkward—albeit for the moment seemingly inevitable—exercise."[90]

Although the universal agreement on the definition of an armed conflict remains tenuous, the significance of the agreement on interpretation of the actions is relevant to status of prisoners of war. Therefore, several scholars proposed characteristics that encompass an international armed conflict. One such commentator stated international armed conflict "... occurs when the armed forces of one party are engaged in hostilities of a reasonably sustained nature against another party, or in cases of total or partial occupation of the territory of another party."[91] Continuing the clarification, the author noted that international law of armed conflict applies "when the armed forces of a State are engaged in reasonably protracted hostilities with a foreign adversary or are in occupation of (a portion of) another State's territory."[92]

---

[87]Protocol Additional to the Geneva Convention of 12 August 1949, and Relating to the Protections of Victims of International Armed Conflict (Protocol I), opened for signature Dec. 12, 1977 U.N. Doc. A/32/144, Annex I, II (1977), reprinted in 16 I.L.M. 1391 (1977) [hereinafter Protocol I].

[88] Int'l & Operational Law Dep't, The Judge Advocate General's Sch., *Operational Law Handbook* 7-13; available at: https://www.jagcnet.army.mil/JAGGCNETInternet/Homepages/AC/CLAMOPublic.nsf/0/1af4860452f962c085256a490049856f/$FILE/Master%20Document.pdf

[89] Canestaro, *supra* note 74, at 91. *as cited in* Drumbl, *supra* note 77, at 48.

[90] *Id. See also*, Dinstein, supra note 27, at 6 ("Still, a single corpus of law applicable to all armed conflicts (inter-State and intra-State) neither exists nor attracts much support.")

[91] Gill et al, *supra* note 51, at 30.

[92] *Id.*

Another commentator noted it is important to establish the type of conflict one is involved in because it determines the issue of status.[93] "Status is inextricably linked to all questions regarding the law of war because status determines the duties owed or owing to people or objects, or who or what may be lawfully targeted."[94] The status of lawful combatant, for example affords the combatant the privilege of combatant immunity.

Similarly, Brooks proposed that the law of armed conflicts assumes five basic principles:

1. Accepts that certain behaviors that are illegal and abhorrent in time of peace are both permissible and desirable in time of war.

2. Purposeful killing of other humans is considered morally abhorrent in peacetime (and would lead to prosecution, trial, and possibly conviction for the crime of murder), but in time of war soldiers are not only permitted, but required, to try to incapacitate members of enemy forces, if necessary by killing them.

3. Combatant immunity flows from the disconnect between appropriate peacetime behaviors and appropriate wartime behavior. In peacetime, the willful killing of another human would normally lead to prosecution, trial and possibly conviction for the crime of murder.

4. Deliberate destruction of appropriation of public or private property is normally punishable in time of peace, but generally permissible in time of war.

5. Combatants taken prisoner by opposing forces may be detained until the cessation of hostilities, but they may not be subject to punishment by opposing forces for their legitimate

---

[93] Major William H. Ferrell, III, *No Shirt, No Shoes, No Status: Uniforms, Distinction, and Special Operations in International Armed Conflict*, 178 Mil. L. Rev. 94 at 97 (2003).
[94] *Id.*

wartime acts, and they must be released and repatriated when hostilities end.[95]

Brooks argued the principles of armed conflict "only offer benefits to those who play by the rules"[96] and reflects the assumption that military violence will be in accordance with these principles. The United States Department of Defense (DoD) also listed six basic purposes and principles of the law of war.[97] According to the DoD manual, the purposes are two-fold: humanitarian and functional. Humanitarian purposes include:

- Protecting both combatants and noncombatants from unnecessary suffering;
- Safeguarding the fundamental human rights of persons who fall into the hands of the enemy; and
- Facilitating the restoration of peace;

Functional purposes include:

- Ensuring good order and discipline;
- Fighting in a disciplined manner consistent with national values; and
- Maintaining domestic and international public support.[98]

The document's mandate declares that the law of war principles shall be applied "to all cases of declared war or any other armed conflicts that arise between the US and other nations, even if the state of war is not recognized by one of them. This threshold is codified in Common Article 2 of the Geneva Convention."[99]

---

[95] Brooks, *supra* note 9, at 692.
[96] *Id. at* 693.
[97] See DOD, Chapter 2, Law of War, p. 12.
[98] Brooks, *supra* note 9, at 12.
[99] *Id.* at 15.

A clear distinction was also created by Jinks[100] who stated that "In a narrow sense, the applicability of the 'laws of war' to these circumstances helps define the scope of the contemplated criminal proceedings against captured al Qaeda and Taliban fighters"[101] because the laws of war are applicable in noninternational armed conflicts and the September 11 attacks breached these laws. He argued that the nature and elements of the attacks, combined with the international reaction to the attacks strongly demonstrate that the attacks prompted or confirmed the existence of an "armed conflict" between the United States and al Qaeda. However, Jinks suggested Common Article 3 of the Geneva Conventions does apply and thus violations amount to "war crimes."[102]

In his discourse, Jinks distinguished two requirements for Common Article 3 to apply: (1) the existence of an armed conflict; and (2) this armed conflict is "not of an international character."[103] In an analysis of the application of the first requirement (existence of an armed conflict), Jinks recognized that there is still no clear definition of an armed conflict; just principles. Therefore, Jinks established the four factors shown above to determine if an armed conflict does exist between the United States and al Qaeda.

Jinks also interpreted the text of Common Article 3 to imply that it is applicable to all armed conflicts not covered by Article 2 of the Geneva Conventions.[104] Jinks concluded that a violation of Common Article 3 constituted a war crime and thus could be prosecuted via military commissions.

Supporting the thesis of Jinks, Goldman and Tittemore[105] opined that "The United States intervention on the side of the Northern

---

[100] Jinks, *supra* note 49.

[101] Brooks, *supra* note 9, at 15.

[102] *Id.* at 9.

[103] Jinks, *supra* note 49, at 20, quoting Geneva Conventions of 1949 for the Protection of War Victims, Aug. 12, 1949, 6 U.S.T. 3114, 75 U.N.T.S. 3 art. 3.

[104] *Id.* ("Can violations of Common Article 3, under the laws of war, serve as the basis for individual criminal liability? If it is deemed a war crime to violate Common Article 3, then those individuals can be prosecuted by military commissions.)

[105] Robert K. Goldman and Brian D. Tittemore, *Unprivileged Combatants and the Hostilities in Afghanistan: Their Status and Rights under International*

Alliance against the Taliban effectively 'internationalized' the conflict and fundamentally changed the nature of the ensuing hostilities."[106] Furthermore, the US intervention complied with the conditions in common Article 2 of the 1949 Geneva Convention for existence of an international armed conflict between the United States and Afghanistan.[107] "In this sense, the Bush Administration is also correct in stating that its global 'war' against al Qaeda is not the kind of armed conflict that was envisioned by the framers of the 1949 Geneva Convention since this new 'war' lacks the necessary parties and other requisites to qualify as either an international or noninternational armed conflict as defined in those treaties."[108] The authors proposed that if al Qaeda launched the attacks on September 11 from a platform on the high seas and were subsequently captured, they would not be prisoners of war, instead they would be treated as common criminals and placed through criminal justice system.[109]

The basic principles of armed conflict address many questions concerning actions of states and non-states, although it does not resolve all issues. Consequently, there is active discourse with regard to the US' actions in the War on Terror and the engagement in an international armed conflict. Some commentators suggested the "War on Terror" is not an international armed conflict in a legal sense.[110] "However, the military operations conducted against the Taliban government and organized units of al Qaeda in Afghanistan and the war in Iraq, both of which are said to be part of the overall worldwide struggle against terrorism, do qualify as international armed conflicts to which the 'laws and customs of war', including the notion of combatant status, must be applied."[111] As noted, it has been widely challenged that

---

Humanitarian and Human Rights Law, The American Society of International Law, Task Force on Terrorism, December 2002 at 6, available at: http://www.asil/org/taskforce/index.htm.

: available at: http://www.asil/org/taskforce/index.htm.

[106] *Id.* at 23.

[107] *Id.* at 23-24.

[108] *Id.*

[109] *Id.* at 29.

[110] Gills *supra* note 51, at 30.

[111] Brooks, *supra* note 9, at 704 ("What constitutes an 'international armed conflict' is not otherwise defined, but the insistence on the irrelevance of declarations of war makes it clear that 'armed conflicts' is to be conceptualized functionally, not formalistically.") See also, Maggs, *Terrorism and The Law*,

if a situation can not clearly be denoted as armed conflict, then the law of armed conflict is not triggered and thus states should deal with these threats through their own domestic criminal law. The global increase in terrorism and individuals involved in terrorist activities challenges the previously held assumptions concerning the law of armed conflict. The following section focuses on key points outlined by supporters and critics of US policy and the War on Terror.[112]

Many in the legal and political field have supported the Bush Administration concerning the belief that the President had the authority to declare America's involvement in an international armed conflict. Critics, however, have decried that an "Act of War" does not exist because the United States is not fighting another nation. Defenders[113] concur that clearly if a nation-state had replicated the exact attacks, there would be no question about whether a state of war existed. Several defenders have compared the action of the al Qaeda organization with actions of a recognized state "because they are very organized, military in nature (training camps), and their primary goal is to spread and enforce their ideological and political objectives."[114] Opponents in the same way have argued that the acts should viewed as criminal acts because they started and ended in the United States and thus should be handled through the domestic laws. Reacting to this point, the government determined that the attacks were planned, organized and financed by a foreign organization[115]and part of a larger campaign.

---

231 (2005) ("The United States generally classified the regular Iraqi army soldiers that it captured during the 2003 invasion of Iraq as prisoners of war under Geneva Convention III. It then released many of them soon after the major combat operations had ended." This dissertation will not focus on those soldiers, it solely focuses on members of al Qaeda and the Taliban.)

[112] Adam Roberts, *Can we define Terrorism?,* Oxford Today, 2002), available at http://www.oxfordtoday.ox.ac.uk/archieve/0102/14_2/04.html. (suggesting that terrorism is difficult to define and the world community has not reached a universal definition.)

[113] See Yoo, *supra* note 7, at 8.

[114] *Id.* at 9.

[115] *Id.* ("the Bali, Madrid, and London episodes, together with the bombings in Iraq, are part of a sustained and coordinated campaign against the United States and our allies by a single network in pursuit of an ideological agenda.")

Similarly, the question of who should be responsible (military or police force) for suppressing the enemy also determines the characteristic of armed conflict. If the military is the organization that must be used to defeat the enemy, for example destroying training camps in Afghanistan, and it has been sent to do so, it is international armed conflict.[116]

Other defenders have responded that in addition to acts of war, the September 11 attacks can equally be considered acts of terrorism because "terrorism almost always involves the deliberate targeting of non-military objectives (here civilians and civilian objects), it would be a 'war crime' even in a declared or legally recognized war."[117] Thus, the attack on 9/11 included violations of criminal law, international law and the law of war, and therefore the United States enjoys all privileges associated with self defense.[118]

Two lines of thought summarize views of proponents' perceptions that the United States is at war.[119] The first reasoning encompasses that America's air strikes against Libya in 1986 were in response to the bombing of a Berlin night club by suspected Libyan terrorists. The United States claimed they were authorized to use self-defense and thus initiate the strikes because a US armed service member had been killed. Similarly, the US invoked the principle of self-defense with the air strikes against Iraq in 1993, after the Iraqi government was suspected of involvement in a conspiracy to assassinate former President Bush during a visit to Kuwait.[120] The rationale involved in these responses presumed the attacks as an armed attack against the United States.

---

[116] *Id.* at 10. (A difference must be noted between what the military can do in war and peace. "The military could not be used to conduct such activities in the United States because it would violate the Posse Comitatus Act. The Posse Comitatus Act prohibits the military from enforcing our laws, with a few narrow exceptions."

[117] Lt. Col (Ret.) US Army H. Wayne Elliot, *Terrorism and the Laws of War: September 11 and its Aftermath*, Crimes of War Project, available at: http://www.crimesofwar.org/expert/attack-elliott.html.

[118] *Id.* Elliot counters that violations of these multitudes of laws grants the US the right to military force without the approval of the UN Security Council, NATO, or any other national body.

[119] Steven R. Ratner, *Terrorism and the Laws of War: September 11 and its Aftermath*, Crimes of War Project, September 21, 2001, available at: http://www.crimesofwar.org/expert/attack-ratner.html

[120] *Id.* at 2.

The second line of thought assumes that the terrorist's acts can be viewed as criminal acts against persons on US soil. Examples of this reasoning include the bombing of the Pan Am Flight 103 in 1998 and the first bombing of the World Trade Center in 1993. In both of these instances, the United States chose not to respond with their military but demanded the (1) the extradition of the suspected terrorist involved in the Pan Am attacks; and (2) prosecution of individuals charged with bombing the World Trade Center.[121]

Collaborating with the international community on extradition and jurisdictional issues has been the usual method to respond to terrorism.[122] However, "...the law enforcement strategy becomes impossible and obsolete if the terrorist organizations are granted a safe haven by one or more countries."[123] Thus, if it is not possible to implement the law enforcement approach due to another nations' sheltering of the terrorist organizations, then it is appropriate to conduct a military operations rescue. The response's purposes is to restore the law and order by coercing the state to withdraw its support from terrorist organizations; punish those responsible for the terrorist attacks; and prevent future terrorist attacks.[124]

In congruence with previous opinions, Joseph Bialke stated an attacked state may respond with military force against the military threat of a stateless organization, even though the laws of armed conflict usually apply to armed conflicts between states.[125]

Joseph Bialke states:

> When hostes humani generis commit acts of international aggression from a rogue state safe haven against the territory

---

[121] *Id.*

[122] Marc Cogen, Bruges Colloquium of October 26-27, 2001. "The Impact of International Humanitarian Law on Current Security Policy Trends." Reprinted in Crimes of war project, available at: http://www.crimesofwar.org/expert/attack-cogen.html.

[123] *Id.*

[124] *Id.* at 2 (The United States may use military force if t he terrorists responsible for the 9/11 attacks are being sheltered and protected by another nation or nations.)

[125] Joseph Bialke, *Al Qaeda & Taliban Unlawful Enemy Detainees, Unlawful Belligerents, and the International Law of Armed Combat*, 55, A.F.L. REV. 1 at 37 (2004).

> of other states, their acts of criminal international aggression may become more than a mere matter of international law enforcement involving an organized international crime force. When such an international attack of hostes generis is of the scope that it amounts to an 'armed attack,' the attacks state may also concurrently deem the aggression of such a stateless organization and non-state actor as an act of war and accordingly respond with military force in individual self-defense or in collective self-defense with allies. Similarly, if such hostes humani generis attackers continue to possess sufficient capabilities to mount further attacks, the attacked state and its allies may regard the hostes humani generis as continuing military threat and accordingly respond with military force to neutralize that military threat.[126]

While not classifying the 9/11 as initiating an international armed conflict or as criminal acts, Gregory Maggs noted the primary purpose of the criminal justice system is to arrest and prosecute criminal suspects.[127] "In the case of international terrorism, these tasks often have proved very difficult as a practical matter."[128] Furthermore, Maggs alluded to the fact that it is difficult to provide a suspected terrorist their Sixth Amendment Constitutional right to a speedy trial because extra precautions must be taken to ensure judges and jurors' protection. The court must be careful not to place so much emphasis on security as to prejudice the accused by signaling he or she is involved in terrorist related activity.[129] The current trend, among other nations, is to deem terrorism as armed aggression versus criminal acts. Afghanistan, Columbia, Israel, Northern Ireland, Russia, Turkey, and the US, for example, have implemented domestic or foreign armed forces against terrorist attacks. Such armed forces seek to attack, detain, interrogate and prosecute suspected terrorists.[130]

---

[126] *Id.* at 44-45.

[127] Gregory Maggs, *Terrorism and the Law*, (Thomson West 2005) at 81. *See also*, Sean D. Murphy, *Terrorism and the Concept of "Armed Attack" in Article 51 of the U.N. Charter*, 43 Harv. Int'l L.J. 41 (2002) as cited in Maggs, at 171.

[128] *Id.*

[129] Maggs, *supra* note 127, at 86.

[130] *Id.* at 159.

The proponents of recognizing the United States was involved in an international armed conflict based their analysis on critical elements of national and international laws. However there were many critics and scholars who disagreed with the Bush Administration's determination that the September 11 attacks initiated an international armed conflict. Opponents argued the appropriate response utilizes the criminal justice system, instead of military force.

Many of these critics acknowledge that the attacks on September 11 were indeed horrific and contained elements associated with a war (the magnitude of casualties). However, in their view, the hijackers on September 11 should be classified as criminals, not enemies,[131] and therefore should be adjudicated through the criminal justice system. Their argument suggests that although treating the perpetrators as criminals will place some constraint on the United States response, in the end, the criminal justice system will better serve the interests of the United States citizens.[132] To that end, cherished American values, like avoiding injuries to innocent civilians, should be considered when thinking of engaging in armed conflict. Additionally, the capture of Bin Laden or terrorists would impact "Our sense of vindication…if bin Laden ends up living out his days in federal prison than if he dies on the wrong end of a cruise missile."[133]

Scholars have also questioned "Who is the enemy in the War on Terror and does this justify the response?" Jordan Paust declared that "Armed attacks by such non-state, non-nation, non-belligerent, non-insurgents actors like bin Laden and members of al Qaeda can trigger the right of selective and proportionate self-defense under the United Nations Charter against those directly involved in an armed attack, but even the use of military force by the United States merely against bin Laden and al Qaeda in foreign territory would not create a state of war between the United States and al Qaeda."[134] In addition, critics

---

[131] *See* Peter Spiro, *Not War, Crime*, Findlaw Commentary September 19, 2001; *See also* Helen Duffy, *The 'War on Terror' and the Frameworks of International Law* (2005) 84 (The attacks on September 11 can not be considered an armed conflict.)

[132] *Id.*

[133] *Id.*

[134] Jordan J. Paust, *Use of Armed Force Against Terrorists in Afghanistan, Iraq and Beyond*, 35 Cornell Int'l L.J. 533 (2002).

propose that the lowest level of warfare or armed conflict to which certain laws of war are applicable is an insurgency and al Qaeda fails to qualify for that category.[135] Therefore, the laws of war are inapplicable to the conflict between the United States and al Qaeda. "Applying the status of war and the laws of war to armed violence below the level of an insurgency can have the unwanted consequence of legitimizing various other combatant acts and immunizing them from prosecution.[136]

Critics contend that the judicial system is the appropriate venue for handling the individuals associated with al Qaeda, where some of their members have already been tried and prosecuted in US federal courts.[137] The government's decision to treat the attacks as acts of war initiated "a highly problematic armed conflict alternative to the criminal law paradigm, which is readily available to combat terrorist acts and threats."[138] Further, it has been suggested that past conduct establishes that terrorist groups who initiated significant and sustained armed violence, were treated as criminals.[139] However, if a state was responsible for those terrorist attacks, it could be defined as an armed attack and implement the right of self-defense under Article 51 of the United Nations Charter. "Where no link to state responsibility exists, terrorists and other criminal non-state actors remain, as a matter of law, at the sub-state level rather than at the inter-state level."[140] This argument continues that the use of force and subsequent detention of terrorists as combatants, rather than criminals, legitimizes terrorism.[141]

---

[135] According to Paust, insurgency can only occur if the insurgent group resembles a government, an organized military force, control of significant portions of territory as its own, and its own relative stable population or base of support within a broader population. Additionally, belligerent status contains the same requirements for insurgency to apply but has one extra condition, outside recognition by one or more states either as a belligerent or a state. Al Qaeda does not satisfy any of these requirements necessary for insurgency or belligerent status.

[136] Paust *supra* note 134, at 327.

[137] Joan Fitzpatrick *Sovereignty, Territoriality, and the Rule of Law*, 25 Hastings Int'l & Comp L. Rev. 303 a 312 (2002).

[138] *Id.*

[139] Mary Ellen O'Connell, *Enhancing the Status of Non-state Actors Through a Global War on Terror*? 43 Colum. J. Transnat'l L. 435 at 445 (2003).

[140] *Id.*

[141] *Id.* at 451. ("This is arguably the situation for Russia in respect to Chechnya, yet even where the Russian government resists, calling the violence civil war,

Thus, according to some scholars, it is more appropriate for the United States to declare "global law enforcement" instead of declaring "global war."[142]

Other scholars are similarly of the opinion that these individuals should be prosecuted but advance the theory that international courts would be the most fitting location[143] and would diminish the risk of bias.[144] These attacks were "non-isolated warlike attacks undertaken against a sovereign state by individuals from other states operating through al Qaeda, a non-state actor that has some command and political structure."[145] Because the U.S. was the target of the September 11 attacks, some may feel our domestic laws are inadequate for these attacks, and the international criminal laws might be more powerful. Furthermore, nationals of eighty-one countries also perished in the attacks making the international court an even more suitable site. This option also presents a basis for verdicts and trials to receive international legitimacy. The United States has accepted this approach as evident in international tribunals for the atrocities in the former Yugoslavia and Rwanda.[146] International tribunals are appropriate for acts that are more than simple criminal acts and the nature of the September 11 attacks demonstrates the seriousness of the crime.

International courts or tribunals additionally offer advantages over domestic criminal courts, such as intelligence security concerns (presence of terrorists in courtrooms),[147]criminal liability imposed for those who "order, plan, instigate, aid or abet the crime, or who act in a common criminal enterprise with those who actually commit the

---

rather than terrorism…..Russia prefers to call these opponents terrorists, rather than combatants.")

[142] *Id* at 457.

[143] Drumbl, *supra* note 77.

[144] Spiro, *supra* note 131.

[145] Drumbl, *supra* note 77, at 4.

[146] *Id.* at 67.

[147] *Id.* (U.S. domestic courts apply discovery rules and important rules may be revealed to suspected terrorist. International tribunals limit discovery procedures and provides for the strict protection of confidential and classified information.)

offense,"[148] and establishment of better international cooperation and coordination (clearly a substantial benefit to the world community due to al Qaeda's transnational nature). However, two primary disadvantages in utilizing international courts have been noted – courts overwhelmed with defendants and funding matters. Despite these problems, it has been suggested that "International criminal law, however, provides a bridge between these two categories" (armed attack or criminal attack) and thus it is the appropriate response the United States should pursue.[149]

The opposing members of the "International Armed Conflict or "Criminal Act" debate clearly interpret the attacks of September 11 and the corresponding response of the United States in different, but equal ways. Defenders of the government's decisions exclaim, "War is violence on a large scale, of the kind we saw on September 11, undertaken for political reasons by a foreign state or entity, which requires a military response"[150] and thus constitute an international armed conflict. Al Qaeda was well financed, organized and focused on destroying Americans. The military, versus the police, is the most efficient organization to deal with them and therefore armed forces should be used. Furthermore, the policy is intended to support the government's assertion when they "declared the attacks to have been 'an act of war,' he [President Bush] was not using the term in its strict legal sense, but for domestic political purposes, and as a warning that the United States was preparing a military response."[151]

Those opposed to this thinking consider the attacks of September 11 as clear criminal acts. Proceeding with the logic of acts of war and its corresponding consequences could diminish civil rights.[152] Some scholars proffer the government needs to be cognizant of individual rights, what our Constitution was based on, and go forth with policies that demonstrate the differences between American values and those attempting to destroy them. Limits on Executive power to identify,

---

[148] Drumbl, *supra* note 77, at 72 as cited in: Rome Statue of the International Criminal Court, art. 25, U.N. Doc. A/CONF/.183/9 (1998), *available at* http://www.un.org/law/icc/statute/romefra.htm

[149] *Id.* at 78.

[150] Yoo, *supra* note 7, at 10.

[151] Ratner *supra* note 119, at 2.

[152] Brooks, *supra* note 9, at 680.

target, detain, and try terrorists must continue to be discussed.[153] Providing fair trials in either domestic criminal courts or international courts could illustrate to the world a high regard for human rights.

As previously noted, whether the September 11 attacks constituted an international armed attack or whether they were criminal acts is a crucial question because of the answer. If the President decided the acts initiated an international armed conflict, military operations would commence and individuals would be captured and detained by the military. However, if the President determined the attacks were criminal acts, individuals could be taken into custody by criminal law enforcement personnel and prosecuted in civilian courtrooms.

On September 18, 2001, Congress authorized the President to use force and thus, resolved the United State's response to the terrorist attacks.[154] In response to Congressional authorization, President Bush deployed troops to Afghanistan.[155] Therefore, the military had the authority to detain individuals captured on the battlefield.[156] A very important aspect to the current conflict with al Qaeda and the Taliban is to define the status applied to these captured individuals. Were they combatants or criminals? A combatant has been defined as "military personnel engaging in hostilities in an armed conflict on behalf of a party to the conflict.[157] Generally, lawful combatants are entitled to prisoner of war status and unlawful combatants are not afforded such privilege. The following section defines these important differences and rights and the evolution of the terminology and respective distinctions.

---

[153] Bradley & Goldsmith, *supra* note 34, at 2.

[154] AUMF *supra* note 52.

[155] While President Bush implemented the services of the armed forces, criminal investigations and subsequent prosecutions also were being conducted for suspected terrorists and supporters. Therefore, the United States response while consisting mainly of military force, also included the criminal justice system.

[156] Helen Duffy, *The "War on Terror' and the Framework of International Law*, at 379 (2005). (Following the commencement of the military campaign in Afghanistan.....the United States, assisted by its allies, began detaining persons in Afghanistan and elsewhere 'for reasons related to the conflict.'")

[157] Department of Defense, Chapter 2, Law of War, p. 17.

SECTION TWO: Lawful and Unlawful Combatants

On November 14, 2001, Vice President Cheney declared "Somebody who comes into the United States of America illegally, who conducts a terrorist operation killing thousands of innocent Americans…is not a lawful combatant…They don't deserve to be treated as prisoners of war."[158] Prior to this speech, many had not heard of this distinction – lawful combatants, and the implied unlawful combatants. However, this is not a new term. Lawful and unlawful combatants, and the distinctions between the two, are evident throughout history.

Designation of lawful combatants was first codified in international law in Article 9 of the 1874 Brussels Declaration.[159] The terms (lawful and unlawful combatants) appear to have been used interchangeably with lawful and unlawful belligerents throughout the decades. Indeed current US military manuals use four terms – 'unprivileged belligerent,' 'detainees,' 'unlawful combatants' and 'illegal combatants' – again apparently interchangeably, to refer to those who are viewed as not being members of the armed forces of a party to the conflict and not having the right to engage in hostilities against an opposing party."[160] In every US conflict, prisoners of war were captured and held for the duration of the conflict. The detention of lawful combatants is not punishment but a way of controlling combatants "*hors de combat* for the duration of the conflict."[161] However, not every captured combatants was detained as a prisoner of war, some were detained as unlawful combatant or belligerent and not provided prisoner of war status).

According to the traditional laws of war, there is an important and significant distinction between lawful belligerency and unlawful belligerency. "The combatant's privilege, and its corollary statuses of privileged and unprivileged (or unlawful) combatants is a hoary and formerly esoteric doctrine *of jus in bello* that has achieved public fame

---

[158] Vice President Dick Cheney speech, U. S. Chamber of Commerce, 14 November, 2001.

[159] Canestaro *supra* note 74, at 100.

[160] Roberts *supra* note 112, at 214, as cited in: International and Operational Law Dep't, the Judge Advocate General's School, US Army, JA-422, Operational Law Handbook (2003), as 12-22

[161] Berman, *supra* note 33, at 9.

in the years since 9/11."[162] This is the present status of the dialogue concerning the privileges afforded the two categories. An historical review of the evolution of key characteristics associated with these terms is the topic of this section.

Several national and international doctrines have defined and clarified the laws of war (concerning the difference between lawful and unlawful belligerents). Casey, Rivkin, and Bartram stated, "Under the traditional laws of war, *jus in bello*, a fundamental distinction was drawn between 'lawful belligerency' and 'unlawful belligerency.'"[163] Lawful combatants can be described as individuals who recognize the burdens and are entitled to the benefits of the laws of war, including to be treated as a prisoner of war, if they served in the armed forces of a sovereign state.[164] Thus, those who *benefit* from the combatant's *privilege*[165] cannot be prosecuted (or brought to trial) for their participation in the ongoing armed conflict; they have immunity from violence attributed during armed conflict.[166]

This supposition is based on the notion that wars (or armed conflicts) are between "public entities, not individuals."[167] Accordingly, specific requirements or mandates for determining that individuals acted in accordance with the laws of war were a primary focus of international laws, first codified in the Hague Convention.[168] Some scholars even propose that the topic of lawful and unlawful combatants can be traced as early as the 17th century,[169] and cite

---

[162] *Id.* at 3 (Berman states that examining the legal doctrines crucial to defining the combatants' privilege is the key concept of *jus in bello.*)

[163] Lee A. Casey, David B. Rivkin, Jr., and Darren R. Bartram, *Unlawful Belligerency and its Implications Under International Law*, The Federalist Society, National Security White Papers, at 2 (2003) (available at http://www.fed-soc.org/Publications/Terrorism/unlawfulcombatants.htm http://www.fed-soc.org/Publications/Terrorism/unlawfulcombatants.htm.

[164] *Id.*

[165] *Id. Emphasis added.*

[166] Berman, *supra* note 33, at 4.

[167] *Id* at 9.

[168] Convention Between the United States and Other Powers Respecting the Laws and Customs of War on Land, Oct. 18, 1907, 36 Stat. 2277 (hereinafter Hague Convention); Regulations Respecting the Laws and Customs of War on Land, Oct. 18, 1907, 36 Stat. 2295 (hereinafter Hague Regulations).

[169] Casey et al., *supra* note 163, at 1.

Emmerich de Vattel, an 18th century international law publicist who stated:

> When a nation or a sovereign has declared war against another sovereign by reason of a difference arising between them, their war is what among nations is called a lawful war, and in form; and as we shall more particularly shew the effects by the voluntary laws of nations, are the same on both sides, independently of the justice of the cause. Nothing of all this takes place in a war void of form, and unlawful, more properly called robbery, being undertaken without right, without so much as an apparent cause. It can be productive of no lawful effect, nor give any right to the author of it. A nation attacked by such sort of enemies is not under any obligation to observe towards them the rules of war in form. It may treat them as robbers. The city of Geneva, after defeating the attempt of the famous Escalde hung up the Savoyards, whom they had made prisoners, as robbers who had attacked them without any cause, or declaration of war. Nobody offered to censure this proceeding, which would have been detested in a formal war.[170]

Although the spirit of the above proposal was adopted by national conferences on the issue of international armed conflicts and combatants and can be clearly seen by standards set forth in first, the Hague Convention, and later embraced by the Geneva Convention III Relative to the Treatment of Prisoners of War,[171] a compelling debate on interpretations of these standards is still active. To be sure, from 1874 to 1949, there were several attempts to define when civilians could legitimately take up arms which has guided most "of the legal controversy in treaty drafting committees and no other problem has 'given rise to as much bitter debate and acrimonious protest.'"[172]

---

[170] Casey et al, *supra* note 163, as cited in: Emmerich de Vattel, *The Law of Nations* 481 (Luke White ed. Dublin 1792).

[171] *Id* at 2. (Indeed Casey et al., note that the United States abided by Vattel's theory as demonstrated by their actions towards 'robbers' in conflicts.")

[172] Canestaro supra note 74, at 90. as cited in: Karman Nabulsi,*Traditions of War: Occupation, Resistance, and the Law*, 41 AT 15 (1999).

As mentioned, the first standard prescribing definition on combatant status was Article I of the 1907 Annex to the Hague Convention (IV) Respecting the Laws of Customs on War On Land, which defined criteria for an individual to be entitled to lawful combatant status and thus treated as a prisoner of war.[173] Article I states: The laws, rights, and duties of war apply not only to armies, but also to militia and volunteer corps fulfilling conditions:

> (1) to be commanded by a person responsible for his subordinates;
>
> (2) to have a fixed distinctive emblem recognizable at a distance;
>
> (3) to carry arms openly; and
>
> (4) to conduct their operations in accordance with the laws and customs of war.[174]

Individuals who fought and did not meet these requirements were designated and detained as unlawful belligerents. As such, they were subject to a different punishment and detainment.[175] As one commentator noted, the Hague Convention codified basic norms that guide the use of military force and were only applicable to wars between state parties.[176]

---

[173] Casey et al., *supra* note 163, Article I of the 1907 Annex to the Hague Convention (IV) Respecting the Laws of War on Land (1-14). (In actuality, the first Hague Convention was signed in 1899 and provided guidelines for the commencement of hostilities, conduct of combatants and it also prohibited the use of certain types of warfare. The second Hague Convention expanded upon the First Convention's rules.)

[174] Hague Regulations, *supra* note 168, art 1.

[175] Casey et al., *supra* note 163 (The authors argue that spies, saboteurs and guerillas fall into this category and that punishment for these unlawful belligerents could be as severe as death.

[176] Canestaro, *supra* note 74, at 81; See also Ferrell, *supra* note 93, at 123. ("Combatants found in enemy controlled territory while wearing civilian clothing may be viewed as engaging in espionage and treated as spies. Spying is not a violation of international laws of war. The combatant caught spying,

In 1864, The Geneva Convention convened to further discuss requirements set forth by the Hague Convention. The authors of the Geneva Convention intended that these laws would closely align with the text of the First Hague Regulation of 1899.[177] According to the International Committee of the Red Cross, the Geneva Conventions and their Additional Protocols are a part of international humanitarian law[178] and are now accepted as customary international law.[179] They provide legal safeguards that address the way wars may be fought and the protection of individuals and were intended to be used only in situations of international armed conflicts.[180] The rules in the first Geneva Convention of 1864 specifically address the care for the wounded soldiers (Convention I for the Amelioration of the Condition of the Wounded and Sick in Armed Forces in the Field).

In 1949, the Geneva Convention expanded upon earlier rules and created the final four Conventions (inclusive of Geneva I Convention) which are used today. These conventions consist of: (1) Convention (I) for the Amelioration of the Condition of the Wounded and Sick in Armed Forces in the Field; (2) Convention (II) for the Amelioration of the Condition of Wounded, Sick and Shipwrecked Members of Armed Forces at Sea; (3) Convention (III) relative to the Treatment of Prisoners of War; and (4) Convention (IV) relative to the Protection of Civilian Persons in Time of War.[181] Article 4(A) of the Third Geneva

---

however, is not entitled to prisoner of war status and is subject to the captured nation's laws." As cited in Michael Bothe, et al., *New Rules for Victims of Armed Conflicts: Commentary on the two 1977 Additional Protocols to the Geneva Conventions of 1949* at 264 (1982).

[177] Evan J. Wallach, *Afghanistan, Quirin, & Uchiyama: Does the sauce suit the gander*? Army Lawyer (Nov. 2003).

[178] Brooks, *supra* note 9, at 691 ("Of the 191 member states of the United Nations, all 191 are party to the Geneva Conventions of 1949, 162 are party to Additional Protocol I, and 157 are party to Additional Protocol II. States Party to the Geneva Conventions and Their Additional Protocols, ICRC (Jan. 6, 2004), available at http://www.icrc.org/eng/party_gc.")

[179] International Committee of the Red Cross, The Geneva Conventions: the core of international humanitarian law available at: http://www.icrc.org/Web/Eng/siteeng0.nsf/html/genevaconventions (Dec. 29, 2006).

[180] Brooks, *supra* note 9, at 712 (Conflicts that are considered internal were only to be applied to Article 3, which is common to all four Geneva Conventions.)

[181] ICRC, *supra* note 179.

Convention specifies who is entitled to prisoner of war status[182] and is the crux of the discussion below. Article 4 of the Geneva Convention III states:

> A. Prisoners of war, in the sense of the present Convention, are persons belonging to one of the following categories, who have fallen into the power of the enemy:
>
> (1) Members of the armed forces of a Party to the conflict, as well as members of militias or volunteer corps forming part of such armed forces.
>
> (2) Members of other militias and members of other volunteer corps, including those of organized resistance movements, belonging to a Party to the conflict and operating in or outside their own territory, even if this territory is occupied, provided that such militias or volunteer corps, including such organized resistance movements, fulfill the following conditions:
>
> (a) that of being commanded by a person responsible for his subordinates;
>
> (b) that of having a fixed distinctive sign recognizable at a distance;
>
> (c) that of carrying arms openly;

---

182 Berman, *supra* note 33, at 4 (While combatants are the primary group entitled to POW status, there are others who qualify for the status as well. For example, POW status is bestowed upon:(p)ersons who accompany the armed forces without actually being members thereof, such as civilian members of military aircraft crews, war correspondents, supply contractors, members of labour units or of services responsible for the welfare of the armed forces, provided that they have received authorization from the armed forces which they accompany, who shall provide them for that purpose with an identity card similar to the annexed model.) Geneva Convention Relative to the Treatment of Prisoners of War, Aug. 12, 1949, art. 4(A)(4), 6 U.S.T. 3316, 75 U.N.T.S. 135 [hereinafter GPW]

(d) that of conducting their operations in accordance with the laws and customs of war

(3) Members of regular armed forces who profess allegiance to a government or an authority not recognized by the Detaining Power.

(4) Persons who accompany the armed forces without actually being members thereof, such as civilian members of military aircraft crews, war correspondents, supply contractors, members of labour units or of services responsible for the welfare of the armed forces, provided that they have received authorization from the armed forces which they accompany, who shall provide them for that purpose with an identity card similar to the annexed model.

(5) Members of crews, including masters, pilots, and apprentices, of the merchant marine and the crews of civil aircraft of the Parties to the conflict, who do not benefit by more favourable treatment under any other provisions of international law.

(6) Inhabitants of a non-occupied territory, who on the approach of the enemy spontaneously take up arms to resist the invading forces, without having had time to form themselves into regular armed units, provided they carry arms openly and respect the laws and customs of war.[183]

B. The following shall likewise be treated as prisoners of war under the Geneva Convention:

(1) Persons belonging, or having belonged, to the armed forces of the occupied country…

---

[183] *Id.* Geneva Convention Relative to the Treatment of Prisoners of War, Aug. 12, 1949, art. 4(A)(4), 6 U.S.T. 3316, 75 U.N.T.S. 135 [hereinafter GPW] art. 4.

Article 5 of the Geneva Convention declares:

> Should any doubt arise as to whether persons, having committed a belligerent act and having fallen into the hands of the enemy, belong to any of the categories enumerated in Article 4, such persons shall enjoy the protection of the present Convention until such time as their status has been determined by a competent tribunal.

In 1977, an international conference seeking to curb aggression created two the Additional Protocols to the Geneva Conventions which were adopted by numerous States on June 8, 1977.[184] Protocol I is entitled, Protocol Additional to the Geneva Conventions of 12 August 1949, and relating to the Protection of Victims of International Armed Conflicts. The second Additional Protocol is entitled, Protocol Additional to the Geneva Conventions of 12 August 1949, and relating to the Protection of Victims of Non-International Armed Conflicts (Protocol II), 8 June 1977. Both of these protocols were widely ratified and expanded the intent of Common Article 3 to include noninternational armed conflicts.[185]

A third Additional Protocol was adopted on December 8, 2005 and is entitled, Protocol additional to the Geneva Conventions of 12 August 1949, and relating to the Adoption of an Additional Distinctive Emblem (Protocol III), 8 December 2005.[186] Additional Protocol I is the most relevant for the discussion on lawful and unlawful combatants. Protocol I only applies "to all cases of declared war or of any other armed conflict which may arise between two or more of the High Contracting Parties, even if the state of war is not recognized by one of them."[187]

---

[184] ICRC Geneva Convention: the core of international humanitarian law. Available at: http://www.icrc.org/Web/Eng/siteeng0.nsf/html/genevaconventions (Dec. 29, 2006).

[185] Protocol Additional to the Geneva Convention of 12 August 1949 and Relating to the Protection of Victims of Non-International Armed Conflicts, June 8, 1977, 1125 U.N.T.S. 609 (hereinafter Protocol II) (extending the human rights guarantees of Protocol I to noninternational armed conflicts.)

[186] ICRC, *supra* note 179.

[187] Canestaro *supra* note 74, at 92.

The Additional Protocols have been ratified by nearly all states except for the United States, Israel, Iran, Pakistan, and Afghanistan.[188] One reason the United States did not ratify the treaties was they believed that the Protocols granted terrorists protections in war even if they did not abide by the laws of war.[189] Former President Reagan stated, "it would grant combatant status to irregular forces even if they do not satisfy the traditional requirements to distinguish themselves from the civilian population and otherwise comply with the laws of war."[190] Others have concurred that the distinction between terrorist and lawful combatants must be clear-cut. "Terrorists are not members of established armed forces for the purpose of the law of war and they do not comply with the acceptable rules as lawful combatants."[191] Therefore, because the US government did not ratify the Protocols, the United States is not legally bound to apply Additional Protocol I and II.

The Hague Convention, Geneva Convention and Additional Protocols are the primary international laws applicable to the detention of captured individuals. While the treaties have been applied to several different conflicts, questions still remain regarding their applicability and the intent of the language, and the scope of the combatant's privileges in *jus in bello* which are always "hotly contested."[192] Several scholars have interpreted the language of these treaties to the question of "lawful and unlawful combatant." "Despite the fundamental nature of the distinction between combatant and non-combatant status, there is little in the way of a detailed definition of combatant status and no explicit reference to the notion of unprivileged belligerency or the status of 'unlawful combatant' which is contained in the relevant provisions of the international humanitarian treaties, although there is considerable treatment of these issues in the literature."[193]

---

[188] Yoo, *supra* note 7, at 25. According to the International Committee of the Red Cross the United States, Israel, Iran, Pakistan, and Afghanistan have not ratified the Protocols, Treaties & Documents, 1949 Conventions & Additional Protocols, available at: http://www.icrc.org/ihl.nsf/CONVPRES?OpenView.

[189] *Id.* at 25.

[190] *Id.* at 36, Message to the Senate Transmitting a Protocol to the 1949 Geneva Conventions, Jan.29, 1987, available at http://www.reagan.utexas.edu/archives/speeches/1987/012987B.htm.

[191] Leonard Cutler. *The Rule of Law and the Law of a War Military Commissions and Enemy Combatants Post 9/11* 2 (2005).

[192] Berman, *supra* note 33, at 6.

[193] Gill et al, *supra* note 51, at 32.

One commentator argued, however, that nations have historically abided by distinctions between lawful and unlawful. They cite "Private individuals who take up arms and commit hostilities against the enemy do not enjoy the privileges of armed forces, and the enemy has, according to customary rule of International Law, the right to treat such individuals as war criminals."[194] Additionally, the Lieber Code, established during the Civil War, clarified "that men, or squads of men, who commit hostilities...without being part and portion of the organized hostile army...are not public enemies, and therefore, if captured, are not entitled to the privileges of prisoners of war."[195]

Historical discussion continues with clear distinctions between the aforementioned combatants during World War II, such as those dissimilar lines between lawful and unlawful belligerents in tribunals created by the Allies after Germany's surrender. These tribunals recognized that unlawful belligerents were not granted the privilege of prisoner of war status and could be punished for being unlawful belligerents.[196] The distinction between lawful and unlawful combatants continues today and in fact "international law...continued to grant the combatants' privilege to most participants even if one side is a state engaged in pure aggression and the other is engaged in self-defense."[197] Others maintain that it is imperative to maintain the distinctions between lawful and unlawful combatants "to do otherwise, would put civilians and combatants in danger."[198]

The following discussions illustrate the many different interpretations of the language found in the treaties, specifically among those who view the individuals involved in September 11 as violators of criminal law and those who support the premise that those individuals are participants in an armed conflict; thus the distinction between lawful and unlawful combatant. If the former, then those

---

[194] Casey et al., *supra* note 163, at 12.

[195] See Article 82 of the Lieber Code, *supra* note 43 (often viewed as the first essential document in the modern codification *of jus in bello* – Berman, *supra* note 33, 14.

[196] *Id* 2.

[197] Berman, *supra* note 33, at 11. See also discussion in Defenders of Acts of War Designation section in Chapter 2 concerning the rights of the United States to defend itself.)

[198] Yoram Dinstein, *Unlawful Combatancy: Combatants and Civilians*, 32 Israel Y.B. H.B. at 174 (2002).

individuals should be entitled to the U.S. criminal procedures and courts but if it is the later, their treatment and status as POW should be viewed under the international law of armed conflict. Arguments will be separated into specific Articles of GPW, beginning with the Hague Conventions implications.

Yoram Dinstein argued that the Hague Conventions are applicable solely to combatants acting on behalf of a state party to the conflict.[199] This is an important condition because it supports the notion that an independent band of guerrillas cannot be observed as lawful combatants, even if they abide by the laws of war, wear a distinctive emblem, and carry their arms openly. "One way or another, 'a certain relationship with a belligerent government is necessary.'"[200] Therefore, according to Dinstein, the Hague Convention distinguished between lawful and lawful combatants and specified only lawful combatants could be detained as prisoners of war.

Many scholars have interpreted the individual requirements detailed in Article 4 of the GPW which specifically addresses when a combatant is entitled to prisoner of war status. This section will summarize key points generated by the discussion concerning provisions of the GPW. The International Committee of the Red Cross Commentaries will be included because it is the most quoted resource on the Geneva Convention, and the most universally accepted to reveal the true intentions of the Conventions.

It is important to clarify the two recognized categories of combatants; the first includes members of the armed forces of a belligerent Party (except medical and religious personnel) and the second category consists of any other persons who take an active part in the hostilities.[201] "Entitlement to the status of prisoner of war – upon being captured by the enemy – is vouchsafed to every combatant. The distinction between lawful and unlawful combatants is a corollary of the fundamental distinction between combatants and civilians: the

---

[199] *Id.* at 163, as cited in Lester Nurick & Roger Barrett, *Legality of Guerrilla Forces under the Laws of War*, 40 AM. J. INT'L. 563, 567-569 (1946).

[200] *Id.* at163, as cited in Denise Bindschedler-Robert, *A Reconsideration of the Law of Armed Conflict, The Law of Armed Conflicts: Report of the Conference on Contemporary Problems of the Law of Armed Conflict* 43 (1971).

[201] Dinstein, *supra* note 27, at 27.

paramount purpose of the former is to preserve the latter."[202] Furthermore, it is recognized under customary international law that any combatant who purposely blends into the civilian population to avoid being detected will be sanctioned – thus deprived the privilege of prisoner of war status. "A person who engages in military raids at night, while purporting to be an innocent civilian by day, is neither a civilian nor a lawful combatant. He is an unlawful combatant."[203]

Interpretations by some legal scholars have determined that it is immaterial how the armed forces are structured or whether their service is voluntary or not.[204] Similarly, according to ICRC Commentary, members of regular forces implies "all military personnel, whether they belong to the land, sea, or air forces."[205] Therefore, a captured lawful combatant (member of the regular force) can be detained as a prisoner of war and accorded all the privileges under the Geneva Convention III.[206] They cannot be punished for taking part in the hostilities. However, they can be prosecuted for violations of the detaining power's law or any violations of international law, which includes the laws of war. If there is a doubt to the lawfulness of the combatant, under Article 5, the third Geneva Convention requires that a combatant will be held as a prisoner of war until a competent tribunal has established their proper status.[207]

The next paragraph in Article 4(A) discusses criterion for irregular forces, including militias, partisan and volunteer corps, to satisfy to be entitled to prisoner of war status. A majority of commentators are of the opinion that Article 4 defines four criteria for a member of an irregular force to satisfy in order to be accorded the privilege of prisoner of war status. However, other commentators have interpreted additional criterion for irregular forces in order to be awarded prisoner of war status. The discussions below first examine the four criteria in Article 4A(2), followed by scholars who have interpreted additional

---

202 *Id.* at 29, cited in T.Meron, '*Some legal aspects of Arab terrorists' CLAIMS TO PRIVILEGED COMBATANCY*, 40 NTIR 47, 62 (1970).

203 Dinstein, *supra* note 27, at 29.

204 *Id.*

205 ICRC Commentary on the Third Geneva Convention Relative to the Treatment of Prisoners 61 (J. Picted ed., 1960) at 51.[hereinafter ICRC Commentary GPW]

206 Roberts, *supra* note 112, at 213.

207 GPW, *supra* note 182, at art 5.

factors for members of irregular forces to satisfy for prisoner of war status. Finally, a discussion on whether members of regular forces are required to satisfy the four requirements will conclude the section.

Scholars generally agree that the framers of this Article wanted to eliminate the possibility of individuals acting on their own accord. "The operation of small units of irregular forces is permissible, provided that the other conditions are fulfilled, but there is no room for individual initiatives."[208] However, it has been noted that specific language relating to this requirement does not elaborate upon the leader's qualifications or how he may obtain this authority.[209] In fact, the ICRC Commentary states that the group's leader or commander can be an officer in the regular armed forces or a civilian.[210] The ICRC notes that the essential factor is for the leader to "be responsible for action taken on his orders…[and]…his competence must be considered in the same way as that of a military commander."[211] Likewise, the United States Army Field Manual states the leader can be a member of the armed forces or another person of "position or authority."[212] The Army Manual also states, "state recognition, however, is not essential and an organization may be formed spontaneously and elect its own officers."[213] Additionally, the ICRC states that in order for this element to be satisfied, the leader must be responsible for both action taken on his orders as well as for action which he was not able to prevent.[214]

Other scholars expand on the meaning and assert that the leader must also discipline his/her subordinates and guarantee their observance with the laws and customs of war,[215] and a chain of command exists which implies an "operative, structured hierarchical system of military good order and discipline acting under an authority that expressly subjects itself to international law."[216] Traditionally, chain of commands train and educate its military to fight according to the laws of armed conflict and enforce such laws. The chain of

---

[208] Dinstein, *supra* note 198.
[209] Goldman & Tittemore, *supra* note 105.
[210] ICRC COMMENTARY GPW, *supra* note 205, at 59.
[211] *Id.*
[212] U.S. DEP'T OF THE ARMY FIELD MANUAL 27-10, THE LAW OF LAND WARFARE, at 27, para. 64 (1956) [hereinafter FM 27-10]
[213] *Id.*
[214] ICRC Commentary GPW, supra note 205, at 59.
[215] Goldman and Tittemore *supra* note 105, at 12.
[216] Bialke, *supra* note 125, at 23.

command must enforce such laws by examining breaches and prosecuting violators. If prosecuted and sentenced, the chain of command must enforce the punishment. This demonstrates that subordinates are not acting on their own but rather are following a chain of command and subsequent orders.[217] Finally, the chain of command controls its forces to avert violations of the law of armed conflict and must be able to order subordinates to respect cease-fires, truce, armistice, or surrender.[218]

A number of concerns have been raised about a seemingly innocuous requirement: a fixed distinctive sign. Several points have arisen about this element. Some have cautioned that the Article intends that the emblem must be fixed, in other words, the force cannot keep changing their emblem. "The fixed distinctive emblem must be worn throughout every military operation against the enemy in which the combatant takes part (throughout means from start to finish, namely, from the beginning of deployment to the end of disengagement), and the emblem must not be deliberately removed at any time in the course of the operation."[219] This emblem should be worn in all locations (e.g., vehicle, ship, aircraft which should also display the emblem) however, the combatants are not required to wear the distinctive emblem when they participating in activities not linked to military operations, such as training.[220] It is also argued whether the emblem must be illuminated at night,[221] primarily so that regular forces in uniforms can distinguish themselves, and thus irregular forces must also distinguish themselves "in ordinary circumstances and in a reasonable fashion" from civilians.[222]

Some contend that the fixed emblem criterion is satisfied by wearing a uniform.[223] However, if the irregular forces choose not to wear a uniform, they must wear a distinctive sign that is recognizable

---

[217] *Id.*

[218] Bialke, *supra* note 125, at 23.

[219] Dinstein, *supra* note 98, 161 as cited in: Howard Levie, *Prisoners of War in International Amred* Conflict, 7 (Howard S. Levie, ed., 1978), (Vol. 59, US Naval War College International Law Studies).

[220] *Id.*

[221] *Id.*at 161.

[222] *Id.*

[223] FM-27-10, US Manual, *supra* note 212, ICRC Commentary GPW, *supra* note 205.

from a distance and plainly distinguishes the combatant from civilians.[224] "The US Army manual states that such a sign could be a 'helmet or headdress' and also suggests that irregulars also wear 'a badge or brassard permanently affixed to [their] clothing.'"[225] Furthermore, the ICRC Commentary explains that the distinctive sign can consist of a "cap…coat, shirt, an emblem or coloured sign worn on the chest."[226] Universal agreement concerning a distinctive sign or a uniform does not currently exist.[227] "Moreover, it is also abundantly clear that there is no treaty-based or customary norm that requires that irregulars in order to distinguish themselves from civilians wear traditional military dress."[228] The contention is that the essential factor to comply with this requirement is that the chosen dress or sign must be clearly visible during the daytime and detectable from a distance without special equipment[229] so as not to incur innocent civilian injuries or death. A lawful combatant may not endanger protected noncombatant civilians by concealing one's combatant status, with perfidious intent, by posing as a protected noncombatant civilian."[230] This essential factor allows the opposing forces to distinguish, and thus protect, noncombatants and combatants.[231]

It is presumed in an armed conflict that opponents will have weapons. This condition requires that these weapons must be visible, primarily to distinguish themselves from civilians or noncombatants and that "irregular combatants do not get unfair surprise in attacks by concealing their weapons on approaching the enemy."[232] The combatant "must carry his arms openly in a reasonable way, depending on the nature of the weapon and the circumstances at hand."[233] "Furthermore, as long as the individual carries his weapon openly, whether it is a machine gun, rifle or pistol, and does not conceal it under his clothing, the requirement is satisfied."[234]

---

[224] Bialke, *supra* note 125.
[225] FM 27-10, *supra* note 212, at 27 para. 64 (b).
[226] ICRC COMMENTARY GPW, *supra* note 205, at 60.
[227] Goldman & Tittemore, *supra* note 105, at 13.
[228] *Id.*
[229] *Id.*
[230] Bialke, *supra* note 125, at 25.
[231] *Id.*
[232] Goldman & Tittemore, *supra* note 105.
[233] Dinstein, *supra* note 198, at 162.
[234] Goldman and Tittemore, *supra* note 105, at 13.

The ICRC elaborates, "The enemy must be able to recognize partisans as combatants in the same way as members of armed forces, whatever their weapons."[235] This Article makes it clear that there must not be any uncertainty among carrying arms openly versus carrying them visibly or ostensibly to distinguish those involved in the conflict.

Several scholars have argued that the fourth condition is the key to lawful combatancy.[236] "Unless a combatant is willing himself to respect the *jus in bello*, he is estopped from relying on that body of law when desirous of enjoying its benefits."[237] Therefore, in order for a combatant to enjoy the protections of the law of war, he must expressly abide by them. "This condition merely reaffirms the most basic notions that combatants in an armed conflict can lawfully engage in acts of violence against the adversary free of the restraints and prohibitions found in the laws and customs of war."[238] The ICRC concurs with this position that irregular forces must abide by treaties prohibiting certain weapons, they cannot directly attack civilians, and they cannot cause unnecessary damage. The ICRC Commentary states, "They may not attack civilians or disarmed persons and must, in all their operations, respect the principles of honour and loyalty as they expect their enemies to do."[239]

Consequences of individual adherence to this mandate, even insignificant ones, do not amount to the entire force losing prisoner of war status.[240] The entire force will lose protection if it is their policy to violate the laws of armed conflict. "According, LOAC (law of armed conflict) instructs that a willful egregious en masse failure by an armed force to follow the four objective Geneva Conventions III requirements

---

[235] ICRC COMMENTARY GPW, *supra* note 205, at 61.

[236] Dinstein, *supra* note 198, Goldman & Tittemore, *supra* note 105, Bialke, *supra* note 125 (Bialke points out, "This fourth requirement is the individual responsibility of every combatant and the collective responsibility of the entire armed force." In order to abide by this requirement, the leaders and their subordinates must strictly follow and obey the customary laws of armed conflict and relevant treaties during military combat operations.

[237] Dinstein, *supra* note 198, at 162.

[238] Goldman & Tittemore, *supra* note 105.

[239] ICRC Commentary GPW, *supra* note 205, at 59.

[240] Bialke, *supra* note 125, at 26.

makes the members of that armed force unlawful combatants, and therefore declines POW status to those forces when captured."[241]

As demonstrated above, there are many different interpretations of the language in Article 4(A)(2). Some scholars have concluded that "By default, then, groups of combatants who do not fulfill these four specified conditions and do not fight in accordance with them are engaging in unlawful belligerency, and are therefore unlawful combatants."[242] Further "in a struggle involving an organization that plainly does not meet the criteria it may be reasonable to proclaim that captured members cannot be considered for POW status. In cases where it is determined that certain detainees are not POWs, they may be considered to be "unlawful combatants."[243]

Others in the discussion have developed theories that expand Article 4 (A)(2). One commentator, Yoram Dinstein, has suggested that although the Geneva Convention repeated the four criteria mentioned in the Hague Convention, two other conditions are implied from the '*chapeau*' of Article 4(A)(2).[244] These two conditions are organization (criteria v) and belonging to a party to the conflict (criteria vi). Furthermore, another condition has been interpreted from case law which is lack of duty to allegiance to the Detaining Power (criteria vii).[245]

Dinstein stresses that the fifth condition (organization), reinforces the first condition. "Lawful combatants must act within a hierarchic

---

241 *Id.* at 29-30. Jiri Torman, *Terrorism and the Regulation of Armed Conflict, International Terrorism and Political Crimes*, 40-41 (M. Cherif Bassiouni, ed., 1973).

242 Bialke *supra* note 125, at 21-23.(Bialke maintains that the laws of armed conflict specify actions a lawful combatant or force may carry out and that these laws are strictly enforced to protect innocent civilians and decrease the amount of destruction. "Specifically, all combat operations must follow the 1949 Geneva Conventions and other basic principles of LOAC, such as: identifying and attacking only military objectives (military necessity); preventing unnecessary suffering and destruction (humanity/chivalry); ensuring that reasonably estimated incidental civilian casualties and collateral damage are not excessive in relation to the military advantage reasonably anticipated (proportionally); and identify and discriminating between combatants and noncombatants in combat targeting, primarily in order to protect the civilian population).

243 Roberts, *supra* note 112, at 230.

244 Dinstein, *supra* note 198, at 160.

245 *Id.*

framework, embedded in discipline, and subject to supervision by upper echelons of what is being done by subordinate units in the field."[246] Application of the sixth condition (belonging to a party to the conflict) was addressed by an Israeli Military Court in the *Kassem* case.[247]

In the *Kassem* case, several people from the organization "Popular Front for the Liberation of Palestine" entered the West Bank for hostile purposes.[248] They were captured and charged with security offenses.[249] The members of the organization argued that they were entitled to prisoner of war status.[250] "The Israeli Military Court held that irregular forces must belong to a party to the conflict."[251] Because no Arab government at war with Israel assumed responsibility for the organization's actions, this condition was not fulfilled.[252]

A possible seventh condition recognized by Dinstein is non-allegiance to the Detaining Power.[253] He acknowledges that while it is not specifically mentioned in the Geneva Convention it has been developed through judicial decisions. The primary judicial opinion on this issue is from the Privy Council in 1967 in the *Koi* case.[254] In *Koi*, Indonesian paratroopers landed and were captured in Malaysia.[255] A number of the paratroopers were Malays. They were all sentenced to death for having unlawfully possessed arms in a security zone. They appealed and argued they were entitled to prisoner of war status.

"The Privy Council held (per Lord Hodson) that nationals of the Detaining Power, as well as other persons owing it a duty of allegiance, are not entitled to such status."[256] The Privy Council held that it was a matter of customary international law and that the Third Geneva

---

[246] *Id.* at 162

[247] *Military Prosecutor v. Kassem*, 42 INT'L L. R. 470 (Israel, Military Court, 1969).

[248] *Id.*

[249] *Id.*.

[250] *Id.*

[251] *Id.* at 476

[252] *Id.* at 477-478.

[253] Dinstein, *supra* note 198, at 163.

[254] *Public Prosecutor v. Koi*, [1967] A.C. 829.

[255] Dinstein, *supra* note 198, at 163.

[256] Dinstein, *supra* note 198, at163, *Public Prosecutor v. Koi*, A.C. 829, 856-58 (1967).

Convention, articles 87 and 100, require that prisoners of war are not nationals of the Detaining Power and do not owe it any duty of allegiance.[257] Therefore, according to Dinstein, case law has created a seventh requirement – non-allegiance to the Detaining Power.

While Dinstein believes there are seven conditions irregular forces must satisfy to be accorded prisoner of war status, other scholars (Goldman and Tittemore) stipulate six conditions to be awarded such status:[258]

1) they must belong to an organized group;

2) the group must belong to a Party to the conflict;

3) the group must be commanded by a person responsible for his subordinates;

4) the group must ensure that its members have a fixed, distinctive sign recognizable from a distance;

5) the group must ensure that its members carry their arms openly; and

6) the group must ensure that its members conduct their operations in accordance with the laws and customs of war.[259]

The first requirement, belonging to an organized group has been interpreted by the ICRC that states, "The implication was that such an organization must have the principal characteristics generally found in armed forces throughout the world, particularly in regard to discipline, hierarchy, responsibility, and honor."[260] The second requirement, that of belonging to Party to the conflict, can be satisfied by a "tacit agreement."[261] In other words, if the Party delivers war material and supplies to the irregular force, the relationship between the two exists. The ICRC Commentary explains that a formal connection is not

---

[257] *Id.* Koi, *Public Prosecutor v. Koi*, A.C. 829, 857 (1967).
[258] Goldman and Tittemore, *supra* note 105, at 11.
[259] *Id.*
[260] ICRC Commentary GPW, *supra* note 205, at 58.
[261] Goldman and Tittemore, *supra* note 105.

necessary, what is essential "...is a de facto relationship between the resistance organization and the party to international law which is in a state of war, but the existence of this relationship is sufficient."[262] Thus, as long as there as a relationship exists between the Party and the irregular forces, this requirement has been satisfied. Goldman and Tittemore offer these two additional requirements in addition to the four detailed in GPW and suggest that "If the members, generally, meet all six conditions all the time, then an individual member who fails to observe any of the last three conditions will not lose his privileged combatant status or prisoner of war status upon capture."[263] Based on leading authorities, they conclude that the entire group must meet the first three requirements and the last three requirements apply to both the group as a whole and to its individual members.

The discussion of Article 4(A)(2) provided key positions on the applicability of these Articles to POW status and therefore unlawful combatants. According to Dinstein, "Unlawful combatants may be tried for violations of ordinary domestic laws and they may also be detained without trial (as long as the hostilities by the force to whom they belong go on)."[264] And finally, he argues that it is imperative to maintain the distinction of lawful and unlawful combatant. To do otherwise, would put civilians and combatants in danger.[265] However, Dinstein does offer a caveat in which Article 4(A)(2) conditions might be alleviated. Such situation is described as situations of "*levee en masse*"[266] or mass uprising.

He suggests that this exception temporarily suspends a few of the conditions to inhabitants of unoccupied territory and if the civilian population must take up arms immediately, without an opportunity to organize themselves, because they are being invaded. They must however, follow two of the seven conditions under Article 4. They must respect the laws of war and carry arms openly. The exception does not last for an extended length of time because one of the three things will inevitably occur: "...either the territory will be occupied (thanks to the 'levee en masse'); or the invading force will be repulsed

[262] ICRC COMMENTARY GPW, *supra* 205, at 59.
[263] Id. *See also* Gill et al, *supra* note 51, at 35.
[264] Dinstein, *supra* note 198, at 174.
[265] *Id.*
[266] *Id.* at165.

(thanks to the 'levee en masse' or to the timely arrival of reinforcements); or the battle of defense will stabilize, and then there is ample opportunity for organization."[267]

Generally it is recognized that Article 4(A) (2) constructs a framework for determining POW status. Roberts states "...in a struggle involving an organization that plainly does not meet the criteria it may be reasonable to proclaim that captured members cannot be considered for POW status. In cases where it is determined that certain detainees are not POWs, they may be considered to be "unlawful combatant."[268] Therefore in Robert's view, it is reasonable to presume that members of an organization that do not meet the criteria for prisoner of war status, may be regarded as unlawful combatants.

A variety of different interpretations to Article 4(A)(2) have been presented in this section. It is apparent that all irregular forces must have a leader responsible for the actions of subordinates, distinguish themselves from civilian population, carry their weapons openly and abide by the laws and customs of war. Another largely debated issue under Article 4 is whether members of the regular force must also satisfy the criteria described in paragraph (A)(2). Many commentators differ whether members of the regular force must satisfy the four criteria. One commentator argues that the drafters of the Third Geneva Convention crafted the four criteria of Article 4(A)(2) "because they believed these criteria were indicative of the characteristics inherent in the regular armed forces of a State."[269] Therefore, it should be logical to assume the four conditions are inherent to regular armed forces because it would be unreasonable to grant prisoner of war status to an organization that met a far lower standard than that met by the regular armed force of a state and those forces must satisfy the four criterion to be accorded prisoner of war status and privileges granted with it. Others clearly have disagreed. These lines of reasoning will be explored in the next section.

According to some in the discussion, there is a presumption that the regular forces will satisfy all the requirements. One such assumption was based on the Privy Council's decision in the *Mohamed*

---

[267] *Id.*

[268] Roberts, *supra* note 112, at 230.

[269] Major Ferrell, *supra* note 93, at 101.

Ali case.[270] The Privy Council held "it is not enough to establish that a person belongs to the regular armed forces, in order to guarantee to him the status of prisoner of war."[271] The Privy Council also held that all members of the armed force must abide by the conditions imposed on irregular forces, even though it is not expressly stated in the Geneva Convention.[272] Others believe that a fundamental premise of the Geneva Conventions has been that to "earn the right to protection as military fighters, soldiers must distinguish themselves from civilians by wearing uniforms and carrying their weapons openly ... Fighters who attempt to take advantage of civilians by hiding among them in civilian dress, with their weapons out of view, lose their claim to be treated as soldiers. The law thus attempts to encourage fighters to avoid placing civilians in unconscionable jeopardy."[273] Therefore, a combatant may forfeit his entitlement to prisoner of war status if he intentionally fails to distinguish himself from the civilian population.

A counter-argument, however, has evolved from the ICRC and others. Based on the above claim, some have noted there is no obligation in international humanitarian law to wear uniforms for distinction with general population[274] and propose that no formal definition exists in international law concerning the composition of a military uniform. They do, however, concur that it is illegal for a combatant to wear civilian clothing if the combatant's motive involves perfidy.[275] This act would indicate that a member of the regular armed

---

270 *Mohamed Ali v. Public Prosecutor*, [1969]1 A.C. 430, 449.

271 Dinstein, *supra* note 198, at 159.

272 *Mohamed Ali v. Public Prosecutor*, 1 A.C. 430, 449-50 (1969).

273 Remarks by Judge Sofar at the Sixth Annual American Red Cross-Washington College of Law "Conference on International Humanitarian Law: A Workshop on Customary International Law and the 1977 Protocols Additional to the 1949 Geneva Conventions" American Journal of International Law and Policy, Vol. 2 (1987) 460.

274 Toni Pfanner, *Military Uniforms and the Law of War*, IRRC March Vol. 86 No. 853 at 114 -115. *See albso*, Duffy, *supra* note 156, at 399 ("...the criteria set forth by Article 4 of the Geneva Convention only apply to irregulars that fight alongside a party to the conflict and not to the armed forces of a party to the conflict itself.")

275 *See also* Commentary Additional Protocol I to the 1949 Geneva Convention July 1977 (discussing Article 37(1)(c), "A combatant who takes part in an attack, or in a military operation preparatory to an attack, can use camouflage and make himself virtually invisible against a natural or man-made

forces cannot forfeit his entitlement to prisoner of war status if he fails to distinguish himself from civilians, unless the intent is to betray the enemy State.

Disharmony over agreement on compliance of the four conditions has also arisen. The ICRC state "The four conditions which these Regulations impose on militias and corps of volunteers were reproduced and it was made clear that these conditions apply to militias and corps of volunteers not forming part of the regular armed forces..."[276] Thus, according to the ICRC Commentary, members of the regular armed forces do not have to satisfy the four requirements to be entitled to prisoner of war status.

Additionally, the ICRC Commentary states that it is unnecessary to specify the sign that armed forces should have to distinguish themselves. "It is the duty of each State to take steps so that members of its armed forces can be immediately recognized as such and to see it to it that they are easily distinguishable from members of the enemy armed forces or from civilians."[277]

Another scholar has presented the opinion that the intent of Article 4(A)(1) is that regular armed forces, including members of militia and volunteer corps, do not have to formally fulfill the four criteria to be entitled to prisoner of war status[278] and further proposing that members of a regular force, if captured, automatically have prisoner of war status because of their relationship to the de jure government.[279] "The very spirit of the Third Geneva Convention is contingent on this relationship which entails that members of armed forces of a State engaged in an international armed conflict are lawfully participating in hostilities and must not be punished for their mere participation in the conflict.[280] Providing historical proof of this application, the author notes that "In the Second World War of 1939-1945, there was no precedent for a general refusal of prisoner of war status for members of the armies

---

background, but he may never feign a civilian status and hide amongst a crowd. This is the crux of the rule." at 438. p. 106 A combatant engaged in espionage and is subsequently captured, is treated and tried as a spy. "Additional Protocol I...explicitly mentions the wearing of uniforms as an essential factor in deciding whether or not a soldier was engaged in spying." Protocol I, art. 46(2).

276 ICRC Commentary GPW, *supra* note 205.

277 *Id.*

278 Toni Pfanner, *supra* note 274, at 114 -115.

279 *Id.*

280 *Id.* at 115.

which failed as a collective unit to comply with one of the four criteria, in particular the obligation to conduct operations in conformity with the laws and customs of war."[281] This precedent supports the contention that all captured members of regular armed forces automatically have prisoner of war status.

The decisive criterion in order to be entitled to such status is solely on the captured individual's member in a regular armed force.[282] "Only non-integrated militias or volunteers would therefore have to undergo what some have termed the 'legal test for prisoner-of-war status' in order to establish that they were operating in accordance with the four above-mentioned conditions."[283] "Neither the 1907 Hague Regulations nor the Third Geneva Convention explicitly stipulate that a member of regular armed forces has to fulfill the four criteria, including wearing a uniform or at least a distinctive sign ..."[284]

As documented above, there are many different interpretations to the language contained in Article 4 of the Third Geneva Convention. The next section discusses scholar's interpretations of the Fourth Geneva Convention and demonstrates the many differing opinions to its intention and applicability to conflicts.

An equally robust dispute has advanced concerning interpretation of the Fourth Geneva Convention.[285] Parties involved in the discussion have examined whether unlawful combatants are protected under the Fourth Geneva Convention and addresses the ICRC's Commentary on the Fourth Geneva Convention, which states unlawful combatants are "protected persons" described in the Convention.[286] The relevant language in Article 4 of the Convention states, "[p]ersons protected by the Convention are those who, at a given moment and in any manner whatsoever, find themselves, in case of a conflict or occupation, in the hands of a Party to the conflict or Occupying Power of which they are not nationals."[287] Furthermore, ICRC Commentary states, "If members

---

281 *Id.* at 117.
282 *Id.*
283 *Id.* at 115 as cited in: Jordan Paust, "There is no need to revise the laws of war in light of September 11th, <http://www.asil.org/taskforce/paust.pdf> at 8ff.
284 *Id.*
285 1949 Geneva Convention IV Relative to the Protection of Civilian Persons in Time of War, Geneva 12 August 1949, art. 4 [hereinafter GPC]
286 Roberts, *supra* note 112, at 215.
287 GPC, *supra* note 285, at art 4, para. 1.

of a resistance movement...do not fill the conditions [for prisoner of war status], they must be considered to be protected persons within the meaning of the present convention."[288]

According to ICRC's Commentary to the Fourth Geneva Convention Relative to the Protection of Civilian Persons in Time of War Treatment of Prisoners of War Commentary, every individual captured by the enemy must have a status under international law.[289] The individual is either protected as a prisoner of war under the Third Convention or a civilian protected by the Fourth Convention. "There is no 'intermediate status'; nobody in enemy hands can be outside the law."[290] This argument, however, has been countered with the interpretation that the four Geneva Conventions recognize in civil wars that detainees may have a different status other than POW or civilian and thus not everyone can fall into the "protected person" category.[291]

The ICRC Commentary for the Fourth Geneva Convention also addresses the definition of protected person under Article 4.[292] They state this article is meant to protect persons of enemy nationality living in the territory of a belligerent State and the inhabitants of occupied territories. "This Article is, in a sense, the key to the Convention; for it defines the people to whom it refers."[293] Concerning paragraph one of Article 4, the Commentary states, "The definition has been put in a negative form; as it is intended to cover anyone who is not a national of the Party to the conflict or Occupying Power in whose hands he is."[294]

Others interpret the Fourth Geneva Convention to exclude nationals of that Party/Power. Therefore, it follows that if an individual is a citizen of X and is captured and detained by X, the Fourth Geneva Convention would not be applicable to him or her. A very broad reading of this language allows civilians and members of the armed forces to be protected. There are, of course, exceptions to Article 4(1). Article 4 paragraph 2 states:

---

[288] ICRC Commentary on the Fourth Geneva Convention Relative to the Protection of Civilian Persons in the Time of War, Geneva 12 August 1949, (J. Picted Ed., 1960) at. 50. [hereinafter ICRC Commentary GPC]
[289] *Id* at 52.
[290] Roberts, *supra* note 112, at 215.
[291] *Id.* at 216.
[292] ICRC Commentary GPC, *supra* note 288, at 46.
[293] *Id.*
[294] *Id.*

> "Nationals of a State which is not bound by the Convention are not protected. Nationals of a neutral State who find themselves in the territory of a belligerent State, and nationals of a co-belligerent State are not protected while the State of which they are nationals has normal diplomatic representation in the State in whose hands they are."[295]

Some have also pointed out that Article 4, section 4 of the Fourth Geneva Convention states that it does not protect persons protected by the first three Conventions.[296] Therefore, all individuals not protected by the first three Conventions, including individuals who do not meet the four conditions set out in the Third Geneva Convention to be entitled to prisoner of war status, are protected by the Fourth Geneva Convention. However, they are only protected if they are not: "nationals of a State which is not party to the Convention; nationals of the Party/Power in which hands they are; or nationals of a neutral State (only if they are in the territory of a belligerent State) or co-belligerent State with normal diplomatic representation."[297]

Further, a State or Power cannot deny a person protection of the Fourth Geneva Convention simply because that person has unlawfully engaged in hostilities.[298] "On the contrary, Article 5 of GC IV, which allows for some derogation – under strict conditions – from the protections of GC IV, uses the term 'protected persons' with regard to persons detained as spies or saboteurs as well as persons definitely suspected of or engaged in activities hostile to the security of the State/Occupying Power."[299] The language of Article 5 from the Fourth Geneva Convention:

> "Where in the territory of a Party to the conflict, the latter is satisfied that an individual protected person is definitely suspected of or engaged in activities in hostile to the security

---

[295] GPC, *supra* note 285, at art. 4, para.2.

[296] Knut Dormann, "*The Legal Situation of Unlawful/Unprivileged Combatants" in International Review of the Red Cross*," IRRC Vol. 85 March 2003 at 49.

[297] *Id.* at 50.

[298] *Id.*

[299] *Id.*

> of the State, such individual person shall not be entitled to claim such rights and privileges under the present Convention as would, if exercise in the favour of such individual person, be prejudicial to the security of such State.
>
> Where in occupied territory an individual protected person is detained as a spy or saboteur, or as a person under definite suspicion of activity hostile to the security of the Occupying Power, such person shall, in those cases where absolute military security so requires, be regarded as having forfeited rights of communication under the present Convention.
>
> In each case, such persons shall nevertheless be treated with humanity and, in case of trial, shall not be deprived of the rights of fair and regular trial prescribed by the present Convention. They shall also be granted the full rights and privileges of a protected person under the present Convention at the earliest date consistent with the security of the State or Occupying Powers, as the case may be."[300]

This language could be interpreted to qualify protected individuals as including those who participate, without entitlement, in hostilities.[301] In other words, unlawful combatants would be protected under Article 5 of the Fourth Geneva Convention.[302] This interpretation is evident in the U.S. Military Manual which contains a provision for persons committing hostile acts and therefore not entitled to be treated as a prisoner of war.[303] Section 73 of the Manual states:

> "If a person is determined by a competent tribunal, acting in conformity with Article 5 [CG III] not to fall within any of the categories listed in Article 4 [CG III], he is not entitled to be treated as a prisoner of war. He is, however, a 'protected person' within the meaning of Article 4 [CG IV]…"[304]

---

[300] GPC, *supra* note 285, art. 5.
[301] Dorman, *supra* note 296, at 52.
[302] *Id.*
[303] *Id.* as cited in US Military Manual FM 27-10, *supra* note 212, at para. 73.
[304] *Id.*

Additionally, another provision in the Manual defined protected persons as those protected by the Fourth Geneva Convention and included individuals who participated in hostile or belligerent activities and were not entitled to prisoner of war status.[305]

Protected persons, detained under the Fourth Geneva Convention are entitled to be treated humanely[306] although they may be prosecuted for serious violations of international humanitarian law and for war crimes.[307] Article 75 of the Protocol I also states that protected persons must be treated humanely in all circumstances and may not be discriminated against based on race, colour and sex among other things.[308] This article "ensures that no person in the power of a Party to an international armed conflict is outside the protection of international humanitarian law."[309] The conclusion appears to confirm that if unlawful combatants meet the Article 4 nationality criteria of the Fourth Geneva Convention, they are thus protected by that convention.[310]

Another scholar comments on unlawful combatants who do not possess prisoner of war status.[311] Such combatants may be protected persons under Articles 2 and 4 of the Fourth Geneva Convention, however, not all unlawful combatants are not automatically accorded protected persons status. Continuing the theory, "They could have this status if they were fighting in an armed conflict between two nations that have signed the Geneva Conventions and they fell into the hands of one of those nations."[312] Protected persons under the Fourth Geneva Conventions do not have the same rights accorded to prisoners of war but they do have limited rights.

Pointing to Article 5 of the Fourth Geneva Convention which states, "[when an] individual protected person is definitely suspected of or engaged in activities hostile to the security of the State, such individual person shall not be entitled to claim rights and privileges

---

305 *Id.* as cited in US Military Manual FM 27-10, *supra* note 212, at para. 247.
306 *Id.*
307 Dormann, *supra* note 296, at 71 as cited in Baxter, "*Unprivileged Belligerency*" at 344.
308 *Id.* at 67, as cited in, Additional Protocol I, *supra* note 87, art. 75.
309 Dormann, *supra* note 296, at 67.
310 *Id.* at 73.
311 Maggs, *supra* note 127, at 232.
312 *Id.*

under the present Convention."[313] The commentator continues that if an unlawful combatant is suspected of participating in hostilities, he or she will no longer be governed by the Fourth Geneva Convention. Such combatants may be protected under Common Article 3 to the Third and Fourth Geneva Conventions, which would afford them minimum humanitarian protections. This scholar is of the opinion that Common Article 3 is inapplicable to unlawful combatants because it only afford protections to "[p]ersons taking no active part in the hostilities."[314]

It is important to also analyze the significance of Additional Protocol I and II in the matter of lawful and unlawful combatants. Some scholars have insisted that the six requirements that an irregular force must meet in order to be held as a prisoner of war are too stringent and almost impossible for an irregular force to satisfy.[315] Therefore, it was necessary to amend the Four Geneva Conventions to alleviate some of the stringent requirements set out previously and Additional Protocol I[316] was created in 1977. "The compromise, reflected in Articles 43 to 47 of Protocol I, was essentially '[to] relax the rigid requirements of the Hague and Geneva Standards sufficiently to provide guerrillas a possibility of attaining privileged combatant status without exposing the forces fighting them to the danger inherent in the use of civilian disguise in order to achieve surprise.'"[317]

It must be noted that the United States has not ratified Protocol I and II, although "the United States...has a long standing policy of implementing those rules."[318] One suggested reason for the nonratification is the perception that the distinction between lawful and unlawful combatant would become blurred. Critics who wish to erase these differences advocate that "the professional soldier, by his very occupation, must accept the risk of possible attack from civilians, whereas the civilian population must never be exposed to such risk."[319]

---

313 *Id. See* GPC, *supra* note 285, at art 5.

314 *Id.*

315 Goldman & Tittemore, *supra* note 105, at 16.

316 Protocol I, *supra* note 87.

317 Goldman & Tittemore, *supra* note 105, at 15-16 as cited in: Solf, *A response to Douglas J. Feith's Law in the Service of Terror – The Strange Case of the Additional Protocol*, 20 AKRON L. REV. 261 at 272 (1986).

318 Roberts, *supra* note 112, at 216; *See also* Bialke, *supra* note 125, at 7.

319 Major J. L. Whitson, *The Laws of Land Warfare: The Privileged Guerrilla and the Deprived Soldier*, April 6, 1984.

The same concern applies to language in the Protocol that could be understood to imply that belligerents involved in insurgent revolutionary type movements are unable to comply with the Geneva Conventions. Those who support this logic (inability to comply with Geneva Conventions) cite three reasons revolutionaries cannot comply: (1) a disadvantage when confronted with superior fire power and mobility of typical counter-insurgent force; (2) nature of tactics require surprise – thus it is essential they disguise themselves as civilians; and (3) during early stages of insurgency there is no other alternative than terror to mobilize effective operations.[320] It is argued that "reducing these requirements is surely an act which moves one step closer to legalization of subversive and terrorist activities in general."[321]

A discussion concerning Additional Protocol primarily focuses on intricacies in Article 43 thru 45, and 75. Article 43 (1) and (2) are important because they offer a new definition of armed forces. Article 43(1) and (2) state:

> 1. The armed forces of a Party consist of all organized armed forces, groups and units which are under a command responsible to that party for the conduct of its subordinates, even if that Party is represented by a government or an authority not recognized by the adverse Party. Such armed forces shall be subject to an internal disciplinary system which, *inter alia*, shall enforce compliance with the rules of international law applicable in armed conflict.[322]
>
> 2. Members of the armed forces of a Party to a conflict (other than medical personnel and chaplains covered by Article 33 of the Third Convention) are combatants, that is to say, they have the right to participate directly in hostilities.

The new definition has led some to interpret that the language abolishes the distinction between regular armed forces and irregular

---

[320] *Id* as cited in: Jay Baird, *From Nuremberg to My Lai* (Lexington: DC Heath and Company, 1972. 260-265.
[321] *Id* at 7.
[322] Protocol I, *supra* note 87.

voluntary corps, militias and other organized movements which puts all members of a party's armed forces on equal legal footing."[323]

Article 44, paragraph 2, states:

> While all combatants are obliged to comply with the rules of international law applicable in armed conflict, violation of these rules shall not deprive a combatant of his right to be a combatant, or, if he falls into the power of the adverse Party, of his right to be a prisoner of war, except as provided in paragraphs 3 and 4.[324]

Some have inferred therefore that even if a combatant does not abide by the laws of war, he does not forfeit his privilege to be treated as a prisoner of war. The second paragraph establishes that anyone who is denied prisoner of war status and will be tried for their participation in the hostilities, may question their right to prisoner of war status before a judicial tribunal. A shift, therefore, is blatant within the Article and the question of the individual's compliance with the laws of war has shifted and the burden of proof is now on the detaining power, and not the individual (a combatant has to establish that he complied with the laws of war, not his group collectively.)[325]

Opponents counter that Protocol I by no means has been accepted universally.[326] They argue that Protocol I in no way suggests that the other requirements for lawful combatant status set out in Article 4 of the Geneva Convention are not applicable. They point to the ICRC Commentary on Protocol I to strengthen their position. "Anyone who participates directly in hostilities without being subordinate to an organized movement under a Party to the conflict, and enforcing compliance with these rules, is a civilian who can be punished for the sole fact that he has taken up arms" and "anyone who takes up arms without being able to claim this status [of a 'lawful combatant'] will be left to be dealt with by the enemy and its military tribunals in the event that he is captured."[327] Based on their interpretation and the ICRC

---

[323] Goldman & Tittemore, *supra* note 105, at 16.
[324] Protocol I, *supra* note 87, at art. 44(2).
[325] *Id.*
[326] Casey et al., *supra* note 163.
[327] *Id.* as cited in: ICRC Commentary to Protocol I, *supra* note 275, at 383.

Commentary, they respond that any dissonance that the status of unlawful belligerent has been eliminated is false.[328]

Articled 44 (3) states:

> In order to promote the protection of the civilian population from the effects of hostilities, combatants are obliged to distinguish themselves from the civilian population while they are engaged in an attack or in a military operation preparatory to an attack.[329]

Again, disagreement as to the interpretation of this article has emerged. Indeed, some have asserted that the US Senate did not ratify this treaty because it was believed, particularly from wording in the article, that persons who did not abide by the laws of armed conflicts had increased protection.[330] The exception provided in Article 44 (3) implies that a combatant can still maintain lawful combatant status even if he does not wear a uniform or a distinctive sign. This article is "highly controversial internationally because it has been construed to overly broaden the category of unlawful combatants to include un-uniformed guerillas, insurgents, and similar groups."[331] In light of these considerations, many feel risks could be increased for noncombatant civilians.

Opponents to this rationale, emphasize that the language in this article does not identify how the combatants must distinguish themselves and even if an individual fails to distinguish himself from the civilian population, they will not lose their privilege to prisoner of war status (although they can be prosecuted and punished for failing to distinguish themselves from the civilian population.[332] However, he can be prosecuted and punished for failing to distinguish himself from the civilian population.[333]

Articles 45 and 75 within Protocol I states that individuals involved in an international armed conflict may have a status other than

---

[328] Casey et al, *supra* note 163, at 4.
[329] Protocol I, *supra* note 87, at art 44, para. 3.
[330] Bialke, *supra* note 125, at 29.
[331] *Id.*
[332] Goldman & Tittemore, *supra* note 105, at 19
[333] *Id.*

prisoner of war, but if denied that status still has legal rights.[334] Article 45 of 1977 Geneva Protocol I states, "Any person who has taken part in hostilities, who is not entitled to prisoner-of-war status and who does not benefit from more favorable treatment…shall have the right at all times to the protection of Article 75 of this Protocol."[335] Article 75 provides basic rights that provide minimum rules of protection for those not entitled to prisoner of war status. The United States has generally implemented these rules.[336] Roberts acknowledges that while the United States is not a party to the 1977 Geneva Protocol I, it has a long standing policy of implementing those rules.[337]

Some scholars have discussed that the language in Protocol I reaffirmed their interpretation of the Fourth Geneva Convention in that unlawful combatants are protected persons if they satisfy the nationality requirements.[338] The language in Article 45, section three of Protocol I clearly makes it evident that the Fourth Geneva Convention applies to some categories of unlawful combatants "otherwise the formulation 'who does not benefit from more favourable treatment in accordance with the Fourth Convention' would be meaningless."[339] ICRC Commentary agrees and state, "In armed conflict with an international character, a person of enemy nationality who is not entitled to prisoner-of-war status is, in principle, a civilian protected by the Fourth Convention, so that there are no gaps in protection…This is one of the reasons why the paragraph under consideration here provides that in the absence of more favourable treatment in accordance with the four Convention, the accused is entitled at all times to the protection of Article 75 of the Protocol."[340]

Further discussion of Article 75 of the Protocol reveals that it is generally viewed as customary law and binds non-parties as well as parties to the instrument.[341] Once it has been determined that an individual is an unlawful combatant and denied prisoner of war status, he does not fall outside the scope of international humanitarian law and

---

[334] Roberts, *supra* note 112, at 216. *See also* Dormann, *supra* note 296, at 50.
[335] Protocol I, *supra* note 87, at art. 45.
[336] Roberts, *supra* note 112, at 216.
[337] *Id.*
[338] Dormann, *supra* note 296, at 50.
[339] *Id* at 51.
[340] ICRC Commentary on Protocol I, *supra* note 275.
[341] Gill et al, *supra* note 51, at 36.

human rights law and the protections that correlate with them. "If a person is not entitled to prisoner of war status on the basis of such a determination, he or she will always be entitled to the fundamental guarantees provided for under Article 75 of Additional Protocol I, unless he or she is entitled to more favourable treatment from other provisions of humanitarian law."[342] Thus, the unlawful combatant will be protected under Additional Protocol I or will benefit from a more favorable status. Therefore it has been interpreted that Additional Protocol I provides for guarantees of humane treatment and fundamental rights for the prisoner, including due process and fair trial by "an impartial and regularly constituted court respecting the generally recognized principles of regular judicial procedure."[343]

The numerous different interpretations of international treaties demonstrate that the laws of war are never black and white. There are many different interpretations of the language provided in the treaties. It can be assumed however a unanimous definition of lawful combatants exists. A lawful combatant can engage in hostilities and cannot be prosecuted for their participation in hostilities and is entitled to be detained as a prisoner of war. On the other hand, the definition and subsequent detainment of an unlawful combatant, as evidenced above, is not so clear. Some historical definitions and notions of unlawful combatant (not pertaining to a particular treaty) are discussed below.

"The uncertainties regarding the status and treatment of people who are involved in hostile activities in various ways, but who fail to meet the criteria for POW status, are reflected in muddled terminology."[344] This sentiment is evident when attempting to find a universally accepted term for persons described in the preceding quotation. Many use the term unlawful combatant (the term chosen by the author). Other terms that are used interchangeably with unlawful combatant are unprivileged belligerent or unprivileged combatant.[345] Additionally, illegal combatant, franc-tireur (meaning free shooter),

---

[342] *Id.*
[343] *Id.* at 38 as cited in: Additional Protocol I, *supra* note 87, art, 75.
[344] Roberts, *supra* note 112, at 214.
[345] Dormann, *supra* note 296, at 45. (Generally these terms are not used in international treaties but are evident in legal literature, military manuals and case law.)

and dishonorable belligerent appear in the literature.[346] One author suggested that "the term unlawful/unprivileged combatant/belligerent is understood as describing all persons taking a direct part in hostilities without being entitled to do so and who therefore cannot be classified as prisoners of war on falling into the power of the enemy."[347]

It is important, as has been proposed throughout this chapter, to determine the status of a combatant as lawful or unlawful. Succinctly put, "The distinction between lawful and unlawful combatants complements the fundamental distinction between combatants and civilians: the primary goal of the former is to preserve the latter."[348] Distinguishing between lawful and unlawful combatants "is a balanced, time-honored, and practical method of encouraging compliance with the laws of armed conflict."[349]

Berman counters that terminology is immaterial. "The legally correct term "unprivileged combatants' suggests the consequences of the failure to meet [those] criteria. Engagement in combat by those not covered by the combatants' privilege, assuming no war crimes were committed, is not illegal per se under international law. Rather, since such acts are not immunized by international law, the contending Parties are free to punish individuals engaged in such activities under their own law." Further, "it is argued that the term 'unlawful combatant' united crime and combat in a manner that short-circuited the alternative between two bodies of law. This seemed to create a category of rightless persons – neither criminal suspects nor prisoners of war, committed to the caprice of unreviewable state power."[350]

Many critics concur with the above opinion and have adamantly questioned President Bush's interpretation of the distinction between lawful and unlawful combatant and his decision to detain al Qaeda and Taliban members in the latter category.

---

[346] Bialke, *supra* note 125, at 10.
[347] *Id.*
[348] Dinstein, *supra* note 198, at 153 as cited in: Theodor Meron, *Some Legal Aspects of Arab Terrorists' Claims to Privileged Combatancy*, 40 NORDISK TIDDKRIFT FOR INT'L RET 47, 62 (1970).
[349] Bialke, *supra* note 139, at 14.
[350] Berman, *supra* note 39, at 13.

SECTION THREE: Appropriate Classification

One of the first public statements concerning the status of al Qaeda and Taliban members was delivered by Secretary of Defense Donald Rumsfeld on January 22, 2002. The Secretary announced that al Qaeda and Taliban members (under the control of the Department of Defense) are not accorded the privilege of prisoner of war status. The detainees, although not prisoners of wars, will still be treated humanely "and to the extent appropriate and consistent with military necessity, in a manner consistent with principles of the Geneva Conventions of 1949.[351]

In February, 2002, Attorney General John Ashcroft penned a letter to President Bush stating that if the President determined that Afghanistan was a failed state, "various legal risks of liability, litigation, and criminal prosecution are minimized."[352] This outcome would assure that the US Armed Forces, intelligence, or law enforcement officers would not be prosecuted for violating the Convention because "the President's decision that the treaty was not in force would be conclusive."[353] An uproar over the United State's decision to not apply the Geneva Conventions arose because of concerns that US Armed Forces or intelligence officers would not be prosecuted for alleged detainee abuse and other such issues.

Shortly afterwards (February 7, 2002), President Bush wrote a memorandum to Vice President Cheney, Secretary of State Powell, Secretary of Defense Rumsfeld, Attorney General Ashcroft, and other administration staff, including Joint Chiefs of Staff General Myers. In this memo, President Bush relied on advice from the Department of Justice and Attorney General Ashcroft, and concluded that none of the provisions of the Geneva Convention are applicable to the conflict with al Qaeda in Afghanistan or anywhere else because al Qaeda is not a High Contracting Party to the Convention. The President also reaffirmed his decision to suspend the Convention between the United States and Afghanistan. President Bush declared that Article 3 of the

---

[351] Department of Defense News Briefing with Secretary of Defense Donald Rumsfeld and General Peter, Jan 22, 2002. available at: http://www.defenselink.mil/Transcripts/Transcript.aspx?TranscriptID=2254 .

[352] Letter to the President, from Attorney General Ashcroft (Feb. 1, 2002).

[353] Yoo, *supra* note 7, at 42.

Geneva Convention did not apply to al Qaeda and the Taliban detainees because common Article 3 applies only to armed conflict not of an international character. The President concluded that al Qaeda and the Taliban detainees were unlawful combatants and as such did not qualify as prisoners of war under Article 4 of the Convention but would be treated humanely and to the extent possible consistent with the principles of the Geneva Convention.[354]

The White House also released a fact sheet on February 7, 2002 about the status of detainees held at Guantanamo Bay. The fact sheet included President Bush's determination that the Geneva Conventions applied to the Taliban detainees, but under the terms of the Convention they were not entitled to prisoner of war status. Furthermore, the Geneva Convention is not applicable to al Qaeda detainees. The fact sheet concluded that "al Qaeda is not a state party to the Geneva Convention; it is a foreign terrorist group. As such, its members are not entitled to POW status.[355]

White House Press Secretary Ari Fleischer, addressed questions regarding the President's decision that Taliban members did not qualify as prisoners of war. Statements regarding Taliban included the decision that they did not qualify as prisoners of war because they did not satisfy the four conditions under Article 4 of the Third Geneva Conventions. More specifically, Fleischer alluded to the fact that they did not wear uniforms, were not visibly identifiable, and did not belong to a military hierarchy. Fleischer also emphasized that the United States would treat all detainees humanely, regardless of their status.[356]

On February 28, 2002, Secretary of Defense Rumsfeld conducted a news briefing and elaborated on the President's decisions regarding the detention of al Qaeda and Taliban members. He stated, "From the beginning, the United States armed forces have treated all detainees, both Taliban and al Qaeda, humanely." He continued that he had "ordered the military to treat all detainees humanely and in a manner

---

[354] Memorandum for the Vice President, Secretary of State, Secretary of Defense…Re: Human Treatment of al Qaeda and Taliban Detainees (Feb. 7, 2002).

[355] Office of the White House Press Secretary. Fact Sheet: Status of Detainees at Guantanamo (Feb. 7, 2002), available at http://www.whitehouse.gov/news/releases/2002/02/20020207-13.html.

[356] White House Press Secretary Ari Fleischer, Press Briefing at the White House (Feb. 7, 2002) available at http://www.whitehouse.gov/news/releases/2002/02/20020207-6.html#3.

that is consistent with the Geneva Conventions. He emphasized that the primary purpose of the Geneva Convention was to "protect innocent civilians by distinguishing very clearly between combatants and non-combatants" and that Taliban members do not distinguish themselves as they do not wear uniforms, nor do they wear distinctive signs, insignias, or symbols. The Secretary expanded "To the contrary, far from seeking to distinguish themselves from the civilian population of Afghanistan, they sought to blend in with civilian non-combatants, hiding in mosques and populated areas." Additionally, the Secretary commented that the Taliban armed forces were not organized military units and therefore did not have an identifiable main command. He concluded that to reward combatants with prisoner of war status, who did not respect the laws of ward, would undermine the conventions incentive system and greatly increase the risk of civilian injuries and death.[357]

The Department of Defense released their definition of enemy combatant on July, 2004. The July Order stated "An enemy combatant…shall mean an individual who is part of or supporting Taliban or al Qaeda forces, or associated forces that are engaged in hostilities against the United States or its coalition partners. This includes any person who has committed a belligerent act or has directly supported hostilities in aid of enemy armed forces."[358]

On July 7, 2006, after much debate and criticism over the Bush Administration's decision to deny prisoner of war status to al Qaeda and Taliban members, the Department of Defense announced that Common Article 3 of the Geneva Conventions does apply to the current situation. The Supreme Court had recently released its opinion on the *Hamdan* case, which held that Common Article 3 to the Geneva Conventions of 1949 applies as a matter of law to the conflict with al Qaeda. The memorandum issued by the Department of Defense stated

---

[357]Press Conference, Dept. of Defense, Secretary Rumsfeld & General Myers, Feb. 8, 2002, available at http://www.defenselink.mil/Transcripts/Transcript.aspx?TranscriptID=2624 [hereinafter RUMSFELD STATEMENT.]

[358] Department of Defense News Briefing, Combatant Status Review Tribunals Order of the Deputy Secretary of Defense , 7 July 2004, available at http://www.defenselink.mil/news/Jul2004/d20040707review.pdf.

that application of Common Article 3 did not change the legal status of the Parties to the conflict.[359]

President Bush's decision regarding the detention of unlawful combatants sparked a massive amount of criticism. Much debate arose over President Bush's decision not to grant detainees the rights under the Geneva Convention. Several scholars, organizations and even politicians were very vocal with their concerns and criticisms of his decision. One of the primary criticisms of President Bush's February, 2002 determination that al Qaeda and Taliban members would not be held as prisoners of war was the lack of information that determined the rationale and reasoning behind his decision. The Bush Administration did not provide much detail about the President's decision. Those who opposed Bush's determination, after repeatedly asking for clarification and denied such information, speculated his reasoning when addressing their criticism. However the government remained tight lipped about his decisions. The following arguments describe supporters or opponents' view of the President's decision.

John Yoo was an attorney at the Office of Legal Counsel (OLC) at the Department of Justice and was a part of the legal team that advised President Bush about the applicability of the Geneva Convention to the present conflict.[360] Yoo with other colleagues at OLC drafted a legal memorandum to President Bush that concluded he had the power "not only to retaliate against any person, organization, or state suspected of involvement in terrorist attacks on the United States, but also against foreign states suspected of harboring or supporting such organizations." The President had the authority to use force abroad without Congressional authorization based prior Justice Departments and attorney general actions in the past. "Nearly all scholars agree that if the United States were attacked, no declaration of war was necessary and the President could immediately respond with armed force. Congressional support was welcome, but in our view it was not constitutionally required."[361]

359 US Department of Defense, Office of the Secretary of Defense, Memorandum for Secretaries of the Military Departments, from US Deputy Defense Secretary Gordon England, Application of Common Article 3 of the Geneva Convention to the Treatment of Detainees in the Department of Defense, July 7, 2006.

360 Yoo, *supra* note 7, at 20.

361 *Id.* at 10-11.

They also advised the President that if the Taliban did not follow the laws of war they could be considered unlawful combatants and thus not afforded the rights granted by the Geneva Convention.[362] Yoo also discussed the President's ability to grant Geneva Convention protections even if the Convention did not require so. It was not a question of law, but one of policy. In the past, the United State's has granted POW status when not legally required to do so (specific examples will be discussed below). On January 18, 2002, President Bush however decided to not grant these detainees the rights granted by the Geneva Convention, but still declared that they be treated humanely. Yoo argued, "Setting policy within the limits of the law would depend on the circumstances."[363]

The OLC provided President Bush with a memorandum which explained why they believed the Geneva Conventions should not apply to al-Qaeda and Taliban members. Some of the lawyers were concerned that if they were given POW status, our ability to apprehend or interrogate their leaders would be hindered. "Geneva's rules were designed for mass armies, not conspirators, terrorists, or spies."[364]

There are many different points of view concerning application of Geneva Convention with the Taliban, and whether they should receive prisoner of war status. Some scholars discussed whether Afghanistan was a failed state and thus the Geneva Convention would not apply to any individuals captured in the area. Although, it is documented that Afghanistan had previously signed the Geneva Conventions, and thus afforded the protections therein, it was challenged by scholars whether Afghanistan continued as a viable state or whether it was a failed state. The determination of whether Afghanistan was a failed state was a question for the President to make. Attorneys in the Office of Legal Counsel created a test to determine whether a state had "failed." They concluded a failed state was indicated by 'the inability of central authorities to maintain government institutions, ensure law and order, or engage in normal dealings with other governments, and by the prevalence of violence that destabilizes civil society and the

---

[362] *Id.* at 21.
[363] *Id.* at 35.
[364] *Id.* at 39.

economy."[365] The OLC believed that "the Taliban did not perform the basic governmental functions of providing minimal services to the Afghani people."[366] Thus, the OLC opined Afghanistan as a failed state and therefore the Geneva Conventions did not govern this conflict.

Secretary of State Powell wrote a memorandum to the President's counsel in January, 2002, urging the President to follow the Geneva Conventions with regards to the Taliban.[367] Powell argued that President Bush had two choices: (1) determine that the Geneva Convention on the treatment of Prisoners of War (GPW) does not apply to the conflict on 'failed state' or some other grounds, announce position publicly, and treat all detainees consistent with the principles of the GWP; and (2) determine that the Geneva Convention does apply to the conflict in Afghanistan, but that members of al Qaeda as a group and the Taliban individually or as a group are not entitled to Prisoner of War status under the Convention, announce this position publicly, and treat all detainees consistent with the principles of the GPW."[368]

Supporters of the Bush Administration's position relate the four requirements under Article 4 of the Geneva Convention to Taliban members. In their determination, the Taliban do not meet the first requirement, being commanded by a person responsible for his subordinates, because they do not have an "organized, identifiable chain of command."[369] Evidence offered to defend this conclusion was based on a number of alleged facts such as the Taliban's outright rejection of the laws of armed conflict. The Taliban's Supreme Leader, Mullah Mohammed, declared that the laws "were merely a manifestation of a false Judeo-Christian Western ideology..." No evidence that the Taliban held any of its members accountable for violations of both the laws or armed conflict and international humanitarian law. Quite to the contrary, the Taliban's actions consistently and openly violated such laws. Furthermore, Taliban

---

[365] Yoo, *supra* note 7, at 27 (Yoo emphasizes that international law did not have a defined criterion for a failed state).

[366] *Id.* at 28.

[367] Memorandum to the Counsel to the President & the Assistant to the President for National Security Affairs, From: Colin L. Powell, Secretary of State, Subject: Draft Decision Memorandum for the President on the Applicability of the Geneva Convention to the Conflict in Afghanistan (Jan. 26, 2002). [hereinafter Powell Memo].

[368] *Id.*

[369] Bialke *supra* note 125, at 30.

command structure was "ambiguous, constantly changing among tribal and warlord alliances, with blurred lines between civilian and military authority."[370] Therefore, the Taliban has repeatedly failed to meet the first requirement.

Applying the remaining requirements to the Taliban, also confirmed the interpretation that the Taliban failed to meet other requirements (e.g., not having a fixed distinctive sign – because Taliban members did not wear a uniform.) Indeed, it was alleged that some members of the Taliban were captured while disguised in traditional female burqas in mosques. The third requirement (carry arms openly) was also not deemed to apply to the Taliban members. Some Taliban members concealed their weapons inside "common civilian clothing to unlawfully feign protected civilian status and blend into the noncombatant civilian population."[371] This requirement is not to be dismissed lightly because "a fundamental premise to the Geneva Convention has been that to earn the right to protection as military fighters, soldiers must distinguish themselves from civilians by wearing uniforms and carrying their weapons openly…Fighters, who attempt to take advantage of civilians by hiding among them in civilian dress, with their weapons out of view, lose their claim to be treated as soldiers."[372] Cultural mores, however, provided a challenge in determining the application of the third requirement because Afghani culture includes carrying firearms openly.

The final requirement, conduct military operations in according with the laws and customs of war, was also not satisfied because "The Taliban adopted and perpetuated an unrestrained, institutionally declared policy and practice of total disregard for LOAC and international humanitarian law."[373] "In stark contrast to the US treatment of enemy combatants detained in Cuba, evidence indicates that the Taliban and al-Qaeda severely beat and murdered the only US service-member they captured during the Afghanistan armed conflict."[374]

---

[370] *Id.*
[371] *Id.*
[372] Remarks by Judge Abraham D. Sofaer, *supra* note 273, at 466.
[373] Bialke *supra* note 125, at 31-32.
[374] *Id.* at 32.

"Because of the Taliban's symbiotic association with and direct support of the al-Qaeda terrorist network, the Taliban surrendered any legitimate claim to de jure nation-state status within the larger international community."[375] Additionally, the Taliban ignored the United Nations General Assembly's request to seize and expel al Qaeda from Afghanistan and they also disregarded the United Nations Security Council's condemnations.[376] Therefore, many defenders determined that the Taliban clearly has not satisfied any of the four requirements set out in Article 4 and as such are not entitled to prisoner of war status.

Opponents argue several of the above points and caution that not every member of the Taliban force falls within the same category. "Ample evidence exists to indicate that many of the rank and file Taliban were orthodox, if not fundamentalist, followers of Islam who had taken up arms only against the Northern Alliance."[377] As to the four requirements set out by the third Geneva Convention, it can be argued that some Taliban units were under a proper command and that they satisfied the distinctive emblem requirement because they wore black head covering of a similar type.[378] Furthermore, they did carry their arms openly, and it is uncertain whether the Taliban complied with the laws and customs of war because there were no real land operations for this to be studied.[379]

Some commentators addressed whether Taliban members were required to distinguish themselves from the civilian population and noted "...the Taliban forces certainly were not standard armed forces and did not wear clothing that resembled traditional military uniforms."[380] On the other hand, other commentators argue that it is well known that Taliban members customarily wear distinctive dark turbans.[381]

---

[375] *Id.*

[376] *Id* at 33-34.

[377] Leslie Green, *Jus in Bello*, 79 International Law Studies, 238 (2003).

[378] *Id.* at 240.

[379] *Id.*

[380] Pfanner, *supra* note 274, at 117.

[381] Goldman & Tittemore, *supra* note 105, at 26. ("Indeed, they may permissibly dress in civilian clothing so long as they also wear some distinctive sign, which can be a cap or an armband that visibly distinguishes them from the civilian population.")

Most states require their armed forces to wear a uniform, however, the question of whether or not a captured member of the regular armed forces who fails to meet the requirement of distinction loses his rights to be treated as a prisoner of war, has not been answered. According to the Privy Council "But State practice and jurisprudence indicate clearly that combatants who do not distinguish themselves from the civilian population while engaged in an attack or in a military operation prior to an attack shall forfeit their rights as prisoners of war."[382]

Other scholars emphasize the US's past in granting combatants prisoner of war status, even if they were not entitled to such. For example, they state that the United States granted prisoner of war status to individual detained during the Korean and Vietnam war who did not comply with the laws of war. They conclude, "consistent with the law and past US practice, members of the Taliban's armed forces should either have been unconditionally granted prisoner of war status, or at a minimum, been presumed to be prisoners of war unless and until subsequently determined otherwise as required by the Third Geneva Convention.[383] Furthermore, according to another scholar, "members of the armed forces who persistently violate the Law of War do not lose their POW status upon capture."[384]

Some who challenge the administration's decision concerning Taliban designation acknowledge the fact that some Taliban members hid in mosques or tried to blend into the civilian population and thus placed innocent civilians in danger. However, they argue that such "shielding" activities by regular armed are punishable, but they cannot divest a combatant's entitlement to prisoner of war status.[385]

Others discuss while only three states recognized the Taliban as the legitimate government of Afghanistan before the September 11 attacks,

---

[382] Pfanner, *supra* note 274, at 120 as cited in: *Osman case*, House of Lords (Privy Council) on Appeal from the Federal Court, cited from Sassoli and Bouvier, *How Does Law Protect War? Cases, Documents and Teaching Materials on Contemporary Practice in International Humanitarian Law, International Committee of the Red Cross, Geneva,* 1999, pp. 923-943 at 773

[383] Goldman & Tittemore, *supra* note 105, at 26.

[384] *Id.* at 10, as cited in: Draper, *The Present Law as to Combatancy*, in REFLECTIONS ON LAW AND ARMED CONFLICTS: THE SELECTED WORKS ON THE LAWS OF WARY BY THE LATE COLONEL G.I.A.C. DRAPER, OBE 197 (Myers & McCoubrey eds., 1998).

[385] Goldman & Tittemore, *supra* note 105, at 10.

there is a serious question as to whether their members ever attained the status of lawful combatant.[386] Therefore, if the Taliban members do not meet any of the four conditions they will not be entitled to prisoner of war status.

Additionally, they stress others ground for detaining Taliban members as unlawful combatants. "Killing prisoners-of-war, massacring civilians, the wanton destruction of civilian property, and treating women as 'the spoils of war' violate both the customary laws of war, and treaty-based norms, including the Geneva Convention of 1949 to which Afghanistan is, itself, a party."[387] If these horrendous acts are conducted by individual elements of an armed force, they are regarded as war crimes and punished on an individual basis. These scholars argue that if it is the policy of the group in question to carry out such horrific activities, they may be held as unlawful belligerents. There is ample evidence to support that the Taliban have killed thousand of innocent civilians and raped several women.[388]

To erase the distinction between lawful and unlawful combatant would in essence undermine the all the effort and intentions in international treaties, which intended to establish rules and legal restraints. Finally, some scholars point out a perilous consequence if the distinction of unlawful and unlawful combatant is erased. "This blurring of distinctions between lawful and unlawful combatants would be tantamount to concluding that there is no difference in the legal rules, applicable to police officers, who discharge their firearms or use other type of force, and criminals, who engage in similar activities. Without a doubt, this blurring of distinctions between a privileged and illegal use of force would destroy an entire 'law and order' system and would undermine the viability of any body that permitted it."[389]

Dinstein points out that before the war the Taliban was in de facto control of Afghanistan, even though most of the international community did not recognize them as such. However, the fact that the Taliban was not recognized as the government does not eliminate the

---

[386] *Id.*

[387] Casey et al., *supra* note 163, at 8.

[388] Casey et al, supra note 163, at 8, as cited in: Neamatollah Nojumi, *The Rise of the Taliban in Afghanistan: Mass Mobilization, Civil War, and the Future of the Region* 229 (2002).

[389] *Id.*

privileges of combatants under customary international law.[390] Regardless of the question of whether the Taliban forces were recognized or unrecognized, they are still bound by the seven requirements of lawful combatancy. "The proper question, therefore, is not whether the Taliban regime was recognized but whether the Taliban forces actually observed all of these conditions."[391] He argues Taliban members are unlawful combatants for two reasons. First, they fall under Article 4(A)(3) of the Third Geneva Convention because they are members of an armed force professing allegiance to a government that is not recognized by the Detaining Power. Such individuals are entitled to prisoner of war status. However, in Dinstein's opinion, to be accorded that privilege, the armed force must still comply with the conditions of lawful combatancy.[392]

Dinstein argues that the Taliban failed to satisfy those conditions. He believes that the Taliban did carry their arms openly but that they did not wear their uniforms or a distinctive emblem.[393] To satisfy the conditions, you must meet all of them, not just one or two. Therefore, Dinstein argues the Taliban is not entitled to prisoner of war status.

A judge at the Iran-US Claims Tribunal, also discussed whether or not Taliban and al Qaeda members were unlawful combatants.[394] Judge Aldrich stated that most questions concerning Taliban and al Qaeda were phrased in terms of entitlement to the status or protection as prisoner of war. However, he believed the proper question was whether or not they were legal or illegal combatants. "In other words, were they persons who had a legal right to take part in hostilities, or, to the contrary, were they persons who could be prosecuted and punished

---

[390] Dinstein, *supra* note 27, at 47.(Dinstein discuses CIA agents in the field – if they were captured without wearing a uniform or distinctive emblem, they would not be entitled to prisoner of war status. "It ought to be emphasized that observance by even ninety-nine percent of the armed forces of a Party to a conflict of the seven conditions of lawful combatancy…does not absolve the remaining one percent from the unshakeable obligation to conduct themselves pursuant to the same conditions.")

[391] *Id.* at 18.

[392] *Id.*

[393] Dinstein, *supra* note 27, at 171.

[394] George H. Aldrich, *The Taliban, al Qaeda, and the Determination of Illegal Combatants, Extract from "Humanitares Volkerrecht*, 96 Am. J. Int'l 891 (2002).

for murder and other crimes under national law simply for their participation in an armed conflict?"[395] Legal combatants are protected under the Geneva Convention and may be detained as prisoners of war but illegal combatants on the other hand, must be charged and prosecuted for their crimes and illegal participation in hostilities.

The judge agreed with the President that there are two separate armed conflicts, one with al Qaeda and another with the Taliban. The Taliban was the effective government of Afghanistan and when the Taliban failed to expel al Qaeda from its safe-haven, an armed conflict was necessary.[396] Because both the United States and Afghanistan were parties to the Geneva Convention of 1949, the armed attack by the US against the armed forces of the Taliban constituted an international armed conflict and therefore the Conventions as well customary international humanitarian law applies. Judge Aldrich discusses the importance of distinguishing between captured al Qaeda and Taliban members, since Taliban members are entitled to prisoner of war status.[397] "As persons who have been combatants in hostilities and are not entitled to POW status, they are entitled, under customary international law to humane treatment of the same nature as that prescribed by Article 3 common to the four Geneva Conventions of 1949 and, in more detail, by Article 75 of Geneva Protocol I of 1977..."[398] The judge argues the threat of prosecution is used to deter illegal combatants.[399]

Another opponent to the Bush Administration's decision to deny prisoner of war status to Taliban members stipulated they are members of an armed force based on Article 43 of Additional Protocol I.[400] Therefore if they are captured they must be treated as prisoners of war and may only be prosecuted for grave breaches and other violations to the Geneva Convention and Protocols. However, one commentator disagreed and stated that even if the United States was a party to the Additional Protocol of 1997, the Taliban would not be entitled to prisoner of war status.[401] More specifically, Article 44(3) in Protocol I

---

395 *Id.* at 892.
396 Aldrich, *supra* note 394, at 893.
397 *Id.*
398 *Id.*
399 *Id.* at 894.
400 Marc Cogen, *supra* note 122, at 4.
401 Bialke, *supra* note 125, at 26-27.

which, erases the requirement for a distinctive sign due to the nature of the hostilities and therefore only requires the combatant to carry arms openly while engaged in hostilities. There is no proof that the nature of hostilities in Afghanistan thwarted the Taliban from acquiring uniforms or a distinctive sign setting them apart from protected noncombatants. "The Taliban armed forces, well funded by al-Qaeda and being in a state of continued internal armed conflict from 1996 forward with the Northern Alliance, could have easily procured and certainly had ample time to affix some form of a distinctive mark by early 2002."[402] Therefore, there are different views as to whether Additional Protocol I, if applicable, would grant prisoner of war status to Taliban members.

Many scholars discussed whether the Geneva Conventions applied to the conflict with al Qaeda and furthermore whether members could be detained as unlawful combatants. Most commentators allude to the fact that the Geneva Conventions are treaties that govern international armed conflicts between parties who have signed them and al Qaeda, as a non-state organization, never signed the Geneva Conventions. "The Geneva Convention even allows a warring power that is not a party to the Conventions to benefit from their protection by voluntarily accepting their terms in a specific war."[403] However, as one commentator noted, al Qaeda has not accepted the Convention's terms. The Conventions are not a law of universal application, they apply only to those who have signed them or abide by the laws of war.

Furthermore, "Al-Qaeda violates every rule and norm developed over the history of war" by specifically targeting innocent civilians.[404] No person or property is immune from their attacks. For example, Osama bin Laden declared in 1998 on American television, "We do not have to differentiate between military or civilian. As far as we are concerned, they are all targets."[405] They do not take prisoners, instead

---

[402] *Id.* at 27.

[403] Yoo, *supra* note 7, at 23.

[404] *Id.*

[405] *Id.* at 17. Yoo also discussed the Judge Advocate Generals (JAGS) disagreement with the Bush Administration decision not to apply the Geneva Conventions to the conflict with al Qaeda. The JAGS argued that the Conventions were now customary international law and thus must apply. Furthermore, despite the fact that al Qaeda is not a Party to the Conventions, "the principles applied to any war and to anyone that the US fought." At 34-35.

they resort to beheading their prisoners and usually televising these atrocious acts.

Bialke argued that because al Qaeda is not confined by any territorial boundaries (as opposed to Taliban operating in almost exclusively in Afghanistan) and because they are not supported or aided by another state, they are stateless. The conduct of stateless armed conflict is not regulated or influenced by a nation, and as such, stateless organizations like al-Qaeda are universally forbidden from participating in armed conflicts. Any participation is unlawful according to international of law. International law forbids private warfare and considers such acts as malum in se, a "wrong in itself."[406]

Furthermore, because al Qaeda is stateless, the Geneva Convention does not grant them all the protections provided to lawful combatants. According to Bialke, an essential prerequisite to be a lawful combatant is that the combatant (in an international armed conflict) must act on behalf of a recognized state or other entity that abides by the laws of armed conflict. Al Qaeda has consistently demonstrated that they do not fight on behalf of a state, rather they fight on behalf of their ideology, their interpretation of Islam. "For instance, Usuama Muhammad bin Awad Laden, al-Qaeda's titular Emir (prince or first-in-command), ordered a fatwa (an Islamic religious dictate) that it is the holy duty of all Muslims to kill all Americans and all their allies, military and civilian, wherever they can be found, especially Zionist Jews."[407]

Bialke also noted that irregardless of al Qaeda's non-state identity and thus exclusion from Geneva Convention protections, al Qaeda consequentially does not qualify as lawful combatant entitled to prisoner of war status because they do not satisfy the four elements stated in the Convention such as al Qaeda members do not have a responsible chain of command and do not wear or display a distinctive sign. Like the Taliban, al Qaeda members repeatedly blend into civilian crowds and do not wear a uniform or any distinctive symbol. The requirement to carry arms openly, is also not met because al Qaeda members usually launch surprise attack by concealing their weapons.

Finally, al Qaeda also does not conduct military operations in accordance with the laws and customs of war. Al Qaeda has repeatedly

---

[406] Bialke, *supra* note 125, at 35.

[407] *Id.* 38, as cited in: Yonah Alexander et al., *Usama bin Laden al-Qaeda: Profile of a Terrorist Network*, APP 1B2 (2001).

violated this requirement due to the fact they have maintained responsibility for firing anti-aircraft against commercial airplanes and members have also been engaged in attempts to assassinate prominent world leaders, including the US President, the Pope and the Egyptian President.[408]

Another scholar addressed whether or not al Qaeda members should be protected under the Fourth Geneva Convention as protected persons.[409] "However, the negotiating history of the Convention is unclear on that question. In any event, the question seems academic in the context of al Qaeda personnel, as the Conventions do not apply to them and as virtually all of them appear to be nationals of States with which the United States has normal diplomatic relations, and such nationals are excluded from the definition of protected persons by Article 4 of the Convention."[410]

Other commentators assert the fact that al Qaeda members were "fighting in an international armed conflict on the side of a state party to the Geneva Conventions against the United States" is essential to determine their combatant status.[411] Furthermore, they argue some al Qaeda members were part of the Taliban armed forces and should not have been denied prisoner of war status. Al Qaeda members who were not part of the Taliban's armed forces, however, must satisfy the requirements set out in the Third Geneva Convention to be detained as a prisoner of war.[412]

Another scholar, argued al Qaeda fighters are categorized as irregular forces under Article 4 of the Third Geneva Convention.[413] Al Qaeda satisfies the requirement of belonging to a Party of the conflict by their relationship with the Taliban. However, al Qaeda members do not meet the conditions expressly required to be entitled to prisoner of war status because al Qaeda members do not wear uniforms or a

---

[408] Bialke, *supra* note 125, at 40.
[409] Aldrich, *supra* note 394, at 203.
[410] *Id.*
[411] Goldman & Tittemore, *supra* note 105, at 29. *See also* Roberts, *supra* note 112, at 211 ("…a key factor in determining whether the lawfulness of a combatant and therefore the entitlement to participate directly in hostilities, is the affiliation of the combatant to a party to the conflict." Taliban was connected to Afghanistan but al Qaeda did not have any connection to a state.)
[412] *Id.* at 30.
[413] Dinstein, *supra* note 198, at 172.

distinctive emblem and more importantly because they do not abide by the laws of war. Thus, they are unlawful combatants and not entitled to prisoner of war status. Furthermore, if captured al Qaeda members owed allegiance to the United States, they could not be expected to be treated as prisoners of war.[414]

One supporter of the Bush Administration opined that the conflict with al Qaeda is not limited to the territory of Afghanistan because it is composed of people from countries all over the world and operates out of different countries. Furthermore, al Qaeda is not in any respect like a State and does not have an international legal personality. Because al Qaeda is not a state, it is not a party to the Geneva Convention or any other international treaty.[415] It follows then that al Qaeda members are illegal combatants and as such cannot be protected by the Geneva Convention and "Its members are properly subject to trial and punishment under national criminal laws for any crimes they commit."[416]

As mentioned by some of the scholars' above arguments, some critics assert that the United State should implement Article 5 of the Third Geneva Convention tribunals to ascertain if a combatant is entitled to prisoner of war status. Article 5 provides for a tribunal if the legal status of a combatant is not evident.[417] The article states, in part, "Should any doubt arise as to whether persons, having committed a belligerent act and having fallen into the hands of the enemy, belong to any of the categories enumerated in Article 4, such persons shall enjoy the protection of the present Convention until such time as their status has been determined by a competent tribunal."[418] One commentary noted since the determination of prisoner of war status is a question of fact and rather than adjudication, a judicial body is not necessary and an administrative board suffices.[419]

Another defender of the government's decision to convene military commissions addressed language in Article 5.[420] The organization of the tribunal is not expressly stated in the Convention and thus defers to

---

414 *Id.*at 173.
415 Aldrich, *supra* note 394.
416 *Id.*
417 GPW, *supra* note 182, at art. 5.
418 *Id.*
419 Gill et al, *supra* note 51, at 33.
420 Bialke, *supra* note 125, at 49.

the detaining party. It is further suggested that the Convention does not stipulate whether the tribunals should be executive or judicial or if a separate tribunal must be conducted for each detainee. The purpose of tribunals is "to ensure that a few displaced civilians or other individual noncombatant captives rounded up by mistake and who are in the proximity of belligerent activity taking place in a combat zone, are then released promptly."[421]

Defenders contend that captured al Qaeda and Taliban members are not entitled to Article 5 tribunals because they have consistently failed to meet any of the four criteria set out by the Convention to be awarded prisoner of war status. "Generally, both the al Qaeda and Taliban detainees now in Cuba were captured without responsible chains of command, without uniforms, with concealed weapons, and without any commitment to or history of compliance with international humanitarian law and LOAC (law of armed conflict)."[422] This repeated failure on their part diminishes any doubt to their unlawful combatant status and thus makes Article 5 tribunals inapplicable and unnecessary.

Other critics urge detainees should be entitled to the Article 5 tribunals on a case-by-case basis to determine lawful vs. unlawful combatant status, as well as "POW versus battlefield detainee" status.[423] However, defenders respond that when an organization repeatedly fails to meet the four requirements for lawful belligerency, there is no requirement under the laws of armed conflict to conduct individual tribunals. Furthermore, "In such cases where there is no doubt or ambiguity as to the entire military organization's unlawful combatant status, LOAC does not prohibit a competent authority from also making a presumptive unlawful combatant status determination as a pertinent statement of fact that would be inclusive of all members of that military organization, thereby formally eliminating any need for individual art.5 tribunals."[424] Therefore, because al Qaeda and Taliban member's actions consistently neglect to abide by laws of armed conflict, the need for Article 5 tribunals is unnecessary.

The government has affirmed that the United States has and will continue to treat all detainees with humanely. Furthermore, the

---

[421] *Id* at 50.
[422] *Id.*
[423] Bialke, *supra* note 125, at 55.
[424] *Id* at 53.

protections afforded to the detainees exceed "that required by customary international law, to the extent appropriate to and consistent with military necessity, and in a manner that conforms to the spirit and principles of the Geneva Convention."[425] Policy makers must balance whether following the Convention would produce any benefits or create a negative outcome. "It would be incorrect, irresponsible, and unwise for the U.S. to afford prisoner of war status to captured members of al Qaeda and the Taliban as they are not entitled to, and are undeserving of this status."[426]

Many are still not convinced that the President's actions are appropriate. One critic noted that "without a doubt the most difficult element to defend of the decisions made by President Bush in February with respect to the status of prisoners in Afghanistan is the blanket, all-encompassing nature of the decision to deny POW status to the Taliban prisoners."[427] Article 5 of the Convention provides for a tribunal if there is any doubt to the combatant's entitlement to prisoner of war status and the appropriate way to ascertain a combatant's status is to conduct Article 5 tribunals.[428] Critics point to the U.S. Army Field Manual on the Law of Land Warfare, which interprets article 5 and states:

> b. *Interpretation.* The foregoing provision applies to any person not appearing to be entitled to prisoner-of-war status who has committed a belligerent act or who has engaged in hostile activities in aid of the armed forces and who asserts that he is entitled to treatment as a prisoner of war or concerning whom any other doubt of a like nature exists."[429]

Scholars argue that the Army Manual's provision clearly demonstrate that should a captive's status be in doubt, a tribunal is necessary if that captive engaged in hostilities and asserts he is entitled

---

[425] *Id.* at 56.

[426] *Id.* at 83. as cited in Paul Butler, Principal Deputy Assistant Secretary of Defense for Special Operations and Low Intensity Conflict, DOD Briefing, Jan. 16, 2004, available at: http://www.dod.mil/cgibin/dlprint.egi? at 3.

[427] Aldrich, *supra* note 394, at 205.

[428] Goldman and Tittemore, *supra* note 105.

[429] Aldrich, *supra* note 394, at 205 as cited in: US Department of the Army Manual FM-27-10, *supra* note 212.

to prisoner of war status. Additionally, they list previous instances where Article 5 was invoked. "It was not until the Vietnam armed conflict that the United States issued directives on the subject and established operational Article 5 tribunals."[430] Article 5 tribunals were also conducted during the Gulf War in 1992.[431] Because of the precedents of the use of Article 5 tribunals, the United State's is under obligations per international human rights and humanitarian law required to afford the detainees minimum standards of human rights protection.[432]

Other critics and supporters expressed objections or endorsements to the Bush Administration's decisions. It is important to discuss these views because they illustrate the importance of the issues and the attention they received by American policy makers. One scholar who endorsed the President's decision noted "President Bush chose the right policy, one that provided the United States with flexibility to develop the rules that should apply to the new enemy of global terrorism, but which, in treating the enemy humanely, maintained American values."[433] However, the ICRC voiced their objections to the Bush Administration's decision.

On October 24, 2001, the ICRC issued a press release which stated all combatants captured by the enemy in the Taliban and US-led coalition were to be treated as Prisoners of War according to the Third Geneva Convention. [434] It also stated that individuals captured were to be treated according to the Fourth Geneva Convention and that the ICRC must be able to visit all captured individuals. Additionally, in November 2002, the ICRC stated that the armed conflict in Afghanistan was no longer an international armed conflict but instead an internal conflict.[435]

One scholar disagreed with the ICRC and argued that they ignored al Qaeda's continuous involvement in Afghanistan and failed to recognize the suggestions in earlier UN Security Council Resolutions

---

430 *Id.*

431 *Id.*

432 *Id.*

433 Yoo, *supra* note 7, at 44.

434 ICRC Press Release 0ct. 24, 2001, available at: http://www.icrc.org/web/eng/siteeng0.nsf/htmlall/57jrl8?opendocument

435 ICRC, Aide-Memoire to US (Nov. 19, 2002).

that the conflict was international. The ICRC statement, "... marked a departure from previous ICRC practice of adopting a low profile approach to the legal characterization of situations with characteristics of both international and internal armed conflict."[436]

The American Bar Association's task force on Treatment of Enemy Combatants preliminary report primarily discussed US citizens detained as enemy combatants.[437] However, the report concedes the "necessity under some circumstances to detain persons in order to prevent them from engaging in future terrorists attacks."[438] The report stated that not every captured individual was entitled to be treated as a prisoner of war. "Persons not entitled to POW status, including so-called 'unlawful combatants,' are nevertheless entitled to protections provided by the Fourth Geneva Convention ..."[439] The report recognized that in some instances, a civilian who has participated in "acts hostile to the security of the State, such individual shall not be entitled to claim such rights and privileges...as would...be prejudicial to the security of each state."[440]

The Department of Defense responded to the ABA's Task Force on the Treatment of Enemy Combatants Preliminary Report on October 2, 2002.[441] The DoD insisted the key purpose of detaining enemy combatants during times of conflict is to gather intelligence and to prevent detained individuals from returning to assist the enemy. The DoD counsel elucidated US practice of detaining enemy combatants and stated, "Then, as now, the purpose of detention was not to punish, but to protect."[442]

---

[436] Roberts, supra note 112, at 196.

[437] Neal R. Sonnett, John S. Cooke, Eugene R. Fidell, Albert J. Krieger, Stephen A. Saltzburg, and Suzanne E. Spaulding. *American Bar Association*: *Task Force on Treatment of Enemy Combatants*, Preliminary Report, 2002. 11 Aug. 2006. available at:
<http://www.abanet.org/leadership/enemy_combatants.pdf>.

[438] *Id.* at 6.

[439] *Id.*. at 13.

[440] *Id.* as cited in, GPC, *supra* note 285.

[441] Haynes, William J. United States. Department of Defense. *DOD Responds to ABA Enemy Combatant Report*. 02 Oct. 2002. 21 Nov. 2006
<http://www.defenselink.mil/releases/2002/b10022002_bt497-02.html>.
[hereinafter Haynes Response to ABA Report].

[442] *Id.*

DoD counsel addressed the President's authority to detain unlawful combatants and alluded to the United States Constitution, Article II which states that the President "shall be Commander in Chief of the Army and Navy of the United States..."[443] Thus, he is vested with the authority to detain enemy combatants and such determination has traditionally been one of the President's most fundamental military judgments. When Congress enacted the AUMF in September, 2001, they specifically authorized the President to use military force, "but also any lesser force needed to capture and detain enemy combatants to prevent them from engaging in continued hostilities against the United States."[444]

DoD's response also addresses the ABA Task Force's criticism that the President cannot detain combatants because Congress did not formally declare we are at war. The DoD asserts that Article II by itself authorizes the President to detain enemies during wartime, in spite of congressional action. "It has long been settled that congressional approval of presidential military action need not take the form of a declaration."[445] Furthermore, in previous US conflicts, presidents have detained enemy combatants in even if Congress did not formally declare war.

One adversary to the Bush Administration's decision opined the reason the United States does not recognize detainees at Guantanamo Bay as prisoners of war is because, "...to do so would limit the United States' ability to try these detainees before military commissions whose decisions are not subject to review in civilian courts."[446] If al Qaeda detainees were treated as common criminals, they would have access to civilian courts, on the other hand, if they were treated as prisoners of war, they could be tried in courts-martial. Either way, they would have full access and rights to appeal in civilian courts. Instead, the United States should prosecute terrorist crimes against Americans in American courtrooms. "To get them here in a military tribunal, you have to call

---

443 U.S. Const. art. II, § 2, cl. 1.

444 Haynes Response to ABA Report, *supra* note 441.

445 *Id.*

446 Harold Koh, *Civil Liberties and National Security, A conversation with Harold Koh, Norman Dorsen, and John Deutch*, Feb. 4, 2002, American Academy of Arts and Sciences, Cambridge Massachusetts, at 6.

them something new to justify not trying them either where they are or in a US court."[447]

Another opponent of the Administration's decisions noted "It seems somewhat strange to have an armed conflict in which one side, by definition, is made up of entirely of 'unprivileged belligerents.'"[448] One commentator recognizes while the Bush administration implemented both law enforcement and the armed forces to fight terrorism threats, "To the extent that the 'law enforcement' arm of the 'war on terror' has been flexed, it has been directed towards information gathering and prevention, rather than criminal prosecution and ensuring that justice was done."[449]

Another major criticism of the Bush Administration's policies was that if the US did not apply the Geneva Conventions to the present conflicts and grant prisoner of war status to captured individuals, other States might not apply the Conventions to captured US soldiers in future conflicts. One commentator responded to such criticisms and noted "Nations at war with the United States will treat American POWs humanely or abuse them based on the imperatives of war, not on what we do against al-Qaeda."[450]

Needless to say, there has been a lot of criticism and support regarding President Bush's decision to deny both al Qaeda and the Taliban members prisoner of war status based on the government's applicability of the Geneva Convention to the current conflicts. Even after President Bush acknowledged in July 2006, that Common Article 3 under the Geneva Convention is applicable to the conflicts with al Qaeda and the Taliban, opponents still fought to grant detainees to prisoner of war privileges. The distinction between lawful and unlawful combatants has been addressed in previous US conflicts. The next section discusses US policy of detaining unlawful combatants in past conflicts. History reveals that in previous conflicts, the United States, as early as the Civil War, differentiated between lawful and unlawful combatants.

---

[447] *Id.*at 15.

[448] Charles Garraway, *Commentary International Law Studies*, Vol 79, 2003 p. 232.

[449] Duffy, *supra* note 156, at 123.

[450] Yoo, *supra* note 7, at 35-36.

SECTION FOUR: Lawful and Unlawful Combatants in U.S. Armed Conflicts

> "Presidents have detained enemy combatants in every major conflict in the Nation's history, including recent conflicts such as the Gulf, Vietnam, and Korean wars."
> William J. Haynes, Department of Defense Counsel
> October 2, 2002[451]

According to John Yoo, "the customary laws of war have always recognized stateless fighters as illegal, unprivileged enemy combatants."[452] Another commentator states "The histories of even the most ancient people are filled with examples of irregular forces harassing and ambushing regular armies."[453] The first clear example of unlawful combatants in conflicts in American history was pirates. "Pirates were the scourge of the oceans, and any nation could capture them; they were never owed the status reserved for legal combatants who obeyed the rules of civilized warfare."[454] Although pirates may be considered one of the first unlawful combatants, they clearly weren't the last and characteristics applying to both lawful and unlawful combatants have existed throughout U.S. history. In point of fact, "The concept and legal implications of privileged combatancy are deeply rooted in the customary law of armed conflict."[455] One case demonstrating these differences was the Hostage Case, also known as, *U.S. v. List*. This case included a Military tribunal and affirmed that there can be no question that a soldier cannot be criminally liable for acts committed in times of war if the act are not prohibited by the

---

[451] William J. Haynes, United States Department of Defense, DoD Responds to ABA Enemy Combatant Report, 02 Oct. 2002 21 Nov 2006, available at http://www.defenselink.mil/releases/2002/b10022002_bt497-02.html.

[452] Yoo, *supra* note 7, at 45.

[453] Canestaro, *supra* note 74, at 77.

[454] Yoo *supra* note 7, at 45.

[455] Goldman & Tittemore, *supra* note 105, at 2-3.

conventional or customary rules of war.[456] The Tribunal also discussed privileged combatants and stated, "It is only this group that is entitled to treatment as prisoners of war and incurs no liability after capture or surrender."[457] Thus, in 1950 the US Military Tribunal recognized there was a group that is not entitled to be treated as a prisoner of war.

In 1776, during the United State's fight for independence in the American Revolution War, the issue of unprivileged belligerent was examined. According to Major J.L. Whitson, many of the American volunteers during this war were farmers during the day or during harvest and soldiers during the night or post-harvest season.[458] The British forces were aggravated because they were unable to determine peaceful civilians from potential combatants. "This frustration was compounded by the fact that they were, themselves, always recognizable and open to attack because of the colorful battle dress they were required to wear."[459]

If the British captured one of the farmers by day/soldier by night individuals, they were not granted legal status as combatants. Instead, the British executed them immediately or they were tried for their "treacherous" acts and then executed.[460] Thus while the United States was fighting for its independence, the distinction between lawful and unlawful combatants was recognized.

In the 1700s, several groups along the southern coastline of the Mediterranean Sea terrorized the sea and plundered the merchant ships of many nations. Due to their piracy acts they became known as the Barbary Pirates.[461] The Barbary Pirates would capture trading ships and their cargo and hold the crew and passengers for ransom.[462] The conflict with the Barbary Pirates was the first non-nation state conflict that the United States used military force against.

---

456 *Id.* at 3, citing: *United States v. List* (The Hostage Case), reported in Trials of War Criminals Before the Nuremberg Military Tribunal 1228, 1238 (1950).
457 *Id.*
458 Whitson, *supra* note 319, at 2.
459 *Id.*
460 *Id.*
461 Constitutional Rights Foundation: The United States and the Barbary Pirates. Available at: http://crf-usa.org/bria/bria18_1.htm#pirates
462 *Id.*

In 1801, President Thomas Jefferson ordered naval warships to the Mediterranean to end the Barbary Pirates' power.[463] In 1802, Congress still refused to declare war against the Pirates but did levy a small war tax and proclaimed "protection of commerce" by the navy.[464] The navy was at that time unsuccessful.[465] In February of 1815, President James Madison, received Congress' authority to use military action against the Barbary Pirates.[466] Jonathon Turley, a George Washington professor stated, "Congress did not actually declare war on the pirates but 'authorized' the use of force against the regencies after our bribes and ransoms were having no effect. This may have been due to an appreciation that a declaration of war on such petty tyrants would have elevated their status."[467] In June of 1815, the United States entered into a peace treaty with the Pirates.[468]

In the early 1802s when the United States was battling the Barbary Pirates, debate arose over what to do with captured pirates.[469] In 1822, members of the Congressional Committee on Naval Affairs cautioned against immediately executing captured pirates instead of giving them a trial because it would be inconsistent with public policy.[470] According to Hoffman, "unlawful belligerents wee entitled to legal protection, but the government was free to choose the means of force used against them, as was asserted long after."[471]

Prior to the Committee on Naval Affairs, in June 1777, Congress considered whether to apply international laws or rules of war applied

---

463 *Id.*

464 Thomas Jewett, *Terrorism in Early America: The US Wages War against the Barbary States to End International Blackmail and Terrorism*, Early America Review, Winter/Spring 2002.

465 *Id.*

466 *Id.*

467 Richard Leiby, *Terrorists by Another Name: the Barbary Pirates*. Washington Post, Oct. 15, 2001: Page C01.

468 *Id.*

469 Michael J. Hoffman, *Rescuing the Laws of War: A Way Forward in an Era of Global Terrorism*, 35 Parameters, US Army War College Quarterly at 31 (2005).

470 *Id.*

471 *Id.* at 31.

to interstate belligerents to captured pirates.[472] "...the Continental Congress took care to distinguish between the rules for maritime warfare that applied in full during interstate hostilities, and rules for the same that would apply only in modified form during military expeditions against pirates."[473] Furthermore, in an undeclared naval war with France, the Attorney General argued that individuals, including officers and crew, found on pirate ships were put through the criminal justice system and prosecuted.[474] Others captured on regularly commissioned and authorized by France as a public or private ship of war will be detained as prisoners, unless they are US citizens.[475]

The United States was involved in civil war from 1861 to 1865.[476] The Civil War began on April 12, 1861 when Confederate soldiers opened fired with 50 cannons at Fort Sumter in Charleston, South Carolina.[477] During the Civil War the distinction between lawful and unlawful combatants was addressed by those who wore a uniform, fought for a nation, and obeyed the rules of war.[478]

The wearing of a uniform created another controversy in this sad time in America's history. The Confederate army declared their right to send their soldiers, dressed in civilian clothes, behind enemy lines to sabotage Union facilities.[479] They also demanded, however, that those soldiers captured behind enemy lines in civilian clothes must be treated as prisoners of war.[480] The Union disagreed. President Lincoln established a special committee to examine this issue in depth and create rules for the conduct of Union soldiers.[481] This was a complex matter for President Lincoln because "Lincoln did not want to recognize the rebellion of the southern states as legitimate, nor was it desirable or feasible to label all Johnny Rebs as traitors subject to

---

[472] *Id.* at 28.
[473] *Id.*
[474] *Id.* at 29.
[475] *Id.*
[476] The History Place, available at: http://historyplace.com/civilwar/ (Dec. 10, 2006).
[477] *Id.*
[478] Yoo, *supra* note 7, at 45.
[479] Whitson, *supra* note 319, at 4.
[480] *Id.*
[481] *Id.*

execution."[482] Lincoln therefore needed a system to handle captured Confederate soldiers as prisoners of war without recognizing the status of the Confederates as a State.[483] Lincoln created a committee to examine these issues and placed Francis Lieber on this committee. Lieber drafted General Orders No. 100, a set of rules commonly referred to as the Lieber Code.[484]

The Lieber Code identified two unconventional forces. The first was the guerrilla prowler and the second was the partisan corps. The guerrilla prowler was classified as an armed bandit who was not entitled to prisoner of war status because his actions consisted of theft, murder and sabotage. On the other hand, the partisan corps was classified as an organization of the regular armed forces and therefore was entitled to protection as a prisoner of war, so long as he abided by the laws of war.[485]

Article 82 of the Lieber Code states:

> Men or squads of men, who commit hostilities...without commission, without being part and portion of the organized hostile army, and without sharing continuously in the war, but who do so with intermitting returns to their homes and avocations, or with the occasional assumption of the semblance of peaceful pursuits, divesting themselves of the character or appearance of soldiers—such men...are not entitled to the privileges of prisoner of war, but shall be treated summarily as highway robbers or pirates.[486]

In *Ex parte Milligan* a unanimous Supreme Court held that President Lincoln did not possess the constitutional authority to suspend the writ of habeas corpus and create a system of military

---

[482] *Id.*
[483] *Id.*
[484] Lieber Code, *supra* note 43.
[485] Whitson, *supra* note 319 as cited in: Phillip Thienel, *The Legal Status of Participants in Unconventional Warfare* (Washington, D.C.: The American University, 1961), at 13-14.
[486] Lieber Code, *supra* note 43, § 83.

justice in areas where civilian courts were open and operating.[487] In *Milligan*, Lambdin P. Milligan a US citizen and resident of the state of Indiana for twenty years was arrested at his home on October 5, 1864.[488] He was arrested on a military order and detained by the military.[489] Later that month, he was brought before a military commission, charged and found guilty and sentenced to be hanged.[490]

Milligan filed a habeas corpus petition in Indiana's Circuit Court alleging that the military commission lacked any jurisdiction to try him because he was a U.S. citizen and was not member of the Rebellion party and thus should have been tried in civilian court with constitutional protections.[491] The Supreme Court held that Milligan could not properly be tried before a military commission on a criminal charge in a state where courts were open and operating. A further discussion of this case and its important implications about the suspension of writ of habeas corpus will be addressed in Chapters Three and Four.

The Spanish American War began in April 1898 and ended in 1899. At that time, Spain controlled many territories in the Caribbean and Philippine Islands. Both of those countries wanted independence. The United States became involved for a variety of reasons; one with the sinking of the U.S.S. Battleship Maine which killed 266 sailors (although controversy still surrounds the cause of the sinking) and human rights issues. President McKinley requested authorization for an armed conflict and a declaration of war ensued in April 1898. The war with Spain successfully concluded on December 1898 with the Philippines, Guam, and Puerto Rico being ceded to the United States and independence for Cuba. However, armed hostilities between American forces and Philippine guerillas began shortly before signing at The Treaty of Paris.

The Philippine President did not want to be a territory of the U.S. and declared the treaty to be a violent and aggressive seizure and

---

487 *Ex parte Milligan*, 71 U.S. 2, 124-25 (1866).
488 *Ex parte Milligan* at 107.
489 *Id.*
490 *Id.*
491 *Ex parte Milligan* at 108.

threatened war. On February 4, 1899, hostilities between the two states broke out after two U.S. soldiers killed three Filipino soldiers in Manila. It is alleged that because of the U.S. soldier's firepower, the Filipinos switched to guerrilla warfare.[492] Several US soldiers were ambushed and those who were captured were executed immediately.[493] "It is because of these actions that American troops began rougher tactics with captured Filipinos, including executions."[494]

During the Philippine Insurrection, according to one commentator, US soldiers had to deal with unconventional guerrilla warfare attacks which required the development of new techniques to deal with such attacks.[495] Although the Army dealt with some type of irregular forces in the Civil War, those conflicts were against soldiers from similar cultures with similar beliefs. "Combat in the Philippines did not include any of these similarities."[496] One group of irregular force, known as the Moros, entered a U.S. military compound while carrying coffins which concealed their weapons. The Moros attacked the soldiers and over three fourths of U.S. soldiers were killed. "In retribution, US soldiers committed atrocities against the guerillas, including summary executions…"[497] This conflict illustrated how the U.S. armed forces adapted to a new kind of enemy and how laws of war were disregarded on both sides.

The Boxer Rebellion also began in November, 1899 and ended in successful victory for the Allies in 1901. The rebellion was propelled with the encroachment of several countries into China. Russia, Japan and several European countries leased and seized portions of China in the early part of the late eighteen hundreds.[498] Anti-foreign sentiment in

---

[492] *Id.*
[493] *Id.*
[494] *Id.*
[495] Major Thomas S. Bundt, *An Unconventional War: The Philippine Insurrection,* 1899, Military Rev. at 9 (2004).
[496] *Id.*
[497] *Id.*
[498] The Boxer Rebellion and the US Navy, 1900-1901. Department of the Navy – Naval Historical Center available at: http://www.history.navy.mil/faqs/faq86-1.htm (Dec. 19, 2006).

China led to the development of a secret society known as I Ho Ch'uan (Righteous Harmonious Fists), but Westerners referred to them as the Boxers.[499] This group wanted to expel all foreigners from China, especially Christian missionaries and recent converts. The Chinese Dowager Empress, Tzu Hsi, did little to prevent the Boxer's rebellious acts and thus Western governments responded to the escalating situation and it became known as the Boxer Rebellion.

On May 30, 1900, foreign ministers at Peking (now Beijing) called for troops to protect foreign individuals and property. As a result, four hundred and thirty sailors and Marines from Great Britain, Germany, Russia, France and the United States arrived in Peking to protect the legations. As the conflict grew, more forces were called from all eight countries. In August 1900, over 20,000 men (including 2,000 Americans) were in China fighting the Boxers. Finally, in February of 1901, the Chinese authorities agreed to abolish the Boxer Society. In September of the same year, the Peace Protocol of Peking officially ended the Boxer Rebellion.[500] The United States was involved in an armed conflict with non-nation states, similar to the Spanish-American War (Philippine Insurgency).

The Mexican Revolution began in November of 1910 when Francisco I. Madero attempted and successfully overthrew the dictator, Porfirio Diaz Mori.[501] In 1913, Madero was forced to resign and the country broke out into civil war as several political and armed groups fought for control. [502] On March 19, 2916, Poncho Villa, a leader in the Revolution, led a raid into Columbus, New Mexico. As a result nine citizens were killed and the town was looted.[503]

The US military responded to Villa's attack and went to Columbus where a battle ensued.[504] Eight soldiers were killed in action. "Whatever law-of-war status Villa's forces may have held in Mexico while fighting in that nation's civil war, they could not lawfully cross

---

499 *Id.*
500 *Id.*
501 Mexican Revolution, wikipedia at: http://en.wikipedia.org/wiki/Mexican_Revolution
502 *Id.*
503 Hoffman, *supra* note 469, at 30.
504 *Id.*

the international border to carry out belligerent acts in the United States."[505] Villa's captured men were not granted prisoner of war status, instead they were turned over to state authorities for trial in civilian court in New Mexico. The United States decided to intervene in the revolution only if Americans or American property were in danger.[506]

During both World War I and World War II, lawful and unlawful combatants were recognized. One example of this distinction that occurred during both wars was the immediate execution of armed persons captured who were not wearing uniforms and considered as outlaws, not combatants.[507] Immediate executions prevailed as the customary action until the pivotal *Ex Parte Quirin* case in which the Supreme Court found that unlawful combatants (saboteurs) who had forsworn the laws of war did not enjoy those laws' protection."[508] (This case will be further examined in Chapters Three and Four). Military commissions were initiated by President Roosevelt[509] as the rightful venue for enforcing laws for persons considered as unlawful combatants and charged with violations of the Articles of War including spying, giving intelligence to the enemy and conspiracy to commit those acts. Their Military Commission took place on July 8, 1942.

The petitioners filed a habeas corpus request in civil court. They claimed that the Executive Branch did not contain any authority to

---

505 *Id.*

506 Mexican Revolution, *supra* note 501.

507 Pfanner, *supra* note 274.

508 Yoo, *supra* note 7, at 44.

509 President Franklin D. Roosevelt (On July 2, 1942, The President ordered the petitioners to be tried by military commission. The President also declared that day, "all persons who are subjects, citizens or residents of any nation at war with the United States or who give obedience to or act under the direction of any such nation, and who during time of war enter or attempt to enter the United States…through coastal or boundary defenses, and are charged with committing or attempting or preparing to commit sabotage, espionage, hostile or warlike acts, or violations of the law of war, shall be subject to the law of war and to the jurisdiction of military tribunals."[509] The President's declaration also stated that all such persons were denied access to the courts.

order military commissions for their offenses and therefore they were entitled to be tried before a civil court and granted constitutional protections. The government argued that the petitioners must not be allowed access to the courts because there are enemy aliens or have entered the United States as enemy belligerents and the President's Proclamation clearly denies such access. The Supreme Court concluded that the Commission has jurisdiction to try the petitioners.

The Supreme Court examined the President's authority to order military commissions and also discussed the differences between lawful and unlawful combatants. They state that the laws of war recognize a difference between lawful and unlawful combatants.[510]

> By universal agreement and practice, the law of war draws a distinction between the armed forces and the peaceful populations of belligerent nations and also between those who are lawful and unlawful combatants. Lawful combatants are subject to capture and detention as prisoners of war by opposing military forces. Unlawful combatants are likewise subject to capture and detention, but in addition they are subject to trial and punishment by military tribunals for acts which render their belligerency unlawful. The spy who secretly and without uniform passes the military lines of a belligerent in time of war, seeking to gather military information and communicate it to the enemy, or an enemy combatant who without uniform comes secretly through the lines for the purpose of waging war by destruction of life or property, are familiar examples of belligerents who are generally deemed not to be entitled to the status of prisoner of war, but to be offenders against the law of war subject to trial and punishment by military tribunals.[511]

---

[510] *Ex parte Quirin*, 317 U.S.1 (1942).

[511] *Id.* at 21 as cited in footnote: Hague Convention No. IV of October 18, 1907, 36 Stat. 2295, Article I of the Annex to which defines the persons to whom belligerent rights and duties attach, was signed by 44 nations. See also Great Britain, War Office, Manual of Military Law (1929) ch. Xiv, §§ 17-19; German General Staff, Kriegsbracuh im Landkreige (1902) ch. 1; 7 Moore, Digest of International Law, § 1109; 2 Hyde, International Law (6th ed. 1940) §

Therefore, the Supreme Court in 1942 distinguished between lawful and unlawful combatants and stated that unlawful combatants are not entitled to be prisoners of war. In their decision, the Court examined U.S. history concerning lawful combatants, specifically application to General Orders No. 11 of April 24, 1863. They compared paragraph 83 to the current distinction. Paragraph 83 states: "Scouts or single soldiers, if disguised in the dress of the country, or in the uniform of the army hostile to their own, employed in obtaining information, if found within or lurking about the lines of the captor, are treated as spies, and suffer death."[512]

The Court also discussed paragraph 84 from the General Order No. 100 which states in part, "Armed prowlers, by whatever names they may be called, or persons of the enemy's territory, who steal within the lines of the hostile army, for the purpose of robbing, killing, or of destroying bridges...are not entitled to the privileges of the prisoner of war."[513]

The Supreme Court decision included an analysis of General Order No. 100 and continued enforcement of the Rules of Land Warfare, established by the War Department. For example, the Court cites Paragraph 9: "names as distinguishing characteristics of lawful belligerents that they 'carry arms openly' and 'have a fixed distinctive

---

107; Bluntschli, Droit International (5th ed. Tr. Lardy) §§ 531-32; 4 Calvo, Le Droit International Theorique et Pratique (5th ed. 1986) §§ 2034-35. footnote 8 quoting Great Britain, War Office Manual of Military Law, ch. Xiv, §§ 445-451; Regolamento di Servizio in Guerra, § 133, 3 Leggi e Decreti del Regno d'Italia (1896) 3184; 7 Moore, Digest of International Law, § 1109; 2 Hyde, International Law, §§ 654, 652; 2 Halleck, International Law (4th ed. 1908) § 4;2 Oppenheim, International Law, § 254; Hall, International Law, §§ 127, 135; Baty & Morgan, War, Its Conduct and Legal Results (1915) 172; Bluntschli, Droit International, §§ 570 bis.

[512] General Order No.100 of April 24, 1863 Paragraph 83.

[513] Lieber Code, General Order No. 100, *supra* note 43, para.84, *See also* Paragraph 100: "A messenger or agent who attempts to steal through the territory occupied by the enemy, to further, in any manner, the interests of the enemy, if captured, is not entitled to the privileges of the prisoner of war, and may be dealt with according to the circumstances of the case."

emblem.'"[514] Furthermore, paragraph of same Rules declares that unlawful belligerents are not entitled to the privileges of war status.[515]

The Rules of Land Warfare, Paragraph 9, which defines lawful belligerent, was implemented by Article 1, Annex to the Hague Convention No. IV of October 18, 1907, which the US signed and adopted.[516] The Court states that because the U.S. government signed the Hague Convention, they recognized a distinction between lawful and unlawful combatants. And thus the US recognizes that there is a class of combatants who are not entitled to prisoner of war status. The Court states that it has been well accepted in our Government that if an individual, during wartime, comes into our territory and discards their uniform upon entry, and has the intent to commit hostile acts has the status of unlawful combatant punishable by military commission. "This precept of the law of war has been so recognized in practice both here and abroad, and has so generally been accepted as valid by authorities on international law that we think it must be regarded as a rule of principle of the law of war recognized by this Government by its enactment of the Fifteenth Article of War."[517]

In a footnote the Court discussed international views of lawful and unlawful combatants. They state that authorities agree that a solider in uniform, who commits such acts as destroying bridges, carrying messages secretly, and committing any hostile act, is entitled to be treated as a prisoner of war. However, if the solider is not wearing his uniform and commits such acts, then those acts are now violations of the laws of war.

The Court in their judgment applied these distinctions to the petitioners in the case. The petitioners entered U.S. territory with the intent to commit hostile acts. They arrived in uniform, but discarded their uniform once they arrived in the United States. "As we have seen, entry upon our territory in time of war by enemy belligerents, including these acting under the direction of the armed forces of the enemy, for the purpose of destroying property used or useful in prosecuting the

---

514 *Ex parte Quirin* as cited in, Rules of Land Warfare (1940) para. 9.
515 *Id.* para.351.
516 *Ex parte Quirin* at 34.
517 *Ex parte Quirin* at 35-36.

war, is a hostile and warlike act. It subjects those who participate in it without uniform to the punishment prescribed by the law of war for unlawful belligerents."[518] Therefore, the Court viewed the petitioners as unlawful combatants.

The petitioners argued that they cannot be unlawful belligerents because they did not actually commit a crime or enter the zone of active military operations. The Court disagreed and found that the petitioners were unlawful belligerents when they passed our military and naval lines or went behind those lines, in civilian dress with hostile intent. "The offense was complete when with that purpose they entered – or, having so entered, they remained upon – our territory in time of war without uniform or other appropriate means of identification."[519] Thus, the Court found it was irrelevant that petitioners had not committed any act when they were taken into custody.

The petitioners also argued that the Court's decision in the *Milligan* case prevents the law of war applying to U.S. citizens "where the courts are open and their process unobstructed."[520] The Court addressed their argument by elucidating that Milligan never was a resident of a state in rebellion and thus was not considered an enemy belligerent; nor was Milligan associated with the armed forces of the enemy. The Court declared Milligan to be inapplicable to the present case and did not define the boundaries of the jurisdiction of military tribunals prosecuting individuals according to the law of war. The fact that the petitioners entered U.S. territory to destroy war materials and remained in our territory without uniform is an offense against the law of war. "We hold only that those particular acts constitute an offense against the law of war which the Constitution authorizes to be tried by military commission."[521]

Another important policy of the United States regarding the detention of individuals is Executive Order 9066 that was implemented during World War II. In that Order, President Franklin Roosevelt

---

[518] *Ex parte Quirin* at 36-37.
[519] *Id.* at 38.
[520] *Id.* citing *Ex parte Milligan*, 71 U.S. 2, 118, 121-32 (1866).
[521] *Ex parte Quirin* at 46.

authorized "curfews and the removal of all people of Japanese descent from the Pacific coast."[522] One curfew order required all persons of Japanese ancestry to remain in their residences from 8 p.m. to 6 a.m.[523] More than 120,000 individuals were transported to "relocation centers" and some remained there for up to four years.[524] The Supreme Court examined the issue in *Korematsu v. United States*.[525] In *Korematsu*, an American citizen of Japanese descent was arrested for violating Exclusion Order No. 34. Order No. 34 stated that all persons of Japanese descent should be excluded from military areas. The Court upheld the exclusion order.[526]

In their ruling, the Court recognized that "hardships are part of war, and war is an aggregation of hardships. All citizens alike, both in and out of uniform, feel the impact of war in greater or lesser measure. Citizenship has its responsibilities, as well as its privileges, and, in time of war, the burden is always heavier."[527] They concluded that Korematsu was denied access to military areas not because of his race. He was excluded from military areas because the United States is at war with the Japanese Empire and the military strongly feared an invasion of the US' West Coast and believed it was necessary to take proper security measures. The Court agreed that the actions were necessary and thus affirmed Korematsu's conviction.[528]

The Korean Conflict occurred before either the United States nor North Korea had ratified the 1949 Geneva Conventions. However, General Douglas MacArthur ordered the troops under his command to follow the "humanitarian principles" of common article 3 and the more

---

[522] John Yoo, *Terrorism, The Laws of War, and the Constitution*: Enemy Combatants and the Problem of Judicial Competence, Hoover Institution Press (Stanford, California) (2005) (ed. Peter Berkowitz) at 9.

[523] *Korematsu v. United States*, 323 U.S. 214, 217 (1944).

[524] *Id*, as cited in: Philip Tajitsu Nash, *Moving for Redress*, 94 YALE L.J. 743, 743 (1985) (reviewing JOHN TATEISHI, AND JUSTICE FOR ALL: AN ORAL HISTORY OF THE JAPANESE AMERICAN DETENTION CAMPS [1984].

[525] *Korematsu v. United States*, 323 U.S. 214 (1944).

[526] *Id* at 219.

[527] *Id*.

[528] *Id* at 224.

detailed requirements of the POW convention.[529] The United States, therefore, granted prisoner of war status to captured members of Communist Chinese and North Korean armed forces despite these forces' rather questionable records of compliance with the laws of war.[530]

During Vietnam, the United States provided prisoner of war status when they were not legally required to do so. Members of the Vietcong were granted prisoner of war status, even though they refused to operate in accordance with the principles of lawful combatant.[531] The United States classified Viet Cong armed forces and Viet Cong as irregular forces.[532] The United States classified them as prisoners of war despite the fact that it was doubtful that both armed forces Viet Cong and irregular forces of the Viet Cong met the four criteria of Article 4 of the Geneva Convention.[533] "Viet Cong irregulars were to be classified as POWs if captured while engaging in combat or a belligerent act under arms, 'other than an act of terrorism, sabotage, or spying.'"[534] The United States implemented the Article 5 tribunals if the status of the captured individual was unclear.[535]

Criteria for classifying detainees in the Vietnam War were described in Annex A of the Directive Number 381-46 of December 27, 1967.[536] The Directive described four categories of forces. The first category was Viet Cong Main Force, which followed by Viet Cong Local Force.[537] The third category included North Vietnamese Army Unit and the final category included Irregulars. Irregulars were composed of guerrillas, self-defense and secret self-defense forces. An

---

529 Yoo, *supra* note 7, at 30.
530 Goldman & Tittemore, *supra* note 105, at 10.
531 Yoo, *supra* note 7, at 30.
532 Roberts, *supra* note 112, at 188.
533 *Id.*
534 *Id.*
535 *Id.* at 188-189.
536 Roberts, *supra* note 112, citing: Annex A, "Criteria for Classification and Disposition of Detainees," part of Directive No. 381-46 of 27, Dec. 1967, as cited in, *Contemporary Practice of the United States* 62 Am. J. Int'l L. 767 (1968). [hereinafter Annex A].
537 Annex A at 766.

individual detained in the first three categories was classified as a Prisoner of War. If a member from the fourth category was detained, they were classified as a prisoner of war, if they were captured while actually engaged in combat or a belligerent act under arms. Furthermore, if the captured individual admits or there is proof he was involved in combat which did not involve terrorism, sabotage or spying, he will be a prisoner of war.[538]

The 'manual' also classified some individuals as Non-Prisoners of War.[539] Those individuals included civil defendants, returnees, and innocent civilians. Therefore, the Vietnam War provides another example of the United States applying prisoner of war status to irregular forces who did not comply with the four requirements set out in Article 4 of the Third Geneva Convention.

During the first Gulf War, the United States Army conducted Article 5 tribunals for any prisoners captured if there was any doubt as to their status.[540] If there was any doubt, the person was detained as a prisoner of war. Additionally, none of the prisoners were prosecuted after the war ended. The Department of Defense determined that 99.9% of the captured individuals were enlisted personnel and most were captured on the battlefield rather than from the occupation of Kuwait. The prisoners were repatriated at the end of the war.[541] The Gulf War provides an example of the United States implementing Article 5 Tribunals if there was a doubt to the captured individual's status.

In the current conflict with al Qaeda and the Taliban, the Bush Administration decision to deny prisoner of war status to both al Qaeda and Taliban members sparked a fury of criticism and debate among scholars. The arguments from the scholars above demonstrate the differences of opinion and the massive attention this policy received. The United States Supreme Court addressed these issues in great detail. The intense debate about the designations of al Qaeda and Taliban

---

[538] *Id.* at 767 Art 4(a)(3).
[539] *Id.* at 767 Art 4(b).
[540] DoD News Briefing: Brayn Whitman available at: http://www.au.af.mil/au/awc/awcgate/dod/t04072003_t407genv.html
[541] *Id.*

members center on the ambiguity of the current national and international laws.

An examination of past US conflicts demonstrates the United States has previously distinguished between lawful and unlawful combatants. The administration has also claimed authority to detain American citizens as unlawful combatants. What are the constitutional rights of these individuals? How does the administration justify their declaration? The framework for chapter three is based on answering these questions.

CHAPTER THREE

United States Citizen Enemy Combatants

> "As this Court sits only a short distance from where the World Trade Center once stood, we are as keenly aware as anyone of the threat al Qaeda poses to our country and of the responsibilities the President and law enforcement officials bear for protecting the nation.
> But presidential authority does not exist in a vacuum..."[542]

September 11, 2001, was one of the "deadliest, most dramatic, and most carefully planned act of terrorism ever to have occurred on American soil."[543] As reflected in the above quote, the United States is acutely aware that a fear of continued terrorist acts permeates the country and the lives of its citizens. These horrendous attacks caused the US government to consider creating new laws that would protect US citizens and deter future attacks from groups such as al Qaeda. One such law was the Authorization to Use Military Force,[544] which was enacted by Congress to grant the President authority to protect the country from future terrorist acts.

The FBI defines terrorism as "the unlawful use of force or violence against persons or property to intimidate or coerce a government, the civilian population, or any segment thereof, in furtherance of a political or social objective."[545] As previously discussed in Chapter 2, members

---

542 *Padilla ex rel. Newman v. Rumsfeld*, 352 F. 3d 695, 699 (2nd Cir. 2003).

543 Joseph T. McCann, *Terrorism on American Soil: A concise History of Plots and Perpetrators from the Famous to the Forgotten,* (2006), Boulder, CO: Sentient Publications, 274.

544 Authorization for Use of Military Force, Pub. L. No. 107-40, 115 Stat. 224 (2001). Available at: http://www.access.gpo.gov/nara/publaw/107publ.html ([hereinafter AUMF].

545 Federal Bureau of Investigation, *Terrorism 2000/2001* (Washington, DC: Federal Bureau of Investigation, 2000/2001), iii.

of al Qaeda and the Taliban who have allegedly been involved in terrorist activities have been designated as unlawful combatants. However, not all members of al-Qaeda are foreign nationalists.

Some US citizens have been accused of associating with these regimes and have also been designated as unlawful enemy combatants. Even though there are less than a handful of cases on this particular issue, this is an especially critical issue, primarily due to the definitive and manifest rights of United States citizens granted by the United States Constitution. One imperative right of US citizens is described in the Sixth Amendment,[546] which grants a citizen the right to counsel when charges have been brought against him or her. Another key right is found in the Fourteenth Amendment,[547] which grants a citizen the right to due process of law.

Much discussion has centered on the AUMF and other laws (such as the USA Patriot Act)[548] with supporters claiming the legislation strengthen the President's ability to fight terrorism, and detractors concerned that civil liberties may be harmed.[549] One issue that has created fierce arguments focuses on the basic question, "Does the President of the United States have the power to detain a United States citizen as an unlawful combatant during the War on Terror?" One

---

[546] U.S. Const. amend. VI (In all criminal prosecutions, the accused shall enjoy the right to a speedy and public trial, by an impartial jury of the state and district wherein the crime shall have been committed, which district shall have been previously ascertained by law, and to be informed of the nature and cause of the accusation; to be confronted with the witnesses against him; to have compulsory process for obtaining witnesses in his favor, and to have the assistance of counsel for his defense.)

[547] U. S. Const. amend. XIV § 1. (All persons born or naturalized in the United States, and subject to the jurisdiction thereof, are citizens of the United States and of the state wherein they reside. No state shall make or enforce any law which shall abridge the privileges or immunities of citizens of the United States; nor shall any state deprive any person of life, liberty, or property, without due process of law; nor deny to any person within its jurisdiction the equal protection of the laws.

[548] USA Patriot Act, H. R. 3162; *supra* note 8, see also Curtis A. Bradley & Jack L. Goldsmith, "*Congressional authorization and the war on terrorism.*" Harvard Law Review 118.7 (May 2005): 2047-2133 InfoTrac.

[549] Stephen J. Schulhofter, *Rethinking the Patriot Act: Keeping America Safe and Free* (New York: The Century Foundation Press, 2005), at 1.

whose case has crystallized the issues involved in the debate is Jose Padilla.

The President designated Jose Padilla as an enemy combatant on June 9, 2002[550] and the government contended that as such he was not entitled to an attorney and may be detained without any charges filed against him. An enemy combatant is defined in the Joint Doctrine for Detainee Operations as an additional classification of detainees who through, their own conduct, are not entitled to the privileges and protection of the Geneva Conventions.[551] Furthermore, as defined by the Department of Defense in 2004, an enemy combatant is "Any person that US or Allied Forces could properly detain under the laws and customs of war. For purposes of the war on terror, an enemy combatant includes, but is not necessarily limited to, a member or agent of al Qaeda, Taliban, or another international terrorist organization against which the United States is engaged in an armed conflict.""[552]

In *Ex parte Quirin*[553] one of the most influential judicial decisions concerning the detention of US citizens, the Supreme Court discussed

---

[550] George W. Bush, *To the Secretary of Defense* (June 9, 2002); available at http://fl1.findlaw.com/news.findlaw.com/hdocs/docs/padilla/padillabush60902det.pdf.

[551] Joint Doctrine for Detainee Operations, Final Coordination, 23 March, 2003; also available at http://hrw.org/campaigns/torture/jointdoctrine/jointdoctrine040705.pdf. (The purpose of this publication is to establish joint level doctrine that will govern detainee operations to support combatant commands, sub-unified commands, joint force commanders, commanders of joint task forces, and subordinate components of these commands), 1-11. The doctrine declares that enemy combatants "although they do not fall under the provisions of the Geneva Conventions, they are still entitled to be treated humanely, subject to military necessity, consistent with the principle of GC, and without any adverse distinction based on race, color, religion, gender, birth, wealth, or any similar criteria, and afforded adequate food, drinking water, shelter, clothing, and medical treatment, allowed the free exercise of religion consistent with the requirement of such detention. There is a comprehensive list of terrorists and terrorist groups identified under the Executive Order 13224, located at http://www.treas.gov/ofac."

[552] Deputy Secretary of Defense global screening criteria, Feb. 20, 2004.

[553] *Ex Parte Quirin,* 317 U.S. 1, 28, 48 (1942) (asserting that the President of the United States may try German-born U.S. residents in a military tribunal without a jury.)

whether US citizens could be tried by military commissions. "Citizenship in the United States of an enemy belligerent does not relieve him from the consequences of a belligerency which is unlawful because it is in violation of the law of war. Citizens who associate themselves with the military arm of the enemy government, and with its aid, guidance and direction enter this country bent on hostile acts, are enemy belligerents within the meaning of the Hague Convention and the law of war."[554] The Supreme Court elaborated that "The offense was complete when with that purpose they [saboteurs] entered – or, having so entered, they remained upon – our territory in time of war without uniform or other appropriate means of identification. For that reason, even when committed by a citizen, the offense is distinct from the crime of treason defined in Article III, § 3 of the Constitution,[555] since the absence of uniform essential to one is irrelevant to the other."[556]

Prior to Padilla's case, few judicial decisions dealt with the President's authorization to detain US citizens during wartime. Two cases however have guided many courts on their decisions. The two most influential cases are *Ex parte Milligan*[557] and *Ex parte Quirin,*[558] which were previously cited. Another important case looked to for interpretations is the case of *In re Territo*, based on an Italian American citizen who was captured by US troops in Italy in 1943 while fighting with the Benito Mussolini's army.[559] Territo was later transferred to a detention center for prisoners of war in the United States and filed a petition for writ of habeas corpus and argued that he could not be held as a prisoner of war because he was a US citizen. The Court of Appeals for the Ninth Circuit held citizenship does not necessarily "affect the status of one captured on the field of battle."[560] The court stated "Those who have written texts upon the subject of prisoners of

---

[554] *Ex parte Quirin*, 317 U.S. 1, 37-38 (1942).

[555] U. S. Const. art. III, § 3 (Treason against the United States, shall consist only in levying war against them, or adhering to their enemies, giving them aid or comfort. No person shall be convicted of treason unless on the testimony of two witnesses to the same overt act, or on confession in open court.)

[556] *Ex parte Quirin* at 38.

[557] *Ex parte Milligan*, 71 U.S. (4 Wall.) 2 (1866).

[558] *Ex parte Quirin*, 317 U.S. 1 (1942).

[559] *In re Territo*, 156 F.2d 142 (9th Cir. 1946).

[560] *Id.* at 145.

war agree that all persons who are active in opposing an army in war may be captured and except for spies and other non-uniformed plotters and actors for the enemy are prisoners of war."[561] Even though he was a US citizen, his request for release was denied and he eventually was deported to Italy.

In *Colepaugh v. Looney*, an American citizen was taken into custody in the United States and was tried and convicted by a military jurisdiction for assisting the German Reich and entering the United States with the purpose of committing espionage and sabotage.[562] President Roosevelt announced that "all persons who are subjects, citizens or residents of any nation at war with the United States or who give obedience to or act under the direction of any such nation, and who during time of war enter or attempt to enter the United States through coastal or boundary defenses, and are charged with committing or attempting or preparing to commit sabotage, espionage, hostile or warlike acts, or violations of the law of war, shall be subject to the law of war and to the jurisdiction of military tribunals."[563] The Court of Appeals held that the charges against the petitioner clearly state an offense of unlawful belligerency and such offense is within the jurisdiction of the Military Commissions and his US citizenship does not divest the Commission of jurisdiction.[564] The Court affirmed the district court's dismissal of his petition for writ of habeas corpus.

In *Ex parte Mitsuye Endo*, the Supreme Court held the power to detain a concededly loyal citizen may not be implied from the power to protect the war effort against espionage and sabotage.[565] Endo was a US citizen of Japanese descent who was detained at an internment camp under the War Resolution Authority, after the President's Executive Order 9066.[566] The government conceded that she was a loyal and law abiding citizen.[567] The Supreme Court stated Endo should be released because "whatever power the War Relocation Authority may have to detain other classes of citizens, it has no

---

[561] *Id.*

[562] *Colepaugh v. Looney*, 235 F.2d 429 (10th Cir. 1956).

[563] *Id.* at 430, U.S. Code Cong. Service 1942, p. 901.

[564] *Id.* at 432.

[565] *Ex parte Mitsuye Endo*, 323 U.S. 283, 65 S.Ct. 208, 89 L. Ed. 243 (1944).

[566] *Id.* at 284.

[567] *Id.* at 294.

authority to subject citizens who are concededly loyal to its leave procedure."[568] Therefore, they ordered for Endo to be released.

All of these cases and rulings are relevant to the current discussion and the question, "Does the President of the United States have the power to detain a United States citizen as an unlawful combatant during the War on Terror?"

SECTION ONE: US Citizens Detained as Enemy Combatants and Enemy Combatants Detained in the United States

Yaser Essam Hamdi was born in Louisiana but spent most of his life overseas. In December of 2001, he surrendered to Northern Alliance forces in Afghanistan and subsequently was turned over to US forces.[569] The government contended that he was armed and was traveling with a military unit of the Taliban. He was initially detained at Camp X-Ray at the Naval Base in Guantanamo Bay in January 2002 but in April 2002 was transferred to a military brig in Norfolk, Virginia after authorities discovered he was a US citizen (he had never renounced his American citizenship).[570] He was subsequently sent to a South Carolina military brig. The United States determined that Hamdi was an enemy combatant and would be detained as such according to the laws and customs of war. The issue examined in Hamdi's is whether the President can detain a US citizen captured in a zone of combat as an enemy combatant in the United States.

---

[568] *Id.* at 298. The Court stated Endo's question is not similar to the one presented in *Ex parte Milligan* and *Ex parte Quirin*, because Endo is not being detained by the military, she is being detained by a civilian agency.

[569] *Hamdi v. Rumsfeld*, 296 F. 3d 278, 280 (4th cir. 2002).

[570] *Id.*

Table 1: Summary of Yaser Essam Hamdi's Procedural History:
Taken into custody in Fall 2001 in Afghanistan

Date	Court	Decision
June 11, 2002	United States District Court for the Eastern District of Virginia	Ordered Hamdi must have unrestricted access to attorney
July 12, 2002	United States Court of Appeals for the Fourth Circuit	Reversed District Court's Remanded to District Court.
August 14, 2002	United States District Court for the Eastern District of Virginia	Ordered the government to provide more details surrounding Hamdi's detention
January 8, 2003	United States Court of Appeals for the Fourth Circuit	Dismissed Hamdi's petition for writ of habeas corpus due
June 28, 2004	United States Supreme Court	The AUMF provides the executive branch with some authority to detain citizens as "enemy combatants" however such individuals have a right to hearing with, at least, an opportunity to present evidence that he was not enemy combatant
August 6, 2004	United States Court of Appeals for the Fourth Circuit	Remands back to Eastern District of Virginia for further proceedings consistent with the Supreme Court's decision
September 17, 2004	Settlement Agreement	Hamdi and US Government agree for Hamdi to be released from military custody and sent back to Saudi Arabia, subject to several conditions

The issue and questions presented in Hamdi's case reached the Supreme Court of the United States.[571] Even though not all the Justices were able to agree on an opinion, two different majorities of Justices held, "that (1) the AUMF provided the Federal Government's executive branch with some authority to detain United States citizens as enemy combatants; but (2) the detained individual in question had the right to a hearing which would afford him, at least, an opportunity to present evidence that he was not an enemy combatant."[572] Justice O'Connor announced the judgment of the court.[573]

The Court addressed the legality of the Government's detention of a US citizen on US soil as an "enemy combatant" and also examined the process that is constitutionally afforded to one who seeks to challenge his classification as an enemy combatant.[574] The court first addressed the detention of a US citizen on US soil. The Court noted there was substantial debate surrounding the scope of the term "enemy combatant" and moreover, the government never provided any court with the full criteria it uses to classify an individual as such. The Court noted however, "It has made clear…for purposes of this case, the 'enemy combatant' that it is seeking to detain is an individual who, it alleges, was 'part of or supporting forces hostile to the United States or coalition partners' in Afghanistan and who 'engaged in an armed conflict against the United States' there."[575] Thus, the Court only answered whether the detention of citizens falling within that definition is authorized.[576]

The Court did not discuss whether the President has the inherent authority under Article II of the United States Constitution to detain enemy combatants because they agreed with the government's alternative position that Congress authorized Hamdi's detention through the Authorization for Use of Military Force. Hamdi argued his detention was prohibited by 18 U.S.C. § 4001(a).[577] However, the

---

[571] *Hamdi v. Rumsfeld*, 542 U.S. 507, S. Ct. 2633; 159 L. Ed. 2d 578 (2004).
[572] *Id.* at 580.
[573] *Id.* Chief Justice Rehnquist and Justices Kennedy and Breyer joined O'Connor's opinion.
[574] *Id.* at 586.
[575] *Id.* at 516.
[576] *Id.*
[577] *Id.* at 591.

Court held the AUMF "is explicit congressional authorization for the detention of individuals in the narrow category we describe (assuming, without deciding, that such authorization is required), and that the AUMF satisfied § 4001(a)'s requirement that a detention be 'pursuant to an Act of Congress' (assuming, without deciding, that § 4001(a) applies to military detentions)."[578]

The AUMF authorized the President to use "all necessary and appropriate force" against "nations, organizations, or persons" connected with the terrorist attacks on September 11, 2001.[579] The Court stated there can be no doubt that those who fight against the United States in Afghanistan as part of the Taliban are individuals Congress intended to target in enacting the AUMF. The Court concluded "the detention of individuals falling into the limited category we are considering, for the duration of the particular conflict in which they are captured, is so fundamental and accepted an incident to war as to be an exercise of the 'necessary and appropriate' force Congress has authorized the President to use."[580]

The Court noted the purpose of detaining enemy combatants is to prevent them from returning to the battlefield and taking up arms once again and therefore their detention is "neither revenge, nor punishment, but solely protective custody..."[581] The Court also acknowledged that there is no bar to the United States from detaining one of its own citizens as an enemy combatant. The Court looked to their decision in *Ex parte Quirin* which stated "[c]itizens who associate themselves with the military arm of the enemy government, and with its aid, guidance and direction enter this country bent on hostile acts, are enemy

---

[578] *Id.* at 591. Authorization for Use of Military Force resolution (AUMF) 115 Stat 224). The government argued that because § 4001(a)'s legislative history and because it is located in Title 18 it only applies to "the control of civilian prisons and related detentions" and thus not to military detentions.

[579] *Id.* at 592, citing 115 Stat 224.

[580] *Id.* at 592. Justice Souter, with whom Justice Ginsburg joins argued the government did not establish why the AUMF authorized Hamdi's detention and therefore § 4001(a) prohibits his detention. (at 607). Furthermore, Justice Souter asserted Congress enacted § 4001(a) to prevent repetition of the World War II internment camps and therefore clear congressional authorization is required before any citizen can be placed in a cell. (at 608).

[581] *Id.* quoting decision of Nuremberg Military Tribunal, reprinted in 41 Am. J. Int'l L. 172, 229 (1947).

belligerents within the meaning of...the law of war."[582] Furthermore, the Court recognized that even though the US citizen in *Quirin* (Haupt) was not tried for violations of the law of war, nothing in their decision suggests that his citizenship would have prohibited his mere detention for the duration of the relevant hostilities. Finally, the Court stated that both an alien and a US citizen can be "part of or supporting forces hostile to the United States or coalition partners."[583]

Based on the aforementioned facts, the Court held it is insignificant that the language in the AUMF does not specifically speak to detention. "Because detention to prevent a combatant's return to the battlefield is a fundamental incident of waging war, in permitting the use of 'necessary and appropriate force,' Congress has clearly and unmistakably authorized detention in the narrow circumstances considered here."[584]

However, Hamdi countered that Congress did not intend to authorize indefinite detentions. The government argued that detentions during World War II were "just as indefinite..."[585] The Court agreed that indefinite detentions are not authorized, but it is a well settled principle of the law of war that the government may not detain an individual once the hostilities end. Moreover, at this point, there remains active combat against the Taliban in Afghanistan. If the record establishes that US troops are actively engaged in combat in Afghanistan, they may detain enemy forces and those detentions are authorized by the AUMF.[586]

The Court determined their decision in the present case concerning the government's ability to detain enemy combatants is not weakened

[582] *Id.* at 592 citing *Ex parte Quirin*, 317 U.S. 1, 37-38 (1942).
[583] *Id.* at 592-93. citing Brief for Respondents 3.
[584] *Id.* at 593. In Justice Thomas' dissent, he stated it is beside the point that the AUMF does not contain specific language to detain enemy combatants "because 'Congress cannot anticipate and legislate with regard to every possible action the President may find it necessary to take or every possible situation in which he might act,' it should come as no surprise that '[s]uch failure of Congress...does not, 'especially...in the areas of foreign policy and national security,' imply 'congressional disapproval' of action taken by the Executive.'" (*Id.* at 633).
[585] *Id.* citing *Ex parte Quirin*, 317 U.S. at 16.
[586] *Id.*

by their holding in *Ex parte Milligan*.[587] The Court stated the fact that Milligan was not a prisoner of war, but a resident of Indiana arrested at his home was vital to their decision. Moreover, the Court stated their holding may have been different if Milligan was captured on a Confederate battlefield, while assisting Confederate soldiers and carrying a weapon against Union troops.[588]

The Court also addressed what process is constitutionally afforded to a citizen who disputes his classification as an enemy combatant. The Court stated the language of § 2241 (habeas challenge) clearly illustrates that Congress intended for habeas petitioners to have some opportunity to present and dispute facts.[589] Moreover, Congress intended for the courts to have some ability to vary the process for a petitioner to present and dispute such facts, especially in cases like the present one.[590]

The government proffered that the Mobbs Declaration completed the required factual finding. They pointed to the Court of Appeals for the Fourth Circuit's opinion which held no further hearing was necessary (other than Mobbs Declaration) because it was undisputed that Hamdi was captured in a war zone.[591] However, the Court rejected this argument because the circumstances surrounding Hamdi's seizure were not undisputed and moreover, the facts proffered in the declaration are insufficient to support his detention.[592] The Court noted that according to the government's definition of an enemy combatant, Hamdi would need to be "part of or supporting forces hostile to the United States or coalition partners" and "engaged in an armed conflict against the United States" to justify his detention.[593] The petition only

---

[587] *Id.* at 594 citing *Ex parte Milligan*, 71 U.S. 2, 4 Wall. 2, 125, 18 L. Ed. 281 (1866). (Lambdin P. Milligan and four others were accused of planning to steal Union weapons and invade Union prisoner-of-war camps and were sentenced to hang by a military court in 1864. However, their execution was not set until May 1865, so they were able to argue the case after the Civil War ended.)

[588] *Id.* at 594.

[589] *Id.* at 596, 28 U.S.C. § 2241.

[590] *Id.* at 597.

[591] *Id.* at 597 citing *Hamdi v. Rumsfeld*, 337 F.3d 335 (CA4 2003).

[592] *Id.* at 597, citing *Hamdi v. Rumsfeld*, 337 F.3d 357 (Luttig, J., dissenting from denial of rehearing en banc).

[593] *Id.* citing Brief for Respondents 3.

states Hamdi resided in Afghanistan, which cannot be a concession that he was "captured in a zone of active combat operations ..."[594]

The Court next addressed the government's argument that any further factual inquiry into Hamdi's case is unwarranted and inappropriate due to the extraordinary constitutional interest at stake.[595] The government contended the court should review a determination that a citizen is an enemy combatant under the "some evidence" standard, which applies great deference to the executive's decision. If the court were to implement the "some evidence" standard, they would assume the facts proffered in the government's Mobbs Declaration were accurate concerning Hamdi's detention and therefore the court would be limited to decide whether the government's basis was a legitimate one.[596] Hamdi argued, on the other hand, that he is entitled to be presented before a neutral tribunal to determine whether the executive's justifications for detaining him are legitimate. Moreover, he argued due process demands that he receive a hearing where he is able to dispute facts in the declaration and produce his own evidence.[597] The Court applied the current case to the due process standard articulated in *Mathews v. Eldridge*.[598] *Mathews* mandates that the "process due in any given instance is determined by weighing 'the private interest that will be affected by the official action' against the Government's asserted interest, "including the function involved" and the burdens the Government would face in providing greater process."[599]

After an exhaustive analysis of both party's interests, the Court concluded that due process demands some system for a citizen detainee to dispute his classification and therefore the government's suggested "some evidence" standard is insufficient.[600] The Court stated "Any process in which the Executive's factual assertions go wholly

---

[594] *Id.* at 597.
[595] *Id.* at 597.
[596] *Id.* at 598.
[597] *Id.* at 598.
[598] *Id.* at 598 citing *Mathews v. Eldridge*, 424 U.S. 319, 47 L. Ed. 2d 18, 96 S. Ct. 893 (1976). (There, the court observed that "the right to be heard before being condemned to suffer a grievous loss of any kind .... is a basic principle of our society.")
[599] *Id.* at 599 citing 424 U.S. at 335, 47 L. Ed. 18, 96 S. Ct. 893.
[600] *Id.* at 604.

unchallenged or are simply presumed correct without any opportunity for the alleged combatant to demonstrate otherwise falls constitutionally short."[601] Therefore, the Court held that a US citizen detainee who seeks to challenge his classification as an enemy combatant "must receive notice of the factual basis for his classification, and a fair opportunity to rebut the Government's factual assertions before a neutral decisionmaker."[602] The parties agreed that this process shall not be implemented on initial captures on the battlefield; but is only due when the government decides to continue to hold the seized combatant.[603]

The Court stated Hamdi has not received the "process" he is entitled to receive under the Due Process Clause. They also recognized the possibility that the standards they have articulated may be satisfied by a military tribunal. However, because at this point of time no such tribunal exists, "a court that receives a petition for a writ of habeas corpus from an alleged enemy combatant must itself ensure that the minimum requirements of due process are achieved."[604]

The Supreme Court's decision was released in June, 2004. The Court ordered for Hamdi to receive an opportunity to hear the government's evidence against him and an opportunity to rebut their allegations. However, on September 17, 2004, the government and Hamdi reached a settlement agreement.[605] In the agreement, Hamdi would be sent to Saudi Arabia and once in Saudi Arabia he would not

---

[601] *Id.* at 604.

[602] *Id.* at 602. The Court also stated "Hearsay, for example, may need to be accepted as the most reliable available evidence from the Government in such a proceedings. Likewise, the Constitution would not be offended by a presumption in favor of the Government's evidence, so long as that presumption remained a rebuttable one and fair opportunity for rebuttal were provided." At 602.

[603] *Id.* at 602.

[604] *Id.* at 605. The Court also addressed Hamdi's argument that the Court of Appeals for the Fourth Circuit erred when they denied him the ability to immediately meet with his counsel. However, the Court notes that since they granted certiorari to this case, Hamdi has been appointed counsel and has had unmonitored meetings with such counsel on several occasions. Therefore, the Court does not consider this issue at this time. (at 605).

[605] *Hamdi v. Rumsfeld* Settlement Agreement (Sept. 2004), available at: http://news.lp.findlaw.com/hdocs/docs/hamdi/91704stlagrmnt.html

be detained by Saudi authorities.[606] Hamdi agreed to reside in Saudi Arabia for five years from the date of their agreement and moreover he may not travel outside Saudi Arabia for such time.[607] The settlement agreement also prohibited Hamdi from filing any claims against the United States concerning his detention.[608] Hamdi and his attorneys signed the agreement on September 15, 2004. US government officials signed the agreement on September 17, 2004.[609] Hamdi was transferred from the South Carolina military brig to Saudi Arabia on October 11, 2004.[610]

The next case discussed is perhaps the most contentious of the cases involving US citizens – Jose Padilla, the alleged "dirty bomber."[611] Padilla was the second United States citizen to be designated and detained in the United States as an enemy combatant. Padilla was born in New York and convicted of murder in 1983 and subsequently convicted on a handgun charge in 1991.[612] He moved to Egypt in 1998 and traveled all over the Middle East. While overseas, it was alleged that Padilla became associated with known members and leaders of al Qaeda.[613] He traveled to Afghanistan in 2001and allegedly became involved in a plot to detonate a "dirty bomb" in the United States.[614] Padilla was taken into custody by Federal Bureau of Investigation (FBI) agents on May 8, 2002 at Chicago O'Hare Airport, where he had just arrived from Pakistan.[615] The agents apprehended

---

606 *Id.* at 2.
607 *Id.* at 3.
608 *Id.* The agreement also prohibited Hamdi from traveling to Afghanistan, Iraq, Israel, Pakistan, Syria, the West Bank, or the Gaza Strip. Hamdi may also not travel to the United States for ten years and after that time, he needs express permission from the Secretary of Defense.
609 *Id.*
610 Department of Defense News Release, Transfer of Detainee Complete (Oct. 2004) available at:
http://www.defenselink.mil/Releases/Release.aspx?ReleaseID=7827
611 Rosa E. Brooks, *War Everywhere: Rights, National Security Law, and the Law of Armed Conflict in the Age of Terror,* 153 U. PA. Rev. 677, 710 (2004).
612 Declaration of Michael Mobbs, Special Advisor to the Under Secretary of Defense for Policy, at 2-3. Unclassified version at
http://news/lp.findlaw.com/hdocs/docs/padilla/padillabush82702mobbs.pdf.
613 *Id.* at 3.
614 *Id.* at 3.
615 *Padilla v. Hanft*, 389 F. Supp.2d 678, 679 (D.S.C. 2005)

Padilla as he stepped off the plane. The agents were executing a material witness warrant issued by the United States District Court for the Southern District of New York.[616] The agents questioned Padilla about his travels. Padilla was under the impression they were questioning him because he had ten thousand dollars in cash, but he only claimed eight thousand. At the end of the interview, the agents placed Padilla under arrest, under a material witness warrant and took him into custody.[617]

Table 2: Summary of Jose Padilla's Procedural History
Taken into custody on May 8, 2002; designated as enemy combatant June 9, 2002

Date	Court	Decision
December 4, 2002	Southern District Court for New York	The President has authority to detain as enemy combatants citizens captured on American soil during a time of war
December 18, 2003	United States Court of Appeals for the Second Circuit	The President lacks the authority to detain Padilla militarily.
June 28, 2005	United States Supreme Court	Dismissed case because Padilla should have filed in South Carolina
February 28, 2005	United States District Court for the District of South Carolina	The President lacks the authority to detain Padilla, Padilla must either be criminally charged or released

---

616 *Id.* at 679.
617 Colleen E. Hardy, *Jose Padilla,* CIP Report, Vol. 4, #8 (2006); available at http://cipp.gmu.edu/research/Padilla-0602Article.php.

Date	Court	Decision
September 9, 2005	United States Court of Appeals for the Fourth Circuit	The President has the authority to detain Padilla under the AUMF
November 17, 2005	United States District Court for the Southern District of Florida	Indictment against Padilla
December 21, 2005	United States Court of Appeals for the Fourth Circuit	Denied the Government's motion to authorize Padilla's transfer from military custody to civilian law enforcement custody.
January 4, 2006	United States Supreme Court	Granted Solicitor General's Application to Transfer Padilla to civilian law enforcement custody.
April 22, 2007	United States District Court for the Southern District of Florida	Padilla's Trial
August 16, 2007	United States District Court for the Southern District of Florida	Jury convicted Padilla of terrorism conspiracy and providing material support to terrorists
January 22, 2008	United States District Court for the Southern District of Florida	Padilla was sentenced to 17 years in prison

Padilla was brought to New York before US District Court Judge Mukasey, who had authorized the material witness warrant and subsequently appointed Padilla an attorney, Donna Newman.[618] On June 9, 2002, Padilla was transferred to Department of Defense custody and held in the Consolidated Naval Brig in Charleston, South Carolina.[619] The next day, Attorney General John Ashcroft stated, "We have captured a known terrorist who was exploring a plan to build and explode a radiological device or 'dirty bomb' in the United States."[620]

The issues and question presented in Padilla's case reached the Fourth Circuit Court of Appeals. The Fourth Circuit answered the question, "whether the President of the United States possesses the authority to detain militarily a citizen of this country who is closely associated with al Qaeda, an entity with which the United States is at war; who took arms on behalf of that enemy and against our country in a foreign combat zone of that war; and who thereafter traveled to the United States for the avowed purpose of further prosecuting that war on American soil, against American citizens and targets."[621] The court of appeals concluded the President does possess such authority pursuant to the AUMF.

It is important to note that the government and Padilla stipulated to the following facts for the court of appeal's decision: (1) al Qaeda operatives recruited Padilla to train for jihad in Afghanistan in Feb. 2000; (2) Subsequently, he met w/ al Qaeda operatives in Afghanistan, received explosives training in an al Qaeda affiliated camp, and served as an armed guard at what he understood to be a Taliban outpost; (3) When US military operations began in Afghanistan, Padilla and other al Qaeda operatives moved from safehouse to safehouse to evade bombing or capture; (4) Padilla was, on the fact w/ which we are presented, "armed and present in a combat zone during armed conflict b/w al Qaeda/Taliban forces and the armed forces of the US;" (5) Padilla eventually escaped to Pakistan, armed w/ an assault rifle. Once

---

[618] *Id.* at 679.

[619] *Padilla v. Hanft*, 389 F. Supp. 2d 678, 680 (D.S.C. 2005).

[620] Attorney General Ashcroft, Transcript of the Attorney General Regarding the transfer of Abdullah Al Muhajir (Born Jose Padilla) To the Department of Defense as an Enemy Combatant (June 10, 200) Available at: http://www.fas.org/irp/news/2002/06/ag061002.html

[621] *Padilla v. Hanft*, 423 F.3d 386, 389 (4th Cir. 2005).

there, he met w/ Khalid Sheikh Mohammad, a senior al Qaeda operations planner, who directed Padilla to travel to the US for the purpose of blowing up apartment buildings, in continued prosecution of al Qaeda's war of terror against the US; and (6) After receiving further training, as well as cash, travel documents, and communication devices, Padilla flew to the US in order to carry out his accepted assignment.[622]

The court of appeals stated Congress enacted the AUMF "in the immediate aftermath of the September 11, 2001, terrorist attacks on the United States."[623] The court of appeals asserted because the AUMF authorized *Hamdi's* detention, it also authorizes Padilla's.[624] The court did not see any difference between Hamdi and Padilla as enemy combatants. Both were associated with forces hostile to the United States in Afghanistan. Moreover, both men took up arms against the United States. "Because, like Hamdi, Padilla is an enemy combatant, and because his detention is no less necessary than was Hamdi's in order to prevent his return to the battlefield, the President is authorized by the AUMF to detain Padilla as a fundamental incident to the conduct of war."[625]

The court of appeals asserted this position is strengthened by the Supreme Court's decision in *Ex parte Quirin.*[626] The Supreme Court stated "citizens who associate themselves with the military arm of the enemy government, and with its aid, guidance and direction enter this country bent on hostile acts, are enemy belligerents within the meaning of ... the law of war."[627] Padilla is similar to Haupt, because both associated with enemy armed forces and with its aid, guidance, and direction and entered the United States bent on committing hostile acts on American soil.[628] Therefore, the court of appeals concluded, "Given that Padilla qualifies as an enemy combatant under both the definition adopted by the Court in *Quirin* and the definition accepted by the controlling opinion in *Hamdi*, his military detention as an enemy combatant by the President is unquestionably authorized by the AUMF

---

[622] *Id.* at 390.
[623] *Id.* at 391.
[624] *Id.* at 391.
[625] *Id.* at 392
[626] *Id.* at 392, citing *Ex parte Quirin*, 317 U.S. 1 (1942).
[627] *Id.* citing *Ex parte Quirin*, 317 U.S. at 37-38.
[628] *Id.* at 392.

as a fundamental incident to the President's prosecution of the war against al Qaeda in Afghanistan."[629]

Unlike the South Carolina district court, the court of appeals held the location where Padilla was taken into custody does not preclude his detention as an enemy combatant. The court stated there should not be a distinction between an enemy combatant captured abroad and detained in the United States, such as Hamdi, and an enemy combatant who escaped capture abroad but was ultimately captured and detained in the United States, such as Padilla.[630]

The court of appeals also disagreed with the district court's assertion that because Padilla can be prosecuted in the criminal justice, he should be. The court of appeals was not convinced that the availability of criminal process is determinative of the power to detain.[631] Criminal prosecution might not achieve the vital purpose for detaining enemy combatants – to prevent such combatants from returning to the battlefield. A criminal prosecution would intrude upon the Executive's efforts to "gather intelligence from the detainee does and to restrict the detainee's communication with confederates so as to ensure that the detainee does not pose a continuing threat to national security even as he is confined – impediments that would render military detention not only an appropriate, but also necessary, course of action to be taken in the interest of national security."[632]

The court of appeals addressed Padilla's argument that *Ex parte Endo* mandates that a clear statement from Congress is necessary to authorize his detention and that the AUMF does not contain such a clear statement.[633] Padilla pointed to language in the Court's decision which stated "the law makers intended to place no greater restraint on the citizen than was clearly and unmistakably indicated by the language [the law makers] used."[634] The court of appeals observed that the Court also stated (in *Endo*) that the "fact that the Act" at issue was "silent on detention [did] not of course mean that any power to detain [was]

---

[629] *Id.*
[630] *Id.* at 393.
[631] *Id.* at 394.
[632] *Id.* at 395.
[633] *Id.* at 395 citing *Ex parte Endo*, 323 U.S. 283, 89 L. Ed. 243, 65 S. Ct. 208 (1944).
[634] *Id.* citing *Ex parte Endo* at 300.

lacking."[635] The court of appeals believed the Court did not adopt and thus require a "clear statement" rule and therefore Padilla's argument fails.

The court of appeals rejected Padilla's argument that the Supreme Court's decision in *Ex parte Milligan* prohibits his detention.[636] The court of appeals looked to the Court's decision in *Quirin* which confirmed that *Milligan* does not extend to enemy combatants because *Milligan* was not "a part of or associated with the armed forces of the enemy."[637] Therefore, *Milligan* is inapplicable to Padilla because Padilla, not like Milligan, associated with and took up arms with an enemy force against the United Stats.[638]

In conclusion, the court of appeals held when Congress enacted the AUMF, they accorded the President all powers necessary and appropriate to protect US citizens from terrorist acts. The Supreme Court has previously held that these powers include the power to detain identified and committed enemies such as Padilla, who is associated with al Qaeda and took up arms against the United States and entered the United States to engage in hostilities against the United States.[639] Therefore, the court concluded that Padilla's detention is fully authorized by an Act of Congress and reversed the judgment of the district court.

The Court of Appeals for the Fourth Circuit issued their opinion on September 9, 2005. Padilla filed a petition for a writ of certiorari to the United States Supreme Court. Shortly after the court of appeals released their opinion, the government determined that Padilla's military custody was no longer necessary.[640] The government announced Padilla was to be transferred to federal law enforcement authorities in Florida to face criminal charges. Padilla was indicted in Miami on November 23, 2005.

---

[635] *Id.* at 395, citing *Endo* at 301.

[636] *Id.* at 396, citing *Ex parte Milligan*, 71 U.S. (4 Wall.) 2, 18 L. Ed. 281 (1866).

[637] *Id.* citing *Ex parte Quirin*, 317 U.S. at 45.

[638] *Id.* at 397.

[639] *Id.* at 397.

[640] *Padilla v. Hanft*, 432 F.3d 582,584(4th Cir. 2005).

Padilla was transferred to federal law enforcement custody in Miami, Florida on January 5, 2006.[641] As mentioned above, in November, 2005 Padilla was indicted by a Miami federal grand jury on criminal charges that he conspired to "murder, kidnap and maim" people overseas.[642] The three charges included: conspiracy to murder U.S. nationals, conspiracy to provide material support to terrorists, and providing material support to terrorists.[643] The charges do not include earlier allegations that he planned to build and detonate a dirty bomb in the United States. Attorney General Alberto Gonzales stated, "Padilla's previous status as an 'enemy combatant' has no legal ramifications for the criminal charges."[644]

Padilla was arraigned on January 12, 2006. He pleaded not guilty to all charges against him and the judge denied his bail due to the seriousness of the charges.[645] His trial began on April 16, 2007. On August 16, 2007 the jury convicted Padilla of conspiracy to murder, kidnap, and maim people overseas as well as two counts of providing material support to terrorists.[646] On January 22, 2008, U.S. District Judge Marcia Cooke sentenced Padilla to prison for 17 years and 4 months.[647] Padilla faced up to life in prison.

---

641 Associated Press, *Alleged al Qaeda Operative in Civilian Court*, FOXNEWS, Jan. 6, 2006, http://www.foxnews.com/story/0,2933,180866,00.html.

642 *United States v. Padilla et al.*, Indictment, Nov. 15, 2005, http://news.lp.findlaw.com/hdocs/docs/padilla/uspad111705ind.pdf. Padilla was also indicted with four other individuals: Kassem Daher (in custody overseas); Adham Hassoun, Mohamed Youssef and Kifah Jayyousi.

643 *Id.*

644 Catherine Herridge and Greg Simmons and AP, *'Dirty Bomb' Suspect Padilla Indicted*, FOXNEWS, Nov. 23, 2005, http://www.foxnews.com/story/0,2933,176361,00.html.

645 Associated Press, *Former 'Enemy Combatant' Padilla Pleads Not Guilty*, FOXNEWS, Jan. 12, 2006 , http://www.foxnews.com/story/0,2933,181431,00.html.

646 Associated Press, *Jury Finds Jose Padilla, 2 Co-Defendants, Guilty on Terrorism Support Charges*, FOXNEWS, Aug. 16, 2007 , http://www.foxnews.com/story/0,2933,293493,00.html.

647 Associated Press, *Accused Al Qaeda Operative Jose Padilla Gets 17 Years*, FOXNEWS, January 22, 2008, http://www.foxnews.com/story/0,3566,324605,00.html

The issues raised in Yasser Hamdi and Jose Padilla's cases focused on the fact they were US citizens who had been declared enemy combatants. However, President Bush designated Ali-Saleh Kahlah al-Marri, a resident alien, also as an enemy combatant, who is still currently detained at the military brig in South Carolina.

The third enemy combatant, Ali Saleh Kahlah al-Marri is not a US citizen but was captured and detained in the United States as an enemy combatant. Presently, he is the only enemy combatant detained in the United States. Al-Marri is a Qatari national. On September 10, 2001, Al-Marri and his family entered the United States. He had previously obtained his bachelors degree from Bradley University in Peoria, Illinois and had returned to the United States to continue his advanced studies to receive his master's degree from Bradley.[648] In December, 2001, US Attorney's Office for the Southern District of New York directed FBI agents to arrest al-Marri as a material witness in the investigation of the September 11, 2001 terrorist attacks.[649] Al-Marri was arrested on December 12 in Peoria and transferred to New York City.[650]

In June, 2003 President Bush designated al-Marri as an enemy combatant[651] and directed that he be transferred to the Department of Defense custody for detention. The US Attorney's Office moved to dismiss the Illinois indictment, which was granted.[652] Al-Marri's counsel asked the district court to stay the case to prevent al-Marri from being transferred from the jurisdiction until he could file a habeas petition.[653] The court stated they no longer had jurisdiction over the case because it had been dismissed and therefore they could not grant a stay. However, the US Attorney's office did agree to inform counsel where al-Marri was to be transferred.[654] Al-Marri was immediately transferred to the Naval Consolidated Brig in Charleston, South Carolina.[655] The issue discussed in al-Marri's case is whether the

---

[648] *Al-Marri v. Bush*, 274 F. Supp. 2d 1003, 1004 (2003).
[649] *Id.* at 1004.
[650] *Id.*
[651] *Id.*
[652] *Id.*
[653] *Id.* at 1004.
[654] *Id.*
[655] *Id.* at 1005.

President has the authority to detain a resident alien taken into custody in the United States as an enemy combatant.

The issue and question presented in al-Marri's case reached the Court of Appeals for the Fourth Circuit.[656] Al-Marri maintains that the President does not have the power to detain him as an enemy combatant and Congress has not authorized his detention.[657] Al-Marri also argued that the Military Commissions Act of 2006 does not authorize his detention.[658] He stated "It does not create any Executive detention authority, but merely limits the class of individuals subject to military commission jurisdiction under the MCA."[659] The government argued that the President has the authority to detain resident aliens as enemy combatants.[660]

The government also argued "Al-Marri was provided ample opportunity to challenge his enemy combatant classification in this habeas action that more than satisfies any due process rights he may have."[661] In November, 2006, the government filed a motion with the court of appeals to send al-Marri's case to the district court with instructions for it to dismiss his case due to the fact that it lacked subject matter jurisdiction over his case.[662] The government proffered "the Military Commissions Act of 2006 removed federal court jurisdiction over pending and future habeas corpus actions and any other actions filed by or on behalf of detained aliens determined by the

---

656 Petitioner-Appellant, *al-Marri v. Wright*, No. 06-7427 (4th Cir. 2007).

657 *Id.* at 12-20.

658 *Id.* at 39 citing Military Commission Act of 2006, Pub. L. No. 109-366, 120 Stat. 2600 (2006) [hereinafter MCA].See also, USA: Government attempts to dismiss appeals of Ali-Saleh Kahlah al-Marri, held in conditions of extreme isolation for over four and a half years, Amnesty International, Dec. 4, 2006 (stating that if the government's motion to dismiss Al-Marri's habeas petition is successful, it will void his present challenge and any other court's potential to review the conditions of his confinement. "He will thus be effectively removed from the protection of the US courts as regards both his detention and his treatment in custody. This will be unprecedented as non-citizens arrested in the USA generally have the right to contest their detention or treatment in the US courts."

659 *Id.*

660 *Id.* at 16.

661 *Id.* at 18.

662 Respondent-Appellee's Motion to Dismiss for Lack of Jurisdiction and Proposed Briefing Schedule, *Al-Marri v. Wright*, No. 06-7427.

United States to be enemy combatants, such as petitioner-appellant al Marri…"[663] Moreover, they argued the MCA applies to al-Marri because he is an alien detained by the United States, as prescribed in the MCA, and the government determined he is properly detained as an enemy combatant.[664] Therefore, because the court no longer has subject matter jurisdiction over the case, it must remand to the district court with instructions to dismiss al-Marri's petition. Both parties agreed that the jurisdictional question should be fully briefed before oral arguments in this case, which are tentatively scheduled for the week of January 31 – February 3, 2007.[665]

The Court of Appeals for the Fourth Circuit heard arguments in al-Marri's case on February 1, 2007.[666] They released their decision on June 11, 2007 and reversed the district court's holding and remanded the case back to the district court.[667] The government petitioned for the court to rehear the case *en banc*, which the court granted in August, 2007.[668] The Court of Appeals for the Fourth Circuit heard arguments in this case on October 31, 2007 and has not released their decision at this time.[669] Al-Marri is currently still detained at the military brig in South Carolina.

The three cases discussed above represent individuals the President has designated as enemy combatants and detained in the United States and the multitude of issues that are associated with such classification.

---

[663] *Id.* at 1; citing Military Commissions Act of 2006, Pub. L. No. 109-366 (2006).

[664] *Id.* at 4. The government also stated that when al-Marri's habeas petition is dismissed, the Department of Defense has ordered that "al Marri be provided with a Combatant Status Review Tribunal (CSRT), in accordance with the existing procedures governing such tribunals. If the CSRT's finding is adverse to al-Marri, he may avail himself of the DTA's (Detainee Treatment Act) exclusive review scheme by filing a claim in the District of Columbia Court." *Id* at 4-5.

[665] *Id.* at 6.

[666] Sari Horwitz, *Detainee Rights at Center of Fight*, Washington Post, Feb. 2, 2007.

[667] *Al-Marri v. Wright*, 487 F.3d 160 (4th Cir. 2007).

[668] *Ali Saleh Kahlah Al-Marri*, Court Cases, Brennan Center for Justice, available at: http://www.brennancenter.org/content/resource/al_marri_v_pucciarelli/

[669] *Id.*

Table 3: Summary of al-Marri's Procedural History
Taken into custody on December 12, 2001

Date	Court	Decision
February, 2002 January, 2003	United States District Court for the Southern District of New York	Indictments
June, 2003	-	President Bush designated al-Marri as an enemy combatant
August 1, 2003	United States District Court for the Southern District of Illinois	Dismissed al-Marri's petition for writ of habeas corpus
March 8, 2004	United States Court of Appeals for the Seventh Circuit	Affirmed District Court's decision to dismiss
July 8, 2005	United States District Court for the District of South Carolina	Al-Marri's detention is authorized by the Authorization to Use Military Force
June 11, 2007	United States Court of Appeals for the Fourth Circuit	Ruled the president may not declare civilians in this country to be enemy combatants and order military to detain them indefinitely
August 22, 2007	United States Court of Appeals for the Fourth Circuit	Court agreed to reconsider the case *en banc*
October 31, 2007	United States Court of Appeals for the Fourth Circuit	Heard arguments in this case

SECTION TWO: US Citizens Detained in Iraq

In October, 29, 2004 Shawqi Ahmad Omar, a naturalized American citizen, was captured and subsequently detained by the Multinational Force – Iraq ("MNF-I") in Iraq.[670] Omar stated he was in Iraq looking for a job when he was captured. Initially, he was not charged with any crime, however in January, 2006 US officials allegedly transferred Omar from Camp Bucca to Abu Ghraib.[671] Omar was later transferred to Camp Cropper, a detainee camp controlled by the Multinational Force – Iraq. On February 2, 2006, US military officials sent an E-mail to Omar's attorneys and notified them that Omar's case would be referred to the Central Criminal Court of Iraq.[672] Omar's attorney immediately filed a motion for an ex parte temporary restraining order that same day.

Mohammad Munaf is an Iraqi-American who immigrated to the United States and became a citizen in 2000.[673] The following year, Munaf and his family moved to Romania. Munaf has split residences between Romania and the United States from 1996 to 2001. Munaf traveled with several Romanian journalists to Iraq in March 2005, however, shortly after they arrived, they were kidnapped by a group claiming to be "Muadh Ibn Jabal Brigade" and held captive for almost two months.[674] In May 2005, military troops under the command of the Multi-National Force-Iraq raided the location where Munaf and the other journalists were being held. Instead of releasing Munaf, however, the MNF-I held him as a prisoner at Camp Cropper.[675]

The issue is Omar and Munaf's case is whether a US citizen, detained in Iraq and in the custody of a multinational force established by the U.N. Security Council, has the right to file a petition for habeas corpus and an injunction in the United States to challenge their detention and to prevent their transfer to Iraqi custody.

---

[670] *Omar v. Harvey*, 416 F. Supp. 2d 19,21 (2006). Omar claims he was in Iraq seeking construction work (at 21 citing Pet. For Writ of Habeas Corpus at 18).
[671] *Id.* at 21.
[672] *Id.* at 21.
[673] *Maisoon Mohammad v. Harvey*, 456 F. Supp. 2d 115, 117 (D.D.C. 2006).
[674] *Id.* at 117.
[675] *Id.*

The district court ruled granted Omar a temporary injunction, preventing his release to the Iraqi government.[676] In February, 2006, District Court Judge Urbina granted Omar's motion because "this controversy presents serious, substantial and difficult questions that give rise to the petitioner's right to present proof to support his claims, because the likelihood the petitioner will suffer irreparable injury is high, and because the public interest strongly favors vigorous application of the writ of habeas corpus."[677]

However, the same court dismissed Munaf's habeas petition.[678] The court held that Munaf is not being held "under or by color of the authority of the United States" or "in violation of the Constitution or laws or treaties of the United States" as required under the habeas statute.[679] Munaf and Omar's cases were consolidated and reached the United States Supreme Court.

The Supreme Court released its opinion in June, 2008 and held that the habeas statute extends to US citizens detained overseas by American forces operating subject to an American chain of command.[680] The Court stated the language in the habeas statute clearly indicates it is applicable to individuals detained "in custody under or by color of the authority of the United States." [681] The Court emphasized the disjunctive "or" implicates that actual Government custody is sufficient for jurisdiction, even if such custody can be described as "under…color of" another authority, such as the MNF-1.[682]

However, the Court held that federal courts may not employ their habeas jurisdiction to prevent the United States from transferring detainees alleged to have committed crimes and detained within the territory of a foreign sovereign for criminal prosecution.[683] The Court stated that neither Omar, nor Munaf, cited a claim in their habeas petitions for which relief can be granted and as a result, their petitions

---

[676] *Omar v. Harvey*, 416 F. Supp. 2d 19, 22 (D.D.C., 2006).
[677] *Id.* at 21.
[678] *Maisoon Mohammad v. Harvey*, 456 F. Supp. 2d 115, 117 (D.D.C. 2006).
[679] *Id.* at 122 citing 28 U.S.C. § 2241 (2006).
[680] *Munaf et al. v. Geren*, No. 06-1666 (U.S. June 12, 2008)
[681] *Id.* at citing 28 U.S.C. §§2241(c)(1).
[682] *Munaf et al. v. Geren*, No. 06-1666, slip op. at 8 (U.S. June 12, 2008).
[683] Id. at 23.

must be dismissed. Both Omar and Munaf asked the court to prevent the Government from transferring them to Iraqi custody.[684] In addition, both admitted that if there were not being detained by the MNF-1, Iraq would be free to arrest and prosecute under the laws of the Iraqi government. The Court held that due to the fact that Omar and Munaf's request would interfere with Iraq's sovereign right to "punish offenses against its laws committed within its borders" their petitions must be dismissed.[685] In conclusion, the Court held that the habeas statute does not prevent the United States from transferring a prisoner to the sovereign authority he concedes has a right to prosecute him.[686]

SECTION THREE: Procedure to Declare Citizen Unlawful Combatant

On February 24, 2004, White House Counsel Alberto R. Gonzales spoke before the American Bar Association about the Administration's policies and procedures surrounding unlawful combatants.[687] Judge Gonzales stated US citizens suspected of being a member of al Qaeda cannot be prosecuted in civilian courts because to do so applies the wrong legal paradigm.[688] Instead, the law of war is applicable to such a citizen. It follows then that "under these rules, captured enemy combatants, whether soldiers or saboteurs, may be detained for the duration of hostilities."[689] They are not detained as a punishment, but rather due to security and military necessity their detention is necessary. "To state repeatedly that detainees are being 'held without charge' mistakenly assumed that charges are somehow necessary or appropriate."[690] However, the laws of war have never required a

---

684 Id at 19.

685 *Id.* at 20 citing *Wilson v. Girard*, 354 U.S. 524, 529.

686 Id. at 28.

687 White House Counsel Alberto R. Gonzales, Addressing Administration Procedures on Unlawful Combatants, Address Before the American Bar Association (Feb. 24, 2004), *in* American Bar Association National Security Law Report, Vol. 26, No. 2 (Summer 2004), at 6-12. It is important to note that Judge Gonzales made his speech prior the Supreme Court's decisions in *Hamdi v. Rumsfeld* and *Rasul v. Bush*.

688 *Id.* at 8.

689 *Id.*

690 *Id.*

country to charge an enemy combatant with a crime, provide them access to an attorney, or allow them to challenge their detention in civilian courts.[691]

Judge Gonzales discussed the Administration's rationale to release minimal facts concerning the designation of US citizens as enemy combatants. He noted the sensitive nature of the information prevented the Administration from revealing most of the information; however, such silence has come at a cost.[692] By not fully articulating their rationale to designate a US citizen as an enemy combatant, the Administration's policy has been criticized and subsequently mischaracterized. Therefore, Judge Gonzales decided to break the silence and offer a glimpse into the Administration's policy and procedures designating an individual as an enemy combatant.[693]

Judge Gonzalez stated that if a US citizen is captured in the United States and it appears he may be an al Qaeda operative and thus he may qualify as an enemy combatant, information on the individual is established and several options are considered by several different agencies.[694] Examples of the options the agencies explore include the possibility for a criminal prosecution, detention as a material witness, and finally detention as an enemy combatant.[695] "Options often are narrowed by the type of information available, and the best course of action in a given case may be influenced by numerous factors including the assessment of the individual's threat potential and value as a possible intelligence source."[696] Judge Gonzales also noted that if based on the available information, criminal prosecution and detention as a material witness are not appropriate, they may conduct an informal process to present their information to an appropriate decision maker, including the question whether an individual might qualify for

---

691 *Id.*

692 *Id.* at 9.

693 *Id.* Judge Gonzales noted that "there is no rigid process for making such determinations – and certainly no particular mechanism required by law. Rather, these are the steps we have taken in our discretion to ensure a thoroughly vetted and reasoned exercise of presidential power." *Id* at 10.

694 *Id.* at 10. Some examples of agencies participating in this procedure include the Department of Defense, the Central Intelligence Agency, and the Department of Justice.

695 *Id.*

696 *Id.*

designation as an enemy combatant.[697] However, before such process can be initiated, the Office of Legal Counsel (OLC) at the Department of Justice must be advised that an individual might qualify as an enemy combatant.[698] Judge Gonzales stated an important consideration is whether the individual has become a member or associated himself with hostile enemy forces.

Many have stridently voiced their opinion that, in the cases of *Hamdi*, *Padilla*, and *al-Marri*, their detentions are unconstitutional[699] and that the government's screening criteria is duplicitous. Their argument is supported by an examination of US citizens who have been suspected of terrorist activities but who have not been designated as enemy combatants. Additionally, the argument continues that individuals of other citizenship, suspected of terrorist activities, have been prosecuted in the United States in the civilian criminal justice system.

SECTION FOUR: Individuals Suspected of Terrorist Activity *not* Detained as Enemy Combatants

As Judge Gonzales noted, not all US citizens alleged to have associated with al Qaeda operatives have been designated as enemy combatants. John Walker Lindh is perhaps the most well known US citizen charged with associating with the Taliban or al Qaeda. Walker Lindh, born in California, was captured as a Taliban fighter in Afghanistan in late 2001. Walker Lindh also allegedly attended al Qaeda training camps.[700] When authorities discovered that Walker Lindh was a US

---

[697] *Id.* at 10.

[698] *Id.* Judge Gonzales noted that on more than one occasion, the OLC advised that information presented does not support classifying the individual as an enemy combatant.

[699] Jesselyn Radack, *How the "Enemy Combatant" Label is Being Used, Part 1*, The Future of Freedom Foundation, available at bhttp://www.fff.org/freedom/fd0501g.asp (May 2005).

[700] Jesselyn Radack, *How the "Enemy Combatant" Label is Being Used, Part 1*, The Future of Freedom Foundation, available at: http://www.fff.org/freedom/fd0501g.asp (May 2005). See also Jesselyn A. Radack, *United States Citizens Detained as "Enemy Combatants": The Right to Counsel as a Matter of Ethics,* 12 Wm. & Mary Bill Rts. J.221 (2003).

citizen, he was transferred to the United States where he was charged in federal district court.

John Walker Lindh entered into a plea bargain with the government in July, 2002. Under the terms of Walker Lindh's plea bargain, Walker Lindh plead guilty to serving in the Taliban militia and carrying a weapon while doing so.[701] The government dropped all other charges filed against Walker Lindh. Additionally, Walker Lindh may not personally benefit financially from telling his story.[702] Walker Lindh will work with the government, including US intelligence officials, providing them with knowledge about the Taliban and Osama bin Laden.[703] Another provision in Walker Lindh's plea bargain included if the he associates with the Taliban or another terrorist organization "the agreement contained in this paragraph shall be null and void, and the United States may immediately invoke any right it has at that time to capture and detain the defendant as an unlawful enemy combatant based on the conduct alleged in the Indictment."[704]

Iyman Faris is another US citizen who has been charged with participating in terrorist activities. Although Faris was born in Kashmir, he entered the United States in May 1994 and became a citizen in 1999. He surrendered to US authorities in March, 2003. Faris, a truck driver, was ultimately indicted for conspiring with other members of al Qaeda to blow up the Brooklyn Bridge[705] and pleaded guilty to providing material support to al Qaeda and to conspiring to do

---

(analyzing the right to counsel of enemy combatants who are US citizens through the lens of the cases regarding Jose Padilla and Yaser Hamdi.)

[701] *US v. Lindh*, Plea Agreement (July 2002) available at: http://fl1.findlaw.com/news.findlaw.com/cnn/docs/terrorism/uslindh71502pleaag.pdf

[702] Bob Franken and John King, '*I Plead Guilty' American Taliban says*, CNN, July 17, 2002, http://archives.cnn.com/2002/LAW/07/15/walker.lindh.hearing/index.html.

[703] *Id.*

[704] *United States v. Lindh*, Plea Agreement P.9 (July 2002) available at: http://fl1.findlaw.com/news.findlaw.com/cnn/docs/terrorism/uslindh71502pleaan/ g.pdf.

[705] *United States v. Faris*, 162 Fed. Appx. 199 (4th Cir. 2005). (Affirming Faris's conviction and 20-year sentence.)

so.[706] In return for his cooperation and guilty plea, prosecutors agreed not to use any of the information he provided against him in other cases and to place him in the Witness Protection Plan if it's determined he faces significant risk of physical harm.[707]

On October 11, 2006, a US federal grand jury indicted Adam Yahiye Gadahn on charges of providing material support to terrorists and treason.[708] According to a Department of Justice news release, Gadahn, who is 28 years old, is a former resident of Orange County, California and he is the first person to be charged with treason[709] since World War II.[710] Gadahn is also known as "Azzam the American" and his current whereabouts are not known.[711] The news release also stated that Gadahn has appeared in several al Qaeda videos, including a video released this summer, and he appeared in a video with al Qaeda leaders Usama bin Laden and Ayman al-Zawahiri.[712] In his first video Gadahn stated he joined al Qaeda "a movement waging war on America and killing large numbers of Americans," and that "the streets of America shall run red with blood."[713] Finally, the news release stated Gadahn has been added to the FBI's Most Wanted List.[714]

Many have interpreted these distinctions (some US citizens as designated as enemy combatants and others as designated as traitorous or criminals) as unclear and have challenged the government's actions

---

[706] CNN.com, *Ohio Trucker Joined al Qaeda Jihad*, available at http://www.cnn.com/2003/LAW/06/19/alqaeda.plea/
[707] *Id.*
[708] First Superseding Indictment, *United States v. Gadahn*, (C.D. Cal. Oct. 2006), No. SA CR 05-254(A).
[709] US Constitution, Article III, Section 3, "Treason against the United States, shall consist only in levying war against them, or in adhering to their enemies, giving them aid and comfort. No person shall be convicted of treason unless on the testimony of two witnesses to the same overt act, or on confession in open court. The Congress shall have the power to declare the punishment for treason, but no attainder of treason shall work corruption of blood, or forfeiture except during the life of the person attainted."
[710] Department of Justice News Release, *U.S. Citizen Indicted on Treason, Material Support Charges for Providing Aid and Comfort to al Qaeda*, Oct. 11, 2006, http://www.usdoj.gov/opa/pr/2006/October/06_nsd_695.html.
[711] *Id.*
[712] *Id.*
[713] *Id.*
[714] *Id.*

concerning individuals prosecuted in civilian criminal justice system and those designated as enemy combatants. Radack[715]compared the designations of Walker Lindh and Faris with other US citizens (Hamdi and Padilla). The commentator noted that neither Walker Lindh nor Faris (who both allegedly trained in al Qaeda camps) were detained as enemy combatants while Hamdi and Padilla were detained as such. In addition, Radack stated that Richard Reid, a British national,[716] was also not deemed an enemy combatant "despite the heinousness of Reid's attempted crime, the massive number of potential victims, and Reid's apparent intent to attack the United States and France by murdering citizens."[717] Included in the discussion also was the case of Zacarias Moussaoui, (French citizen) the alleged "20th hijacker," who admitted pledging allegiance to al Qaeda and participating in the September 11 attacks, was not charged as an enemy combatant.

The argument continues with an explanation that Padilla and al-Marri were taken into custody on a "material witness" warrant and detained in a federal civilian jail.[718] Moreover, although the government claimed Hamdi was a tremendous threat to national security, prosecutors agreed to his release provided he abided by certain conditions including that he resides in Saudi Arabia ("a hotbed of al Qaeda activity").[719] Based on the similarities in the factual circumstances of those placed through the criminal justice system and those designated as enemy combatants, Radack concluded "There is simply no principled way to justify the government's use of the 'enemy combatant' label."[720]

Several opponents to the Administration's policy concerning enemy combatants argued that Walker Lindh's settlement agreement demonstrates that the US criminal justice system is robust enough to

---

[715] Jesselyn Radack, *How the "Enemy Combatant" Label is Being Used, Part 2*, The Future of Freedom Foundation,
available at http://www.fff.org/freedom/fd0502g.asp (May 2005).
This article was also published on CNN, Oct. 15, 2004,
http://cnn.com/2004/LAW/10/15/radack.enemy.combatant/index.html.

[716] Richard Reid, *Who is Richard Reid:* "The Shoe Bomber," BBC.com. available at http://news.bbc.co.uk/1/hi/uk/1731568.stm

[717] *Id.*

[718] Radack, *supra* note 700.

[719] *Id.*

[720] *Id.*

handle terrorism cases and thus there is no need for military tribunals. However, many other legal scholars have supported the government's distinction of enemy combatants between US citizens.

Another supporter of the special circumstances of designation, Jane Mayer[721] compared Walker Lindh's case with Hamdi's, and asserted that Hamdi was actually captured on the same day and at the same location as Walker Lindh was in Afghanistan.[722] However, whereas Walker Lindh spoke to the press and to US interrogators, Hamdi refrained from making statements and thus did not provide any self-incriminating evidence. Walker Lindh's statements, it was argued, provided the government with enough information to indict him.[723]

Mayer also discussed issues concerning the appropriateness of the criminal justice system for handling individuals accused of terrorism and stated that it apparent that "information gleaned from our open court system can be used against us"[724] (for example, in the prosecution of the first World Trade Center bombing, government experts say terrorists were able to learn vital information about structural weaknesses in the buildings, as well as other bits of strategically useful information). Therefore, prosecuting terrorists has potential risks, yet our Constitution provides a defendant with certain rights which creates an "ingrained and serious tensions in these prosecutions, and, it seems, society has yet to find a comfortable solution."[725]

The arguments continue about the appropriate designation of US citizens who are alleged to be involved with organizations focused on causing harm to the United States. Some scholars have asserted that the government should charge US citizens suspected of terrorist activity with treason. For example, Benjamin A. Lewis argued that the government should prosecute American citizens detained during the

---

721 Jane Mayer, *Measuring Betrayal*, The New Yorker Online Only, March 3, 2003, http://www.newyorker.com/printables/online/030310on_onlineonly02. (This was an online discussion with The New Yorker's Amy Tubke-Davidson about John Walker Lindh's case with Jane Mayer, an investigative journalist.)

722 *Id.*

723 *Id.*

724 *Id.*

725 *Id.*

War on Terror and later designated as enemy combatants with treason.[726]

Lewis noted that in Justice Scalia's dissent in *Hamdi v. Rumsfeld*, he stated "that when the United States government accuses one of its own citizens of waging war against it, 'our constitutional tradition has been to prosecute him in federal court for treason or some other crime.'"[727] Thus, he is of the opinion that the treason clause has been successfully used in the past and there are no substantive reasons why it should not be applied in the War on Terror.[728] Lewis emphasized that the application of the treason clause in a criminal court will be a more beneficial form of prosecution for the government concerning Hamdi and Padilla's case.[729]

In discussions of the Gadahn, the US citizen accused of treason, Deputy Attorney General Paul J. McNulty stated "The War on Terror is a fight for hearts and minds, and Gadahn gave himself to our enemies in al Qaeda for the purpose of being a central part of their propaganda machine. By making this choice, we believe Gadahn committed treason – perhaps the most serious offense for which any person can be tried under our Constitution."[730] According to one news report, Gadahn is believed to be in Pakistan.[731] Deputy Attorney McNutly addressed why Gadahn was charged with treason instead of being charged for crimes similar to John Walker Lindh's or to be designated as an enemy combatant, and stated that the government hopes to use publicity to

---

[726] Benjamin A. Lewis, *An Old Means to a Different End: The War on Terror, American Citizens…And The Treason Clause*, 34 Hofstra L. Rev. 1215 (2006).
[727] *Id.* at 1215 citing *Hamdi v. Rumsfeld*, 542 U.S. 507, 554 (2004).
[728] *Id.* at 1216.
[729] *Id.* at 1251.
[730] *Id.*
[731] Catherine Herridge and Ian McCaleb and AP, *American al Qaeda Members to be Indicted for Treason*, FOXSNEWS, Oct. 12, 2006,

capture Gadahn.[732] Moreover, he stated the last video Gadahn appeared in provided sufficient evidence for him to be indicted.[733]

Therefore, several legal scholars and American observers have thoroughly discussed the President's decision to detain US citizens as enemy combatants and to detain a resident alien as an enemy combatant in the United States. They have also addressed other options for suspected terrorists, for example charging them with terrorist related activity or charging them with treason.

SECTION FIVE: Conclusion

The Founding Fathers were gravely aware of the country's dire need for a government that encompassed checks and balances to prevent the formation of a government with limitless power. The American people wished to be free from a government that exercised unrestricted power and answered to no one. To this end, the framers established three branches and accorded each branch with different authority and responsibilities. The three different branches also included the ability to provide checks and balances to ensure that one branch did not over exceed its breadth of authority. However, caution is required so that one branch does not infringe upon the authority of the other.

The Founding Fathers accorded the executive branch with authority, among other things, to conduct the country's foreign affairs. However, they also accorded the judicial branch the authority to ensure the American citizen's liberty is not comprised or jeopardized without cause. The cases discussed above illustrate the balancing act of the executive branch's ability to respond to the War on Terror and the judicial branch's responsibility to ensure the executive's response has not exceeded it authority.

The question continues to be debated if the current laws are robust enough to handle the new threats facing the United States. The

---

732 Dan Eggen and Karen DeYoung, *U.S. Supporter of al Qaeda is Indicted on Treason Charge*, Washington Post, Oct. 12, 2006 at AO3, http://www.washingtonpost.com/wp-dyn/content/article/2006/10/11/AR2006101101121.html?nav=rss_nation/nationalsecurity.

733 *Id.* The authors noted a previous indicted against Gadahn, not including a charge of treason, had been sealed.

individuals included in the above charts are a small selection of those who may need to avail themselves of the rights and laws of the United States. It is also evident that the balance between one branch encroaching upon another is not set in stone. The judicial branch generally accords deference to the executives' military decisions. However, if those decisions infringe upon the rights of citizens, the judicial branch is more likely to interject and analyze the executive's and/or legislative decisions.

The President's designation of US citizens as enemy combatants and the subsequent detention of those individuals designated as such triggered several questions about the scope of the executive's authority. For example, does the executive branch have the authority to detain a US citizen as an enemy combatant, without charge and holding him incommunicado? Does that executive decree need congressional authorization to detain US citizens as enemy combatants? Does the Authorization to Use Military Force authorize such detentions? What rights are accorded to those designated as enemy combatants? Does the executive have the authority to detain a resident alien as an enemy combatant and detain him in the United States without charge? Can US citizens detained in Iraq by the multinational force mandated by the U.N. Security Council challenge their detentions in the United States?

The Supreme Court of the United States addressed one of the questions generated from the President's designation of US citizens as enemy combatants. However the Supreme Court did not resolve all of the related issues. In *Hamdi v. Rumsfeld*, the Supreme Court held the Authorization to Use Military Force authorized the President to designate US citizens as enemy combatants.[734] However individuals detained as enemy combatants must be provided an opportunity to present evidence that they are not an enemy combatant. Whether the Supreme Court's holding is limited to the circumstances surrounding Hamdi's capture has yet to be seen. The Supreme Court did not specifically address the circumstances surrounding Padilla's detention because Padilla failed to file the case in the proper jurisdiction. Padilla was transferred to Miami before the Supreme Court had the opportunity to hear his case the second time around. The Supreme Court may address the President's authority to designate individuals as enemy

[734] *Hamdi v. Rumsfeld*, 542 U.S. 507 (2004)

combatants if al-Marri's case is presented to them. However, questions still remain as to who may be designated as an enemy combatant and once designated as such, what rights are accorded to them. In October 2006, the President signed into law the Military Commission Act of 2006[735] which addresses the remaining questions.

All three branches of the United States government have played a key role in the United States' response to the tragic events on September 11, 2001. The executive determined that it is necessary to detain some US citizens and resident aliens as enemy combatants to prevent such individuals from returning to assist the enemy. Moreover, the executive deemed it essential to gather as much information and intelligence from these individuals as possible. The information these individuals may provide has great potential to prevent future attacks on American soil. Congress enacted the Authorization to Use Military Force and permitted the President to use force against al Qaeda's threat. The Supreme Court has affirmed the executive's ability to detain enemy combatants because they deemed the AUMF provided the President with such authority. Therefore, every branch provided an essential part to the United State's response and has acted in accordance with the powers afforded to them by the Founding Fathers.

---

[735] Military Commission Act of 2006, *supra* note 390.

CHAPTER FOUR

Non-US Citizens Detained at Guantanamo Bay

> "It is a rare occasion when a President can sign a bill he knows will save American lives. I have that privilege this morning. The Military Commissions Act of 2006 is one of the most important pieces of legislation in the War on Terror ... And now, in memory of the victims of September the 11th, it is my honor to sign the Military Commissions Act of 2006 into law."
> - President George W. Bush, 10/17/06

After the terrorist attacks on September 11, President Bush, as authorized by Congress, launched missile and air strikes against the Taliban rulers of Afghanistan who were protecting and harboring members of al Qaeda. Since the initial deployment in November 2001, the United States and its allies have captured thousands of al Qaeda and Taliban fighters.[736] Some individuals were released or detained in Afghanistan or Iraq, depending on where they were captured. Hundreds of individuals, however, designated to be enemy combatants were sent to Guantanamo Bay, a US naval base in Cuba. Based on the law of armed conflict, these individuals detained at Guantanamo and designated as enemy combatants were not accorded rights associated with the status of prisoners of war.

The detainees held at Guantanamo Bay and the several issues that emerged from US policy surrounding their detention ignited massive debates and discussions. The focus of this chapter is on the rights and privileges afforded to the detainees and the United State's response to judicial decisions regarding the detainees, as well as Congressional authorization.

[736] 29 Harvard Society for Law & Public Policy, Harvard Journal of Law & Public Policy (Fall, 2005). 159.

SECTION ONE: History of Guantanamo Bay

In 1903, the United States entered into a Lease Agreement with the newly independent Republic of Cuba, created as a result of the Spanish-American War.[737] President Theodore Roosevelt signed the Lease Agreement in February, 1903.[738] Pursuant to the Lease Agreement, "the United States recognizes the continuance of the ultimate sovereignty of the Republic of Cuba over the [leased areas]," while "the Republic of Cuba consents that during the period of the occupation by the United States...the United States shall exercise complete jurisdiction and control over and within said areas."[739] Thirty years later, the United States and the Republic of Cuba entered into a treaty which stated that "absent an agreement to modify or abrogate the lease, the lease would remain in effect '[s]o long as the United States of America shall not abandon the...naval station of Guantanamo Bay.'"[740]

Guantanamo Naval Base is the oldest American naval base outside the continental United States and occupies 45 square miles.[741] The naval base previously housed migrant camps, assisting Haitian and Cuban refugees in the 1990s.[742] On January 10, 2002, after President Bush sent US armed forces into Afghanistan, the United States transported alleged members of the Taliban an al Qaeda to Guantanamo Bay.[743] As will be discussed further, these individuals were designated

---

737 *Rasul et al., v. Bush*, 542 U.S. 466, at 471,124 S. Ct. 2686, 159 L.Ed. 2d 548 (2004).

738 Alfred De Zayas, *The Status of Guantanamo Bay and the Status of the Detainees*, 37 U.B.C. L. Rev. 277, 289 (2004).

739 *Id.* citing Lease of Lands for Coaling and Naval Stations, Feb. 23, 1903, U.S.-Cuba, Art. III, T.S. No. 418 [hereinafter 1903 Lease Agreement].

740 *Id.* citing Treaty Defining Relations with Cuba, May 29, 1934, U.S.-Cuba, Art. III, 48 Stat 1683, T.S. No. 866 [hereinafter 1934 Treaty].

741 Alfred De Zayas, *The Status of Guantanamo Bay and the Status of the Detainees*, 37 U.B.C. L. Rev. 277, at 288 (2004).According to De Zayas, the base is roughly the size of Manhattan Island.

742 Guantanamo Bay, Global Security Organization, *available at*: http://www.globalsecurity.org/military/facility/guantanamo-bay.htm.

743 Alfred De Zayas, *supra* note 741, at 309. The detainees were first kept in a facility known as Camp X-Ray (a quickly erected facility) which exposed detainees to outdoor elements. On April 28, 2002, Camp Delta was created for the detainees. Camp Delta is divided into separate areas, and detainees are remanded to appropriate level according to security issues. Levels 1, 2, and 3

as enemy combatants and some were ordered to be prosecuted by military commissions. Military commissions have been used in almost every war the Untied States was involved with and have historically been used to prosecute enemy combatants who have been accused of violating the laws of war.[744] The last time the United States convened military commissions was during World War II. The following section briefly discusses the history of the utilization of military commissions.

SECTION TWO: History of Military Commissions

The United States has a long history of implementing military commissions to "try those accused of '[v]iolations of the laws and usages of war' dating back to the early years of the Republic.'"[745] Military commissions were thus implemented before the adoption of the United States Constitution and are sometimes referred to as the American Common Law War Courts.[746] History demonstrates that military commissions were used in twelfth century England "where the Court of the Constable and the Marshal were 'established for control of the King's Army, appeals of death penalties for murder committed out of the country, and the rights of prisoners taken in war.'"[747]

It has been noted that, "The laws of war have long recognized that military commissions can be convened to prosecute war crimes during

---

are rated maximum security; Level 4 is medium security (Harvard J. L. & Public Pol'y, *supra* note 736, 161.

[744] US Department of Defense, Fact Sheet, Military Commissions, Oct. 16, 2006, *available at*: http://www.defenselink.mil/news/Oct2006/d20061016factsheet.pdf.

[745] Christopher M. Evans, *Terrorism on Trial: The President's Constitutional Authority to Order the Prosecution of Suspected Terrorists by Military Commission*, 51 Duke L.J. 1831, 1836 (2002).

[746] Heather Anne Maddox, *After the Dust Settles: Military Tribunal Justice for Terrorists After September 11, 2001*, 28 N.C.J. Int'l L. & Com. Reg. 421 (2002), citing The United Nations War Crimes Commission, Law Reports of Trials of War Criminals, 111 (William S. Hein & Co., Inc. 1997) (1947).

[747] *Id.* at 424 citing Harold L. Kaplan, *Constitutional Limitations on Trials by Military Commissions* 3 (1943) (unpublished Doctor of Juridical Science dissertation, New York University School of Law) (available in microfiche at the University of North Carolina School of Law Library).

an armed conflict."[748] The United States convened military commissions during the Revolutionary War to try enemy spies.[749] The United States Supreme Court in *Ex parte Quirin* noted several individuals were tried during the Revolutionary War before military commissions.[750] The Court also noted instances of individuals tried before a military tribunal during the War of 1812 as well as the Mexican War.[751] Additionally, the Court stated "During the Civil War a number of Confederate officers and soldiers, found within the Union lines in disguise, were tried and convicted by military commission for being spies."[752]

One scholar noted 4, 271 military commissions convened during the Civil War and 1, 435 took place during Reconstruction.[753] President Andrew Johnson ordered military commissions to prosecute the conspirators involved in the assassination of President Abraham Lincoln.[754] The Secretary of War and the Attorney General argued the men should be tried by military courts because Lincoln was the Commander in Chief. Other government officials argued the conspirators should be tried in civilian courts.[755] The conspirators were tried by a military commission and all were found guilty and several were executed.[756]

Military commissions continued to be used through the World Wars.[757] After World War I, the United States and the Allies tried war criminals before military tribunals; their right to do so was recognized

---

748 Evans, *supra* note 745, at 1836, citing William Winthrop, *Military Law and Precedents*, 330 (2d ed. 1920).
749 *Id.* at 1836-37.
750 *Ex parte Quirin*, 317 U.S. 1, 42 n.14 (1942).
751 *Ex parte Quirin*, 317 U.S. at 42 n.14.
752 *Ex parte Quirin*, 317 U.S. at 32 n.10, citing General Orders cited in 2 Winthrop, Military Law (2d ed. 1896) p. 1298, *supra* note 748.
753 David Glazier, *Precedents Lost: The Neglected History of the Military Commission*, 46 Va. J. Int'l L. 5, 40 (2005) citing Mark E. Neely, Jr., *The Fate of Liberty: Abraham Lincoln and Civil Liberties* 168-73, 176-77 (1991).
754 Trial of the Conspirators at http://www.spartacus.schoolnet.co.uk/USACWtrial.htm. (Last visited Feb. 2, 2007).
755 *Id.*
756 *Id.* Thee individuals were pardoned by President Andrew Johnson in 1869.
757 Maddox, *supra* note 746, at 424.

by the peace treaties ending the war.[758] In addition, numerous military commissions were held after World War II.[759] The Nuremberg tribunals (military tribunals) were conducted by the United States, the United Kingdom, France and Russia to try individuals who had committed severe violations of law.[760] During these tribunals and the other tribunals conducted solely by the United States, the United States Supreme Court was flooded with habeas corpus petitions.[761] Thus, the United States Supreme Court "has had a number of opportunities to 'consider at length the sources and nature of the authority to create Military Commissions.'"[762]

In *Ex parte Milligan*, the Supreme Court held that a military commission did not have jurisdiction to prosecute a US citizen, who was not a prisoner of war nor a resident of a rebellion state, if civilian courts were open and operating.[763] In 1942, the Supreme Court held in *Ex parte Quirin*, that the President's appointed military commissions were lawful to prosecute unlawful combatants who entered the United States bent on committing hostile acts against the United States.[764] The Court held that under the laws of war, unlawful combatants were subject to trial and punishment by military tribunals for acts which render their belligerency unlawful.[765] Finally, the Court stated "It has long been accepted practice by our military authorities to treat those who, during time of war, pass surreptitiously from enemy territory into our own, discarding their uniforms upon entry, for the commission of

---

[758] *Id.* citing *In re Yamashita*, 327 U.S. at 12 n.1 (citing Art. 128 of Treaty of Versailles, June 28, 1919; Art. 173 of Treaty of St. Germain, Sept. 10, 1919; Art. 157 of Treaty of Trianon, June 4, 1920).

[759] *Id.* at 424. Military Commissions were authorized but not used during the Korean War. Daryl A. Mundis, *The Use of Military Commissions to Prosecute Individuals Accused of Terrorists Acts*, 96 Am. J. Int'l L. 320, 321 (2002) citing General Headquarters United States Command, Tokyo Japan, AG 000.5 (28 October 50) JA (Oct. 28, 1950).

[760] Holocaust Encyclopedia, War Crimes Trials, available at: http://www.ushmm.org/wlc/en/index.php?ModuleId=10005140.

[761] Maddox, *supra* note 746, at 425.

[762] *Id.* at 435, citing The United Nations War Crimes Commission, Law Reports of Trials of War Criminals at 111 (William S. Hein & Co., Inc. 1997) (1947).

[763] *Ex parte Milligan*, 71 U.S. 2, 18 L. Ed. 281 (1866).

[764] *Ex parte Quirin*, 317 U.S. 1 (1942).

[765] *Id.* at 13.

hostile acts involving destruction of life or property, as unlawful combatants punishable as such by military commission."[766]

In *In re Yamashita*, the Supreme Court stated unless there was an express suspension of the writ of habeas corpus by the Executive Branch, Article III courts retained the power and, in fact, the duty to examine the authority of military commissions if such petitions were made.[767] However, the Court stated their duty to examine such petitions was limited to cases where commissions were held on US soil or in a place where the United States exercises sovereignty.[768] Moreover, the Court observed that they were not authorized to review military tribunals' judgments.[769] The Court examined another important case concerning the right of an individual tried before a military commission to file a habeas corpus petition in *Johnson v. Eisentrager*.[770]

The Court stated if the military tribunals have lawful authority to hear, decide and punish, their action is not subject to judicial review simply because they have made a wrong decision on disputed facts.[771] Instead the Court held "Correction of their errors of decision is not for the courts but for the military authorities which are alone authorized to review their decisions."[772] However, the Court did not say that they could not review military commission verdicts or procedures for potential constitutional problems, and in fact the Courts have the authority to review the order itself establishing the military commissions for constitutional violations.[773] Thus, the Court stated they would respect the military commissions "so far as they do not conflict with the commands of Congress or the Constitution."[774]

In *Johnson v. Eisentrager*, the Court held it would not review military commission findings of fact.[775] One scholar noted *Johnson*

---

[766] *Id.* at 14.
[767] Maddox, *supra* note 746, at 436 citing *In re Yamashita*, 327 U.S. 1, 9 (1946).
[768] *Id.*
[769] *Id*, citing *In re Yamashita*, 327 U.S. 8.
[770] *Johnson v. Eisentrager*, 339 U.S. 763 (1950).
[771] Maddox, *supra* note 746, at 437.
[772] *In re Yamashita*, 327 U.S. 1, 9 (1946).
[773] Maddox, *supra* note 746, at 437.
[774] *In re Yamashita*, 327 U.S. at 16.
[775] Maddox, *supra* note 746, at 436.

can be cited as authority for the proposition that "Article III Courts should not afford trials to al Qaeda terrorists living outside the United States who nonetheless travel to the US to commit violations of the law of war. Rather they would presumably be triable by military commissions."[776] As the Court stated "The nonresident enemy alien, especially one who has remained in the service of the enemy, does not have even this qualified access to our courts, for he neither has comparable claims upon our institutions nor could his use of them fail to be helpful to the enemy."[777] The author concluded the distinction between lawful and unlawful combatants (or belligerents) has been important for the United States Supreme Court to determine who may be lawfully subject to trial by military commissions.[778]

These incidents clearly reveal that the United States and the international community as a whole have a long history of implementing military commissions. Military commissions have been utilized in every major armed conflict involving the United States. The United States Supreme Court has heard several cases about the appropriateness and process of military commissions. The next section discusses litigation and issues concerning military commissions implemented during the current War on Terror.

SECTION THREE: The War on Terror & Guantanamo Bay

The Department of Defense announced on January 11, 2002 that 20 individuals captured in Afghanistan were on a plane to Guantanamo Bay.[779] Individuals sent to Guantanamo Bay were not detained as prisoners of war but instead as unlawful combatants and therefore were not accorded all of the privileges prisoners of war were entitled to. To assuage concerns of many who questioned this decision, President Bush stated that all detainees shall be treated humanely and afforded

---

[776] *Id.* at 442.
[777] *Johnson v. Eisentrager*, 339 U.S. at 776.
[778] Maddox, *supra* note 746, at 442.
[779] US Department of Defense, News Briefing, Secretary of Defense Donald Rumsfeld & General Myers, January, 11, 2002.

certain protections from the Geneva Convention.[780] Rights currently appropriated to Guantanamo detainees include: three meals a day that meet their cultural dietary requirements;[781] adequate shelter and clothing (including shoes, uniforms and hygiene items);[782] opportunity to worship and provision of "prayer beads, rugs, and copies of the Quran in their native language."[783] (the "Muslim call to prayer is broadcast for the detainees…five times a day…" and each cell block has a painted arrow which points toward Mecca, Saudi Arabia;[784] afforded the means to send and receive mail and also are provided with books and other reading materials; and[785] provision of excellent medical care.[786]

Additionally, although individuals detained at Guantanamo Bay are subject to interrogations by the US government,[787] interrogators are prohibited from using certain interrogation methods on the detainees (detainees must at all times be treated humanely).[788]

---

780 Memorandum for the Vice President, Secretary of State, Secretary of Defense, Re: Human Treatment of al Qaeda and Taliban Detainees (Feb. 7, 2002).

781 Guantanamo Today, July 2006, 2. The report noted that "Detention personnel also pay respect to Islamic holy periods, like Ramadan, by modifying meal schedules in observance of religious requirements." *Id.* at 3.

782 *Id.* Each detainee is provided with basic items (toothpaste, soap, shampoo, plastic flip flops, and cotton underwear, shorts, pants and a shirt). Guards are not allowed to remove basic items but they are allowed to take away comfort items for behavior infractions. Kathleen T. Rhem, *Detainees Living in Varied Conditions at Guantanamo*, American Forces Information Service, Feb. 16, 2005.

783 *Id.*

784 *Id.* at 3. The report stated that once the prayer call sounds, the detainees receives 20 minutes, during which they may not be interrupted, to practice their faith. Additionally, "DoD detention personnel schedule detainee medical appointments, interrogations, and other activities mindful of the prayer call schedule." *Id.* Kathleen T. Rhem, *Detainees Living in Varied Conditions at Guantanamo*, American Forces Information Service, Feb. 16, 2005.

785 *Id.*.at 2. The report noted that Agatha Christie and Harry Potter books in Arabic are among the most popular.

786 *Id.*

787 US Department of Defense, Guantanamo Detainees, April 2004, available at: http://www.defenselink.mil/news/Apr2004/d20040406gua.pdf.

788 *Id.* at 3.

The International Committee of the Red Cross (ICRC) regularly visits the detainees at Guantanamo Bay. As of June, 2004, more than 8,500 messages were facilitated through the ICRC to detainees at Guantanamo.[789] The ICRC delegates speak to the detainees in total privacy and such delegates also inspect the detainee's cells and other facilities.[790] The ICRC also meets with a detainee before he is released to make certain that if the detainee has any concerns about returning to his home State, that such concerns are known both to the ICRC and the US government.

On November 13, 2001, President Bush issued a Military Order which authorized the trial of noncitizens suspected of terrorist activity, including members of al Qaeda, to be tried before specially convened military commissions.[791] President Bush reaffirmed that his constitutional authority as Commander in Chief of the Armed Forces of the United States and the laws of the United States, in addition the AUMF, provided him with the authority to order trial by military commissions.[792]

President Bush's Military Order recognized that the September 11th attacks were on a scale that created a state of armed conflict which required the use of the United States Armed Forces.[793] Moreover, President Bush acknowledged the individuals involved in the attacks "if not detected and prevented, will cause mass deaths, mass injuries, and massive destruction of property, and may place at risk the continuity of the operations of the United States Government."[794] The President declared military tribunals were essential to protect the United States and American citizens and given the danger to the safety of the United States, the principles of law and rules of evidence generally applied in

---

789 US Department of Defense, News Transcript, International Committee of the Red Cross Interaction with the Department of Defense on Detainees, June 24, 2004 at 3. Their first visit was on January 18, 2002.

790 International Committee of the Red Cross, Operational Update, US Detention Related to the Events of 11 September 2001 and its Aftermath – The Role of the ICRC, Dec. 12, 2006.

791 Military Order of November 13, 2001: Detention, Treatment, and Trial of Certain Noncitizens in the War Against Terrorism, 66 Fed. Reg. 57, 833 (Nov. 13, 2001) [hereinafter Military Order].

792 *Id.*

793 *Id.* at § 1(a).

794 *Id.* at § 1(c).

criminal cases are not applicable to current military commissions.[795] The President defined those subject to his Military Order as noncitizens and determined that:

> (1) there is reason to believe that such individual, at the relevant times: (i) is or was a member of the organization known as al Qaida; (ii) has engaged in, aided or abetted, or conspired to commit, acts of international terrorism, or acts in preparation therefore, that have caused, threaten to cause, or have as their aim to cause, injury to adverse effects on the United States, its citizens, national security, foreign policy, or economy; or (iii) has knowingly harbored one or more individuals described in subparagraphs (i) or (ii) of subsection 2(a)(1) of this order; and
>
> (2) it is in the interest of the United States that such individual be subject to this order.[796]

The Military Order emphasized that all detainees will be treated humanely, afforded adequate food, and allowed the free exercise of religion consistent with the requirements of such detention.[797] A detainee tried before the military commission may only be convicted by two-thirds of the members of the commission present at the time of the vote.[798] Individuals subject to this Military Order are under the sole jurisdiction of the military tribunals and therefore the individual is not able to seek any remedy or any other proceeding in: (i) any court of the United States, or any State thereof; (ii) any court of any foreign nation; or (iii) any international tribunal.[799]

The Constitution of the United States provides the President with the authority to establish military commissions under the president's commander in chief powers.[800] However, such authority is not

---

[795] *Id.* at § 1(e) and (f).
[796] *Id.* at § 2(a)(1) and (2).
[797] *Id.* at §3(a)-(e).
[798] *Id.* at §4(6).
[799] *Id.* at §7(3)(b)(1) and (2).
[800] Evans, *supra* note 745, at 1837. See U.S. Const. art. II, § 2.

unlimited.[801] As one scholar noted "The Constitution vests the president, as commander in chief, with the power to wage war that Congress has declared, and to execute all laws passed by Congress defining and punishing offenses committed against the law of nations, including those governing the conduct of war, the jus in bello."[802] Moreover, Article 21 of the Uniform Code of Military Justice ("UCMJ") states that military commissions have "concurrent jurisdiction with respect to offenders or offenses that by statute or by the law of war may be tried by military commissions...or other military tribunals."[803] Therefore, according to some scholars, the president is limited in his capacity as commander in chief, to establish military commissions for violations acts found in statutes defining certain acts as violations of the law of war.[804] In addition, it has been well settled that Congress also has the ability to mandate the trial by military commission of war criminals.[805]

President Bush's Military Order establishing military commissions for those detained in connection with terrorist activity is similar to courts-martial yet includes some important distinctions. For example, according to one scholar, courts-martial are appealable on all issues of fact and law and encompass the strict rules of evidence.[806] Military commissions, to the contrary, follow evidentiary guidelines promulgated by Secretary of Defense.[807] Discussion on the primary differences between a court-martial and a military commission rely on the assumption that general courts-martial are governed by the Military Rules of Evidence, which mirror the Federal Rules of Evidence.[808]

Some have noted President's Bush's decision to convene military commissions was "predicated upon the belief that terrorist acts amount

---

[801] *Id.*

[802] *Id.* at 1837-38 citing *Ex parte Quirin*, 317 U.S. at 26.

[803] *Id.* at 1837 citing 10 U.S.C. § 821 (2000).

[804] *Id.* at 1838.

[805] Maddox, *supra* note 746, at 445, citing 78 Am. Jur. 2d War 35 (2002) (citing *Application of Yamashita*, 327 U.S. 1 (1946).

[806] Christopher M. Evans, *Terrorism on Trial: The President's Constitutional Authority to Order the Prosecution of Suspected Terrorists by Military Commission*, 51 Duke L.J.1831 (2002).

[807] *Id.* at 1832.

[808] Robinson O. Everett & Scott L. Sillman, *Forums for Punishing Offenses Against the Law of Nations*, 29 Wake Forest L. Rev. 509, 516-517 (1994).

to acts of war, and that, accordingly, suspected terrorists should be treated as war criminals."[809] Supporters of President's Bush's Military Order assert his power over foreign affairs provides the president the authority to convene military commissions.[810] However, objections debating the legality of the United States' war status impact whether President Bush was acting in the realm of "external affairs" when he issued the Military Order on November 13, 2001.[811]

Although some have argued that while President Bush's Military Order meets the constitutional requirements set forth in *Ex parte Quirin*, they argue that it is not consistent with international law, of which the laws of war are a subset.[812] Some have argued that current international law is only applicable to states recognized as having legal "personality"—that is, the capacity to hold rights and to be subject to obligations within the international legal system.[813] According to one scholar, the laws of war only apply to state actors and do not apply to individuals and only individuals acting as agents of a recognized state may be tried and punished for offenses against the laws of war.[814] The author noted under President Bush's Military Order those responsible for the attacks on September 11 would be tried before military commission.[815] However, because those individuals were not acting as agents of a recognized state, but rather members of an independent terrorist organization the author stated "the suspects cannot, consistent with existing international law, be tried before military commissions for violating the laws of war."[816]

In addition, others argued that President Bush's Military Order is an attempt to rapidly change customary international law so that it applies to nonstate actors like al Qaeda members. Current customary international law results from a consensual process of consistent and

---

[809] Christopher M. Evans, *Terrorism on Trial: The President's Constitutional Authority to Order the Prosecution of Suspected Terrorists by Military Commission*, 51 Duke L.J. 1831, 1832 (2002).
[810] *Id.* at 1839.
[811] *Id.* citing *United States v. Curtiss-Wright Export Corp*, 299 U.S. 304, 319 (1936).
[812] *Id.* at 1851.
[813] *Id.* citing Michael Byers, *Custom, Power and the Power of Rules*, 75 (1999).
[814] *Id.* at 1852.
[815] *Id.*
[816] *Id.*

general practice among states and the United States cannot effectuate a change unilaterally.[817] Even if the proposition that the laws of war are applicable to nonstate actors becomes customary international law, it cannot be applied retroactively through the November 13 Military Order.[818] Therefore, "to characterize members in terrorist organizations as unlawful combatants and recognize them as subject to the laws of war could mean that, in certain instances, members of terrorist groups might be entitled to combatant and prisoner of war status." To do so, would grant political legitimacy and respectability upon such groups where it is neither warranted nor prudent.[819] Thus, it has been concluded by some who support this argument that the President's Military Order is authorized under the constitution but is inconsistent with existing international law because it applies to nonstate actors.

On July 3, 2003, President Bush determined that six enemy combatants detained by the United States were subject to his Military Order of November 13, 2001.[820] The Department of Defense listed several factors that are considered before a detainee is charged and such factors include: 1) "the quality of evidence, 2) the completeness of intelligence gathering and, 3) our desire to bring closure to individual cases."[821] Furthermore, DoD included as criterion evidence of attendance at terrorist training camps and involvement in financing al Qaeda, protection for Usama bin Laden, and recruitment of future terrorists.[822]

On December 3, 2003, the Department of Defense announced that one of the detainees, David Hicks, was assigned a military defense counsel.[823] Hicks was the first detainee at Guantanamo to be assigned a military lawyer. The first military commission was convened on

---

817 *Id.* at 1852.

818 Evans, *supra* note 806, at 1854.

819 *Id.*

820 US Department of Defense News Release, President Determines Enemy Combatants Subject to his Military Order, July 3, 2003.

821 *Id.*

822 *Id.*

823 US Department of Defense, News Release, DoD Assigns Legal Counsel for Guantanamo Detainee, Dec. 3, 2003. Additionally, Hick's Australian lawyer met with Hicks later that month. Associated Press, *Lawyer Says Cuba Appeal Prompted Pentagon*, New York Times, Dec. 9, 2003, available at: http://www.pegc.us/archive/Press/NY_Times/nyt_digest_2003.txt.

August 24, 2004.[824] Salim Achmed Hamdan was charged with conspiracy to commit violations of the law and was present at the trial.[825] The next day, David Hick's trial by military commission convened.[826] Two other military commissions convened within the next months.

However in December 2004, action on all military commissions was suspended due to a November 2004 federal district court order which stayed further proceedings in the case of Salim Ahmed Hamdan.[827] On July 15, 2005, the US Court of Appeals for the District of Columbia reversed the district court's order.[828] On July 18, 2005, the Defense Department announced military commissions would resume within the following weeks.[829] Federal district courts were granted jurisdiction to hear habeas corpus petitions from detainees at Guantanamo Bay due to the Supreme Court decision's in *Rasul v. Bush* in 2004.[830]

In *Rasul*, the United States Supreme Court determined whether alien enemies detained outside of the United States had the right to file a petition for a writ of habeas corpus. As noted above, the detainees held at Guantanamo Bay were designated as enemy combatants and as such were not granted prisoner of war status under the Third Geneva Convention. While they were not afforded all of the prisoner of war protections, they were provided with significant amount of protections and privileges. However, the question became whether the detainees held at Guantanamo Bay had the right to file a petition of habeas corpus in US federal courts challenging their detention. This question has sparked a massive amount of debate regarding the rights of enemy aliens not detained in the United States. This topic has been one of the

---

824 US Department of Defense, News Release, First Military Commission Convened at Guantanamo Bay, Cuba, August 24, 2004.
825 *Id.*
826 US Department of Defense, News Release, Australian is the Second Commissions Case, August 25, 2004.
827 US Department of Defense, News Release, Military Commissions to Resume, July 18, 2005.
828 *Hamdan v. Rumsfeld*, 415 F. 3d 33 (D.C. Cir. 2005).
829 US Department of Defense, News Release, Military Commissions to Resume, July 18, 2005.
830 *Rasul v. Bush*, 542 U.S. 466, 124 S. Ct. 2686, 159 L. Ed. 2d 548 (2004).

most contentious issues concerning the rights granted to Guantanamo Bay detainees.

On June 28, 2004 (same day the Court released their opinion in *Hamdi v. Rumsfeld*[831]) the Supreme Court issued their decision in *Rasul v. Bush.*[832] Several detainees held at Guantanamo Bay had filed petitions for habeas corpus relief in District Court of the District of Columbia challenging their detention. The petitioners in *Rasul* included two Australian citizens and twelve Kuwaiti citizens who claim they were never involved in any acts of aggression against the United States.[833] The District Court for the District of Columbia dismissed their cases for want of jurisdiction stating "aliens detained outside the sovereign territory of the United States.[834] The Court of Appeals affirmed the District Court's dismissal.[835]

The United States Supreme Court held, however, that detainees held at Guantanamo Bay may file petitions in federal district court to challenge their detentions. Justice Stevens delivered the opinion of the Court. Justice O'Connor, Souter, Ginsburg and Breyer, JJ joined in Justice Steven's opinion. Justice Stevens stated that over the past two centuries, the habeas statute has expanded habeas corpus "beyond the limits that obtained during the 17th and 18th centuries."[836]

One scholar commented that with this decision the Court reversed 54 years of precedence by opening up the federal court system to detainees currently held at Guantanamo Bay and likely beyond.[837] He asserted by allowing detainees held at Guantanamo Bay to file habeas corpus petitions and challenge their detentions deprives the President of one of his most necessary wartime powers, "the ability to effectively prosecute the War on Terror unimpeded by litigation from our enemies, and the consequences of that litigation."[838] The hurdles that the

---

[831] *Hamdi v. Rumsfeld*, 542 U.S. 507 (2004).

[832] *Rasul v. Bush*, 542 U.S. 466, 124 S. Ct. 2686, 159 L. Ed. 2d. 548 (2004).

[833] *Id.* at 472. The Court also granted certiorari to two British citizens but since then they have been released from custody. Id n.1.

[834] *Id.* citing *Rasul v. Bush*, 215 F. Supp. 2d 55, 68 (DC 2002).

[835] *Id.* at 473 citing *Rasul v. Bush*, 335 U.S. App. D.C. 189 (CADC 2003).

[836] *Id.* at 474 citing *Swain v. Pressley*, 430 U.S. 372, 380 n.13, 51 L.Ed. 2d 411, 97 S.Ct. 1224 (1977).

[837] Captain Christopher M. Schumann, *Bring it On: The Supreme Court Opens the Floodgates with Rasul v. Bush,* 55 A.F. L. Rev. 349 (2004).

[838] *Id.* at 350.

President will now face due to the Court's decision include opening the door to the potential of an unlimited number detainees and prisoners of war around the world, both present and future, to challenge their detention by US forces.[839]

Moreover, it has been stated that the Court's decision will "impose an unnecessary burden on commanders and soldiers in the field by requiring them to simultaneously engage in both combat and prepare for potential litigation surround that combat."[840] Their decision will hinder the intelligence community's efforts to gather intelligence from the detainees because their interrogation capabilities are limited due to the premature introduction of the litigation process. "While our soldiers in the field already go to great lengths to ensure proper targeting and minimal collateral damage, they will now be expected to collect evidence throughout the battle in preparation for the potential litigation that will likely arise should they take prisoners."[841]

These decisions from the Court, however, do not limit itself only to Guantanamo Bay, "because the logic used to justify the decision can easily be applied to enemy combatants detained in placed like Kabul, Baghdad, Tehran, or North Korea."[842] Conversely, because in their holdings the Supreme Court did not articulate the process and procedure necessary to meet their demand, their decision could result in further litigation.[843] Many have argued that the matter should be left to

---

839 *Id.* at 367. Captain Schumann also stated "By opening our courts to our enemies and allowing them to essentially place our soldiers on trial, aid and comfort is provided to our enemies and the war effort is undoubtedly harmed." *Id* at 370.

840 *Id.*

841 *Id.* at 368. Additionally, "This Court's decision will now hamper that ability to collect intelligence and discover future plans of our enemies, because resources will need to be shifted to defend the very detention itself. This is truly a unique proposition unheard of in the history of warfare, and could result in this nation paying a very high price." *Id.* at 369.

842 *Id.* at 369. Associated Press, Saddam Lawyer Wants Supreme Court Intervention, (9 Jul 04), at http://www.foxnews.com/printer_friendly_story/0,3566, 125164.00.html (Saddam Hussein, before his trial and execution, filed an appeal to the United States Supreme Court asking the Court for permission to file an indigent appeals on his behalf)

843 *Id.* Captain Schumann also addressed Justice Kennedy's concern over the length of detention and stated "While it would be helpful to know just how long

Congress and that "Congress should revise the federal *habeas* statute and specifically state that its application does not extend to enemy aliens detained by our military forces overseas, and they must do it without further delay."[844]

In response to the Supreme Court's decision in *Hamdi v. Rumsfeld* and *Rasul v. Rumsfeld*, the government created a review process for detainees at Guantanamo Bay. On July 7, 2004 the Department of Defense announced the creation of Combatant Status Review Tribunals ("CSRT").[845] The order establishing the CSRTs stated they are only applicable to foreign nationals held as enemy combatants in DoD control at Guantanamo Bay.[846] The order also established that each detainee will be assigned a military officer, with the appropriate security clearance, who will assist the detainee with their review process.[847] The personal representative may provide the detainee with information about his designation, however, may not share classified information with the detainee.

The order also stated if the Tribunal determined that the detainee should no longer be classified as an enemy combatant, the written report of its decision must be forwarded to the Secretary of Defense or

---

this war will last, a close review of history will show that Adolf Hitler was not magnanimous enough to set an end date for his aggression during World War II. Neither has al Qaeda." *Id* at 369.

[844] *Id.* at 370.

[845] Order Establishing Combatant Status Review Tribunal, July 7, 2004, available at:
http://www.defenselink.mil/Releases/Release.aspx?ReleaseID=7530

[846] Memorandum for the Secretary of the Navy, Order Establishing Combatant Status Review Tribunal, July 7, 2004. The order defined enemy combatants as: "an individual who was part of or supporting Taliban or al Qaeda forces, or associated force that are engaged in hostilities against the United States or its coalition partners. This includes any person who has committed a belligerent act or has directly supported hostilities in aid of enemy forces. Each detainee subject to this Order has been determined to be an enemy combatant through multiple levels of review by officers of the Department of Defense." *Id* at p.1.

[847] *Id.* at (c). The personal representative will also be able to review any "reasonably available information in the possession of the Department of Defense that may be relevant to a determination of the detainee's designation as an enemy combatant, including any records, determinations, or reports generated in connection with earlier determinations or reviews, and to consult with the detainee concerning that designation and any challenge thereto." *Id.*

his designee.[848] The Secretary of Defense will notify the Secretary of State, who will coordinate the detainee's transfer for release to the detainee's country of citizenship or another destination that is consistent with domestic and international obligations and the foreign policy of the United States.[849] The memorandum concluded by stating that the order is intended to improve management at Guantanamo Bay concerning the DoD's detention of enemy combatants. The order is not "intended to, and does not, create any right or benefit, substantive or procedural, enforceable at law, in equity, or otherwise by any party against the United States, its departments, agencies, instrumentalities or entities, its officers, employees or agents, or any other person."[850]

The Senior Defense Official also stated CSRTs differ from the administrative reviews accorded to Guantanamo Bay detainees. The administrative reviews are an annual review to determine whether the detainee continues to be a threat to the United States, and if he does not continue to be a threat, to determine if he can be safely released. Therefore, the difference between CSRTs and the administrative review is that the CSRT focuses on the detainee's status as an enemy combatant, whereas the administrative review focuses on the threat posed by the detainee, not on his status as an enemy combatant.[851]

In October, 2004, the Defense Department held a Special briefing with Secretary of the Navy, Gordon R. England to discuss the implementation of the tribunals.[852] He stated as of October 1, 2004, the Defense Department has conducted 115 tribunals and currently has 350 cases open.[853] Of the 115 tribunals, 71 detainees personally appeared. All 115 tribunal decisions were sent to Admiral McGarrah for his review.[854] As of that date, Admiral McGarrah had reviewed 64 of the decisions and disagreed with the finding of one (that is, that the detainee was an enemy combatant).[855] That detainee was transferred to

---

[848] *Id.* at i.

[849] *Id.*

[850] *Id.* at j.

[851] *Id.* p.3.

[852] Special Defense Department Briefing, Secretary of the Navy Gordon England, Oct. 1, 2004.

[853] *Id.*

[854] *Id.*

[855] *Id.* According to American Forces Information Service, the man did not call any witnesses during his tribunal hearing, but he did participate in the process.

Pakistan in September, 2004. Secretary England also stated he hoped the Annual Review Boards would begin shortly. The CSRTs were completed by March 2005.

On September 15, 2004, the Department of Defense announced that Secretary England signed the implementing directive for the administrative review procedures for enemy combatants detained at Guantanamo Bay.[856] The directive established the administrative review board (ARB), which will be convened on a yearly basis, will conduct necessary proceedings to determine whether there is reason to believe that the enemy combatant continues to pose a threat to the United States or its allies.[857] Moreover, the review board will examine the enemy combatants' intelligence value in the Global War of Terror.

According to this document, there are three possible outcomes to the review: (1) the enemy combatant will be released without limitations to his home State or a third State as appropriate; or (2) he may be transferred to his home State (or a third State as appropriate) with conditions agreed upon between that State and the United States; or finally; (3) the enemy combatant will continue to be detained as an

---

The man was removed from the detainee population in Guantanamo Bay and is being held in a transitional status elsewhere on the island. The State Department is responsible to coordinate his release to his home country. Secretary England noted that 150 detainees have been released from Guantanamo Bay "either because they were determined to not be enemy combatants or they were determined to no longer be threats to the United States. But, he noted, some of those individuals have subsequently been captured again fighting US forces." Kathleen T. Rhem, *Tribunal Finds Guantanamo Detainee Not Combatant; Man to Be Sent Home*, American Forces Information Service, Sept. 8, 2004.

[856] US Department of Defense News Release, Administrative Review Implementation Directive Issued, Sept. 15, 2004.

[857] *Id.* A memorandum defined enemy combatant as: "an individual who was part of or supporting Taliban or al Qaeda forces, or associated forces that are engaged in hostilities against the United States or its coalition partners. This includes any person who has committed a belligerent act or has directly supported hostilities in aid of enemy armed forces." Memorandum for Secretaries of the Military Departments, Chairman of the Joint Chiefs of Staff, Under Secretary of Defense for Policy, Subject: Revised Implementation of Administrative Review Procedures for Enemy Combatants Detained at US Naval Base Guantanamo Bay, Cuba July, 14, 2006 at 1. [hereinafter July 14, 2006 Memorandum].

enemy combatant in US control.[858] The detained enemy combatant is provided with advance notice of the review board and also supplied with a written unclassified summary of the information concerning his detention.[859] The ARB panel consists of three military officers and a military officer is assigned to the enemy combatant to assist him throughout his ABR process.[860] Before the ARB convenes, the Department of Defense solicits information on the detainee from other US government agencies and from the family and national government of the detainee.

During the review proceeding, the detainee may appear in person and is provided with the opportunity to be heard and present information supporting his release.[861] However, he will be excluded from the review if classified information is discussed or presented.[862] The enemy combatant has the choice to participate in his review proceeding, he is not required to do so.[863] The ARB proceedings are not governed by the Federal Rules of Evidence and witnesses may not

---

[858] *Id.* at Encl (3). *See also*, US Department of Defense News Release, Defense Department Conducts First Administrative Review Board, December 14, 2004.

[859] July 14, 2006 Memorandum, *supra* note 1560, at 2 and Encl (3) p.2. Moreover, the detainee will be prohibited from attending a classified session of the review board.

[860] *Id.* Each three-member panel will consist of a Presiding Officer (PO) and at least one office with intelligence experience. Panel members consist of individuals with a grade of 0-4 or higher (except for the Presiding Officer), a minimum security clearance of Top Secret and may be selected from among all the military services. The Assisting Military Officer (AMO) is not an advocate for or against the combatant's continued detention. *Id* at Encl (3) p2. Additionally, Admiral McGarrah stated there is no presumption of confidentiality between the AMO and the detainee. Kathleen T. Rhem, *Hearings Determine Detainee's Threat Status*, American Forces Information Services, March 30, 2005.

[861] US Department of Defense News Release, Defense Department Conducts First Administrative Review Board, December 14, 2004. In March, 2005, Admiral McGarrah stated "Some (detainees) are already represented by…counsel in the federal courts, and in many cases the counsel has advised their client not to participate in any of these processes." Kathleen T. Rhem, *Hearings Determine Detainee's Threat Status*, American Forces Information Service, March 30, 2005.

[862] July 14, 2006 Memorandum, *supra* note 1560, at Encl (3) p.2.

[863] *Id.* at Encl (3) p. 3.

be called.[864] However, the military officer assisting the detainee may submit written information gathered from the enemy combatant's home State and his relatives.[865] The panel members will make an assessment using several factors including the nature and circumstances surrounding the enemy combatant's apprehension and subsequent detention, any intelligence gathered about him since he was taken into custody, and any statements he made prior to or while he was detained (whether corroborated or uncorroborated by other information).[866] They must also examine information provided by the enemy combatant's relatives.[867]

After the ARB takes place and the panel assesses all the necessary information concerning the detainee, they make a recommendation to the Designated Civilian Official (DCO). The ARBs "shall conduct such proceedings as necessary to make a written assessment of whether the enemy combatant continues to pose a threat to the United States or its allies in the ongoing armed conflict against al Qaeda and its affiliates and supporters, and/or whether there are other factors bearing upon the need for continued detention."[868] The DCO makes the final

---

864 *Id.* Additionally, the "ARB may consider any reasonably available information that is relevant to its determination of whether the enemy combatant poses a continuing threat to the United States or its allies in the ongoing armed conflict against al Qaeda and its affiliates and supporters, and any other factors bearing upon the need for continued detention."

865 *Id.* at Encl (3) p. 2.

866 *Id.* at Encl (3) p. 5. Other factors the panel may use to make their final assessment include: "Corporation of the enemy combatant with US Government or allied representatives; Conduct, including misconduct, while in detention, insofar as it bears on the question whether the enemy combatant poses a current threat; Information provided by the enemy combatant's home State, including whether the home State will or will not accept return of the enemy combatant and the circumstances of, or any conditions related to such return; Information provided by other relevant US government agencies; Any US Government psychological or behavioral assessments conducted of the enemy combatant; The enemy combatant's age, work history, health, education, marital and family status; The likelihood of the enemy combatant again taking up arms against the United States or its allies; Any statements made by or on behalf of the enemy combatant at the ARB proceedings; and Any other information as deemed appropriate by the ARB."

867 *Id.*

868 *Id.* at Encl (3) p.2.

determination whether to release, transfer or continue to detain the individual.[869] If the DCO deems it necessary to continue to detain the enemy combatant, he will remain in DoD control and a new review date will be scheduled to ensure an annual review.[870] The DCO established the Office for the Administrative Review of the Detention of Enemy Combatants (OARDEC).[871]

The Administrative Review Boards began in December, 2004.[872] In July, 2005 Rear Admiral McGarrah spoke at a Defense Department Special Briefing and provided information on the success of the review boards.[873] Admiral McGarrah emphasized that the combatants were being detained not to as a punishment, but to prevent them from continuing to fight against the United States and its allies, as well as to obtain intelligence in the ongoing global war on terrorism.[874] Admiral McGarrah also noted that the ARBs are not required by the Geneva Conventions, nor are they required by domestic law. "But because of the unique nature of this global war on terrorism, we've taken what we believe is a historic and unprecedented action to establish this process to allow enemy combatants to be heard while a conflict is ongoing."[875]

In addition to the Department of Defense's action in response to the Supreme Court's decision in *Rasul*, members of Congress also responded by drafting legislation concerning the rights to detainees. Furthermore, reports[876] of detainees receiving abusive and inhumane

---

[869] *Id.*

[870] *Id.*

[871] Memorandum for Secretaries of the Military Departments, Chairman of the Joint Chiefs of Staff, Under Secretary of Defense for Policy, Subject: Revised Implementation of Administrative Review Procedures for Enemy Combatants Detained at US Naval Base Guantanamo Bay, Cuba July, 14, 2006 at 2.

[872] Guantanamo Today, July 2006 at 5.

[873] US Department of Defense, News Transcript, Defense Department Special Briefing on Administrative Review Boards for Detainees at Guantanamo Bay, Cuba, July 08, 2005, Presenters: Director, Office for the Administrative Review of the Detention of Enemy Combatants, Rear Adm. James McGarrah.

[874] *Id.*

[875] *Id.*

[876] MSNBC Interactive The Associated Press, Reuters and NBC News, *U.N.: U.S. Torture Guantanamo Detainees*, MSNBC, Feb. 13, 2006, available at: http://www.msnbc.msn.com/id/11333496/. The U.N. investigation concluded the United States committed acts amounting to torture at Guantanamo Bay. Examples of torture included force feeding detainees and subjecting them to

treatment surfaced and Congress took action to ban torture.[877] Additionally, one scholar noted that there was confusion concerning what interrogation methods interrogators were allowed to use and which methods they were prohibited from implementing.[878] The author noted that some methods were approved for certain detainees, depending on their classification, while other methods were prohibited. Congress addressed this issue by applying a blanket prohibition on the use of cruel, inhuman or degrading techniques.[879]

In response to allegations[880] that detainees were being subject to torture and inhumane treatment, Senator John McCain introduced an amendment which prohibited the use of cruel, inhuman or degrading

---

"prolonged solitary confinement." The report recommended the United States close the naval base and revoke all special interrogation methods authorized by the DoD. Finally, the report stated a detainee could only be kept in isolation for a maximum of 30 days and that some detainees at the naval base for in "quasi-isolation for up to 18 months."

877 Kathleen T. Rhem, *Naval Official Reports Review of Detainee Operations*, American Forces Information Service, May 14, 2004. After photographs of detainees in Iraq's Abu Ghraib being abused were released, Secretary Rumsfeld ordered a review of operations at Guantanamo Bay and the South Carolina Brig. Vice Admiral Albert T. Church, the Navy's inspector general "reported that he found 'eight minor infractions involving contact with detainees' going back to 2002."

878 Araslan M. Suleman, Recent Developments, *Detainee Treatment Act of 2005*, 19 Harv. Hum Rts. J. 257, 258 (2006).

879 *Id.*

880 Steven Donald Smith, *Guantanamo Detainees Being Held Legally, Official Says*, American Forces Information Services, Feb. 15, 2006. A state Department legal adviser commented on a draft of the U.N.'s report regarding the detainees at Guantanamo, and stated "We think that the report is fundamentally flawed in its procedures and is riddled with inaccuracies and really was done in a way, frankly, that discredits the report overall and the work of the rapporteurs in this effort." He also criticized the U.N. for writing the report without even visiting the naval base, despite the fact that they had been invited to visit. Furthermore, he asserted the U.N. based their conclusions on statements made by members of al Qaeda or the Taliban who had been released or from their defense counsel. He also commented on the allegation that force-feeding amounted to torture and stated "It's a little bit difficult to understand how the U.N. rapporteurs, without having interviewed anybody in the U.S. government, would accept at face value the assertions of the defense counsel that this definitely amounted to torture."

treatment against any individual in the custody or physical control of the Unite States.[881] Other members of Congress additionally introduced amendments concerning federal court's jurisdiction to entertain habeas petitions filed by detainees at Guantanamo Bay. For example, Senators Graham, Levin, and Kyl introduced an amendment which would prevent a district court from having jurisdiction to consider or hear an application for a writ of habeas corpus filed by or on behalf of a detainee at Guantanamo Bay.[882] After intense debates, portions of the Senator's amendments became known as the Detainee Treatment Act (DTA) of 2005, which was part of the Department of Defense Appropriations Act, 2005.[883] President Bush signed the Detainee Treatment Act on December 30, 2005.[884]

The DTA restricts the interrogation methods used on detainees and also limits federal court from reviewing habeas corpus petitions from detainees held at Guantanamo Bay. For example, § 1002(a) states: No person in the custody or under the effective control of the Department of Defense or under detention in a Department of Defense facility shall be subject to any treatment or technique of interrogation not authorized by an listed in the United States Army Field Manual on Intelligence Interrogation.[885] The DTA also prohibits the use of cruel, inhuman or degrading treatment or punishment to any individual under custody or physical control of the United States Government.[886]

Section 1005 discussed procedures for status review of detainees held outside the United States. One section stated "Except as provided in section 1005 of the Detainee Treatment Act of 2005, no court, justice, or judge shall have jurisdiction to hear or consider" applications for a writ of habeas corpus filed by or on behalf of any alien detained by the Department of Defense or any other action against the United

---

[881] Human Rights First, Congress Puts Bush Administration on Notice to Stop Using Abusive Interrogation Methods; but Struggle Continues to Keep Torture Evidence out of Court, available at: http://www.humanrightsfirst.org/us_law/etn/misc/tort_court.htm

[882] S. 1042, 109th Cong. § e (2005).

[883] Detainee Treatment Act of 2005, Jurist, Dec. 31, 2005.

[884] Detainee Treatment Act of 2005 (DTA), Pub. L. 109-148, §§ 1001-1006 (2005), *available at* http://jurist.law.pitt.edu/gazette/2005/12/detainee-treatment-act-of-2005-white.php

[885] Detainee Treatment Act, *supra* note 884, § 1002(a).

[886] Detainee Treatment Act, *supra* note 884, § 1003(a).

States concerning the detainee's detention at Guantanamo Bay.[887] However, the following section was limited to those in military custody or who "has been determined by the United States Court of Appeals for the District of Columbia Circuit in accordance with the procedures set forth in section 1005(a) of the Detainee Treatment Act of 2005 to have been properly detained as an enemy combatant."[888]

The DTA also granted the United States Court of Appeals for the District of Columbia jurisdiction to determine the validity of any final decision of a Combatant Status Review Tribunal that a detainee is properly classified as an enemy combatant.[889] However, the Court of Appeals' jurisdiction is limited to determine whether the procedures used in the combatant's CSRT was consistent with the standards and procedures specified by the Secretary of Defense for Combatant Status Review Tribunals and whether the use of such standards and procedures are consistent with the Constitution and the laws of the United States.[890]

The language in the DTA, specifically the language restricting a federal court's jurisdiction to entertain a detainee's petition for the writ of habeas corpus, came under intense debate in the following year. Salim Ahmed Hamdan filed a petition for a writ of habeas corpus before the DTA was signed into law and the question became whether the DTA applied to petitions filed after the DTA's enactment or whether it applied to pending petitions. The issue made its way to the Supreme Court of the United States, who heard arguments on March, 28, 2006 and issued their decision on June, 29, 2006.

Salim Ahmed Hamdan, a Yemeni national, was captured by militia forces in November 2001 in Afghanistan.[891] Hamdan was turned over to the US military and in June, 2002 he was sent to Guantanamo Bay.[892] On July 3, 2003, President Bush deemed him eligible for trial by military commission, but did not specify the charges against him. On July 13, 2004, Hamdan was charged with one count of conspiracy

---

887 *Id.* at § 1005(e)(1) & (2).

888 *Id.* at § 1005(e)(2)(B).

889 *Id.* at § 1005(e)(2)(A).

890 Detainee Treatment Act, *supra* note 884, § 1005(e)(2)(C)(i)-(ii).

891 *Hamdan v. Rumsfeld*, 548 U.S. 557, 126 S.Ct. 2749, at 2759, 165 L. Ed. 2d 723 (2006).

892 *Id.*

"to commit ...offense triable by military commission."[893] Hamdan's charge sheet stated the basis for the military commission jurisdiction (the November 13 Military Order).[894] His charge sheet also included a background description of al Qaeda. The last two paragraphs of his charge sheet provided the allegations against Hamdan. They stated that "from on or about February 1996 to on or about November 24, 2001," Hamdan "willfully and knowingly joined an enterprise of persons who shared a common criminal purpose and conspired and agreed with [named members of al Qaeda] to commit the following offenses triable by military commission: attacking civilians; attacking civilian objects; murder by an unprivileged belligerent; and terrorism."[895] In April, 2004, Hamdan filed a petition for a writ of habeas corpus and mandamus, challenging the President's decision to try Hamdan by a military commission.

Hamdan argued that a courts-martial constituted in accordance with the Uniform Code of Military Justice (UCMJ) had the authority to prosecute him.[896] Moreover, Hamdan alleged the military commissions lacked the authority to try him because "neither congressional Act nor the common law of war supports trial by this commission for the crime of conspiracy—an offense Hamdan says, is not a violation of the law of war."[897] Hamdan also argued "the procedures that the President has adopted to try him violate the most basic tenets of military and

---

[893] *Id* citing Application to Petition for Certiorari 65a.
[894] *Id.* at 2760.
[895] *Id.* at 2761, citing App. To Pet. For Cert. 65a. Paragraph 13 of Hamdan's charge sheet detailed four "overt acts" he is alleged to have committed sometime between 1996 and November 2001 in furtherance of the conspiracy: "(1) he acted as Osama bin Laden's 'bodyguard and personal driver,' 'believ[ing]' all the while that bin Laden 'and his associates were involved in' terrorist acts prior to and including the attacks of September 11, 2001; (2) he arranged for transportation of, and actually transported weapons used by al Qaeda members and by bin Laden's bodyguards (Hamdan among them); (3) he 'drove or accompanied [O]sama bin Laden to various al Qaeda sponsored training camps, press conferences, or lectures,' at which bin Laden encouraged attacks against Americans; and (4) he received weapons training at al Qaeda sponsored camps." *Id* at 2761 citing App. To Pet. For Cert. 65a-76a.
[896] *Id.* at 2759.
[897] *Id.*

international law, including the principle that a defendant must be permitted to see and hear the evidence against him."[898]

In November, 2005, the Supreme Court of the United States granted certiorari to determine whether the military commission convened to try Hamdan had the authority to do so and whether Hamdan could rely on the Geneva Conventions in those proceedings.[899] In February, 2006, the government filed a motion to dismiss the writ of certiorari because the Detainee Treatment Act of 2005 prevented the court from hearing the writ.[900] The Supreme Court released their opinion in June, 2006. The Supreme Court held that the military commissions convened to try Hamdan lacked the power to proceed because such commissions' structure and procedures violated both the UCMJ and the Geneva Conventions.[901] Furthermore, four Justices held that conspiracy was not an "offsen[e] that by…the law of war may be tried by military commissions."[902]

The Court first discussed the government's motion to dismiss concerning the Detainee Treatment Act of 2005 ("DTA"). The government asserted that §§1005(e)(1)[903] and 1005(h) had the "immediate effect, upon enactment, of repealing federal jurisdiction not just over detainee habeas actions yet to be filed but also over any such actions then pending in any federal court—including this Court", thus they argued the Court lacked the jurisdiction to review the Court of Appeal's decision.[904] Hamdan argued, if the Government's interpretation is indeed correct, then Congress has unconstitutionally suspended the writ of habeas corpus.[905] The Court stated it was not

---

[898] *Id.*

[899] *Id.* at 2762.

[900] *Id.* Detainee Treatment Act of 2005 (DTA), Pub. L. 109-148, 119 Stat. 2739.

[901] *Id.* at 2760.

[902] *Id.* citing 10 U.S.C. §821.

[903] *Id.* Subsection (e) of §1005, "Judicial Review of Detention of Enemy Combatants" states "Except as provided in section 1005 of the Detainee Treatment Act of 2005, no court, justice, or judge shall have jurisdiction to hear or consider—(1) an application for a writ of habeas corpus filed by or on behalf of an alien detained by the Department of Defense at Guantanamo Bay, Cuba; or…"

[904] *Id.* at 2763.

[905] *Id.* at 2764.

necessary to discuss any of Hamdan's arguments because "Ordinary principals of statutory construction suffice to rebut the Government's theory—at least insofar as this case, which was pending at the time the DTA was enacted..."[906]

The DTA is silent about whether paragraph (1) of subsection (e) "shall apply" to claims pending on the date of enactment.[907] The Court admitted in the past they have "applied intervening statutes conferring or ousting jurisdiction, whether or not jurisdiction lay when the underlying conduct occurred or when the suit was filed."[908] However, the Court stated the more accurate "presumption" is nonapplication. In other words, the Court applied the presumption against retroactivity unless clear congressional intent favoring such a result.[909] After examining members of Congress' statements during hearings concerning the DTA, the Court concluded §1005(e)(1) did not strip federal courts' jurisdiction over cases pending on the date of the DTA's enactment.

The Court next addressed the government's claim that even if the Court has jurisdiction to hear the case, they should apply the "judge-made rule that civilian courts should await the final outcome of on-going military proceedings before entertaining an attack on those proceedings."[910] The government relied on the Court's decision in *Councilman*, where an army officer was charged under the UCMJ for selling, transferring and possessing marijuana.[911] The officer filed a suit in Federal District Court to enjoin his proceedings because he argued the alleged offenses were not "service connected."[912] The Court noted that the officer did not question the lawfulness of the courts-martial, nor did he question the procedures.[913] Instead, officer argued the subject matter of his case did not fall within the scope of courts-martial authority.[914] The Court did not address the merits of whether

---

[906] *Id.*

[907] *Id.* at 2763. Justice Scalia, in his dissent, stated the meaning of §1005(e)(1) is entirely clear. *Id* at 2813 (Scalia J., dissenting).

[908] *Id.* at 2764 citing *Landgraf v. USI Film Products*, 511 U.S. 244 (1994).

[909] *Id.* at 2765 citing *Landgraf*, 511 U.S. at 280.

[910] *Id.* at 2769 citing Brief for Respondents 12.

[911] *Id.* citing *Schlesinger v. Councilman*, 420 U.S. 738 (1974).

[912] *Id.* at 2770 citing *Councilman*, 420 U.S. at 740.

[913] *Id.*

[914] *Id.* citing *Councilman*, 420 U.S. at 741, 759.

the marijuana charges were sufficiently "service connected" to place them within the subject matter jurisdiction of a courts-martial. "Instead, we concluded that, as a matter of comity, federal courts should normally abstain from intervening in pending courts-martial proceedings against members of the Armed Forces, and further that there was nothing in the particular circumstances of the officer's case to displace that general rule."[915]

The Court observed that *Councilman* established two factors of comity that favor abstention pending completing of an ongoing court-martial proceeding against service personnel:

> "(1) military discipline and, therefore, the efficient operation of the Armed Forces are best served if the military justice system acts without regular inference from civilian courts; and
>
> (2) federal courts should respect the balance that Congress struck between military preparedness and fairness to individual service members when it created 'an integrated system of military courts and review procedures, a critical element of which is the Court of Military Appeals, consisting of civilian judges 'completely removed from all military influence or persuasion…'''"[916]

The Court concluded that neither of the comity consideration described above suggest abstention in this case. The Court maintained that Hamdan was not a member of the US Armed Forces and thus concerns about the military discipline did not apply.[917] Additionally, the military commission established to try Hamdan is not part of the integrated system of military court.[918] Therefore, the Court rejected the

[915] *Id.* citing *Councilman*, 420 U.S. at 740, 758.

[916] *Id* at 2770 citing *Councilman*, 420 U.S. at 752, 758 (quoting H.R. Rep. No. 491, 81st Cong. 1st Sess., p. 7 (1949)).

[917] *Id.* at 2771.

[918] *Id.* The Court observed that Hamdan's military commission did not consist of independent review panels that Congress had established. Moreover, they stated Hamdan did not posses the right to appeal any possible conviction to civilian judges of the Court of Military Appeals (now called the United States Court of Appeals for the Armed Forces (Pub. L. 103-337, 108 Stat. 2831)). Id at 2771.

government's assertion that they refrain from reviewing the case before Hamdan's military commission takes place.[919] Finally, the Court noted that the government failed to identify a "important countervailing interest" that would prevent a federal court to depart from their general "duty to exercise the jurisdiction that is conferred upon them by Congress."[920] Therefore, the Court rejected the government's argument to refrain from entertaining Hamdan's petition.

The Court subsequently examined the merits of Hamdan's challenge. The Court observed that military commissions are not mentioned in the Constitution nor are they created by statute.[921] Instead, the Court stated military commissions were born of military necessity.[922] In examining the history of military commissions, the Court noted that during the Civil War, military commissions usually "took jurisdiction over ordinary crimes, war crimes and breaches of military orders alike."[923] Additionally, the Court noted Chief Justice Chase's decision in *Ex parte Milligan*.[924] Chief Justice Chase stated:

> "...Congress cannot direct the conduct of campaigns, nor can the President, or any commander under him, without the sanction of Congress, institute tribunals for the trial and punishment of offences, either of soldiers or civilians, unless in cases of a controlling necessity, which justifies what it compels, or at least insures acts of indemnity from the justice of the legislature."[925]

---

[919] *Id.* at 2771. The Court noted their decision in Ex parte Quirin also supported their conclusion. As the Court of Appeals stated Quirin "provides a compelling historical precedent for the power of civilian courts to entertain challenges that seek to interrupt the processes of military commissions." *Hamdan v. Rumsfeld*, 415 F. 3d at 36 (*Ex parte Quirin*, 317 U.S. 1 (1942).

[920] *Id.* at 2772 citing *Quackenbush v. Allstate Ins. Co.*, 517 U.S. 706, 716 (1996).

[921] *Id.* at 2772-73.

[922] *Id.* See W. Winthrop, Military Law and Precedents 831 (rev. 2d ed. 1920). [hereinafter Winthrop].

[923] *Id.* at 2773.

[924] *Id.* at 2773 citing *Ex parte Milligan*, 71 (4 Wall) 2 (1866).

[925] *Id.* at 2773-74 citing *Milligan*, 71, at 139-140.

The Court noted Chief Justice Chase's suggestion that the President may constitutionally convene military commissions "without the sanction of Congress" in cases of "controlling necessity" may be correct, however the Court has never answered it definitively.[926] The Court did not address such suggestion in the present case because of their decision in *Quirin* where they held that Congress had, through the Article of War 15, sanctioned the use of military commissions in such circumstances.[927] The Court in *Quirin* recognized that Article 15 (currently Article 21 of UCMJ) was not a sweeping authorization for the President to "invoke military commissions when he deems them necessary."[928] Moreover, the Court disagreed with the government's argument that the AUMF or the DTA established the overriding authorization for the military commission convened to try Hamdan.

The Court stated that neither of those congressional Acts provided the President with authority to convene military commissions. As for the AUMF, the Court held that the Act activated the President's war powers, which include the power to convene military commissions in appropriate circumstances, but "there is nothing in the text or legislative history of the AUMF even hinting that Congress intended to expand or alter the authorization set forth in Article 21 of the UCMJ."[929] Additionally, the DTA was enacted after the President had established Hamdan's commission and it lacks any language authorizing that tribunal or any other at Guantanamo Bay.[930] Thus, the Court stated the AUMF and the DTA at most recognized a general Presidential authority to establish military commissions "in circumstances where justified under the 'Constitution and laws,' including the law of war."[931] Therefore, the Court turned to determine whether Hamdan's military commission was justified.

The Court stated that historically, military commissions have been used in three situations. The first situation is when the commission substituted for civilian courts during times (and in places) where

---

926 *Id.* at 2774.
927 *Id.* citing *Ex parte Quirin*, 317 U.S. at 28.
928 *Id.* citing Brief for Respondents 17.
929 *Id.* at 2775 citing *Hamdi v. Rumsfeld*, 542 U.S. 507, 518 (2004), *Ex parte Quirin*, 317 U.S. at 28-29.
930 *Id.* at 2775.
931 *Id.*

marital law has been declared.[932] The second situation consists of commissions established to try civilians "as part of a temporary military government over occupied enemy territory or territory regained from an enemy where civilian government cannot and does not function."[933] The final situation in which military commissions have historically been used is as an "incident to the conduct of war" when there is a need "to seize and subject to disciplinary measures those enemies who in their attempt to thwart or impede our military efforts have violated the law of war."[934] The Court concluded that because Guantanamo Bay was not enemy-occupied or under martial law, the law-of-war commission is the appropriate model for the present case.

The Court examined Hamdan's charge sheet, which alleged he was involved in a conspiracy from 1996 to November 2001 which is before the conflict with al Qaeda was initiated.[935] The Court noted that none of the overt acts alleged against Hamdan violates the laws of war. More importantly, the offense alleged against Hamdan, conspiracy, is not triable by law-of-war military commissions.

The Court observed that the conspiracy "has rarely if even been tried as such in this country by any law-of-war military commission not exercising some form of jurisdiction, and does not appear in either the Geneva Conventions or the Hague Conventions—the major treaties on

---

[932] *Id.*

[933] *Id.* at 2776 citing *Duncan v. Kahanamoku*, 327 U.S. 304, 314 (1946).

[934] *Id.* at 2776 citing *Quirin*, 317 U.S. at 28-29. The Court also noted the this type of military commission's jurisdiction is "limited to offense cognizable during time of war, but its role is primarily a factfinding one—to determine, typically on the battlefield itself, whether the defendant has violated the law of war." Id at 2776.

[935] *Id.* at 2778. In Justice Thomas' dissent, he stated the duration of the conflict with al Qaeda dates back (at least) to Usama bin Laden's "Declaration of Jihad Against the Americans" in August 1996. And moreover, under the Executive's description of the conflict with al Qaeda, "every aspect of the charge, which alleges overt acts in 'Afghanistan, Pakistan, Yemen and other countries' taking place from 1996 to 2001, satisfies the temporal and geographic prerequisites for the exercise of law-of-war military commission jurisdiction." Finally, he stated "the starting point of the present conflict (or indeed any conflict) is not determined by congressional enactment, but rather y the initiation of hostilities." *Id* at 2826 citing App. To Pet. for Cert. 64a.

the law of war."[936] Moreover, according to Winthrop, "it is not enough to intend to violate the law of war and commit over acts in furtherance of that intention unless the overt acts either are themselves offenses against the law of war or constitute steps sufficiently substantial to qualify as an attempt."[937]

The government argued that the saboteurs in *Quirin* were charged with conspiracy and thus it has been charged against the law of war before. However, the Court noted that the Court in *Quirin* "declined to address whether the offense actually qualified as a violation of the law of war –let alone one triable by military commission."[938] Furthermore, the Court in *Quirin*, was careful in its decision to identify an overt, "complete" act and thus observed the saboteurs' argument "that there can be no violation of a law of war—at least not one triable by military commission—without the actual commission of or attempt to commit a 'hostile and warlike act.'"[939] And finally, the Court stated international sources affirm their decision that conspiracy is not a recognized violation of the law of war.[940] Therefore, because the Court held that conspiracy is not a violation of the law of war, Hamdan's charge sheet

---

936 *Id.* at 2780-81.

937 *Id.* at 2781, citing Winthrop, *supra* note 1353, at 841. The government also argued Winthrop identified conspiracy as an offense "prosecuted by military commissions" and another military historian, Charles Roscoe, also listed conspiracy "to violate the laws of war by destroying life or property in aid of the enemy" as an offense triable in violation of the law of war during the Civil War. Id at 2781 citing Brief for Respondents 27-28 (citing C. Howland, Digest of Opinions of the Judge Advocates General of the Army 1071 (1912) (hereinafter Howland)). The Court noted that all of the judicial decisions Howland pointed to did not provide support for the inclusion of conspiracy as a violation of the law of war (at 2783) and the government cannot rely on Winthrop's statement, which was in a footnote, as supporting their conclusion that conspiracy is a crime that can be triable under the laws of war. *Id* at 2783.

938 *Id.* at 2781.

939 *Id.* at 2781 citing *Ex parte Quirin*, 317 U.S. at 37-38.

940 *Id.* at 1784. The Court noted "The International Military Tribunal at Nuremberg, over the prosecution's objections, pointedly refused to recognize as a violation of the law of war conspiracy to commit war crimes and convicted only Hitler's most senior associates of conspiracy to wage aggressive war. Id at 2784 citing 1 Trial of the Major War Criminals Before the International Military Tribunal; Nuremberg, 14 November 1945—1 October 1946, p. 225 (1947)

does not support the commission's jurisdiction and thus the commission lacks authority to try Hamdan.[941]

Additionally, the Court held that Hamdan's charge sheet must also fail because the Executive did not "satisfy the most basis precondition—at least in the absence of specific congressional authorization—for establishment of military commissions: military necessity."[942] The Court supported this conclusion by observing that Hamdan's commission was not appointed by a military commander in the field of battle and moreover, Hamdan was not charged with an "overt act for which he was caught red-handed in a theater of war and which military efficiency demands be tried expeditiously…"[943] The crimes Hamdan is alleged to have commit may well be crimes, but they are not offenses triable by a military commission.[944] And finally, the Court stated "none of the overt acts alleged to have been committed in furtherance of the agreement is itself a war crime, or even necessarily occurring during time of, or in a theater of war."[945]

Irregardless of whether the charges against Hamdan provided a military commission with jurisdiction, the Court held, the procedures the government established to govern Hamdan's trial by commission violated the UCMJ and thus are unlawful.[946] "The UCMJ conditions the President's use of military commissions on compliance not only with the American common law of war, but also with the rest of the UCMJ itself, insofar as applicable, and with the 'rules and precepts of the law of nations' including the four Geneva Conventions signed in 1949."[947] The Court stated that Order No. 1, which explained the procedures to be used during the military commissions, violated all the aforementioned laws. The Court expressed concern over provisions that would ban the accused from parts of his trial and provisions that would allow hearsay evidence to be considered.[948]

---

[941] *Id.* at 2875.

[942] *Id.*

[943] *Id.*

[944] *Id.*

[945] *Id.*

[946] *Id.* at 2786.

[947] *Id.* at 2786 citing *Ex parte Quirin*, 317 U.S. at 28.

[948] *Id.* citing Commission Order No. 1 (amended on Aug. 31, 2005) at §§6(B)(3) and 6(D)(1).

In examining Hamdan's procedural challenge, the Court noted that procedures governing trials by military commissions have historically been similar to those governing courts-martial.[949] However, the Court stated the uniformity principle is flexible and does not forbid all departures from the courts-martial procedures, but that any department must be tailored to the exigency that necessitates it.[950] The Court looked to the language in Article 36 of the UCMJ to support their conclusion. In interpreting the language in Article 36, the Court stated it creates two restrictions on the President's power to promulgate rules of procedures for courts-martial and military commissions.[951]

The first restriction to the President's power to promulgate rules of procedures is that "no procedural-rule he adopts may be 'contrary to or inconsistent with' the UCMJ—however practical it may seem."[952] The second restriction provides that the rules adopted must be "uniform insofar as practical" meaning that the rules applied to military commissions must be identical to those applied to courts-martial "unless such uniformity proves impracticable."[953] Hamdan asserted that Commission Order No. 1 violates both restrictions because they are inconsistent with the UCMJ and the government has failed to explain why it was necessary to deviate from the courts-martial procedures.[954]

---

[949] *Id.* The Court observed that the military commissions established to try General Yamashita differed greatly from courts-martial procedures. The Court stated the reaction to the drastic deviations in his military commission procedures prompted the UCMJ to expand the category of persons subject to it to include defendants such as Yamashita and Hamdan. Thus, "The most notorious exception to the principle of uniformity, then, has been stripped of its precedential value. *Id* at 2790, citing *In re Yamashita*, 327 U.S. 1 (1946). The Court noted that "Article 2 of the UCMJ now reads: (a) The following persons are subject to [the UCMJ]: (9) Prisoners of war in custody of the armed forces; (12) Subject to any treaty or agreement to which the United States is or may be a party or to any accepted rule of international law, persons within an area leased by or otherwise reserved or acquired for the use of the United States which is under the control of the Secretary concerned and which is outside the United States and outside the Commonwealth of Puerto Rico, Guam, and the Virgin Islands." 10 U.S.C. §802(a). Id at 2790 n. 47.

[950] *Id.* See Winthrop, *supra* note 748, at 835, n. 81.

[951] *Id.*. at 2790.

[952] *Id.*

[953] *Id.*

[954] *Id.*

The government argued that the UCMJ contains nine articles that expressly mention "military commissions" and the procedures established in Commission Order No. 1 are not "contrary to or inconsistent with" any of the nine provisions.[955] Secondly, "military commissions would be of no use if the President were hamstrung by those provisions of the UCMJ that govern courts-martial."[956] And finally, the government argued the President's decision that "the danger to the safety of the United States and the nature of international terrorism" makes it impracticable to apply "the principles of law and rules of evidence generally recognized in the trial of criminal cases in the United States district courts."[957] Thus, the government proffered the President's November 13 Order provides the explanation for any deviation from court-martial procedures.[958]

The Court agreed with Hamdan and held that the President's determination of "practicability" is insufficient to justify variances from the procedures governing courts-martial.[959] The Court once again examined the language in Article 36 of the UCMJ and stated subsection (a) requires the rules the President establishes for "courts-martial, provost courts, and military commissions alike conform to those that

---

[955] *Id.* at 2791. The Court listed the nine Articles of the UCMJ that touch upon military commissions. The first two, 21 and 36 were discussed supra. The last sever include: (1) Article 28 (requiring appointment of reporters and interpreters); (2) Article 47 (making it a crime to refuse to appear or testify 'before a court-martial, military commission, court of inquiry, or any other military court or board'); (3) Article 48 (allowing a 'court-martial, provost court, or military commissions' to punish a person for contempt; (4) Article 49(d) (permitting admission into evidence of a "duly authenticated deposition taken upon reasonable notice to the other parties' only if 'admissible under the rules of evidence' and only if the witness is otherwise unavailable'); (5) Article 50 (permitting admission into evidence of records of courts of inquiry 'if otherwise admissible under the rules of evidence,' and if certain other requirements are met); (6) Article 104 (providing that a person accused of aiding the enemy may be sentenced to death or other punishment by military commission or court-martial); and (7) Article 106 (mandating the death penalty for spies convicted before military commission or court-martial). *Id* at 2791 n. 49.

[956] *Id.*

[957] *Id.*

[958] *Id.* citing Brief for Respondents 43-47 and n.22.

[959] *Id.* at 2791.

government procedures in *Article III courts*, '*so far as he considers* practicable.'"[960] Moreover, section (b), added after World War II, "demands that the rules applied in courts-martial, provost courts, and military commissions—whether or not they conform with the Federal Rules of Evidence—be 'uniform *insofar as practicable*.'"[961] Thus, the Court interpreted the language to require the Manual for Courts-Martial to apply to military commissions unless impracticable.[962]

President Bush determined that it is impractical to apply the rules and principles of law that govern "the trial of criminal cases in the United States district courts" to Hamdan's military commission.[963] The Court defers to the President's determination in that regard. However, the Court held the President did not make a similar official determination that it is impractical to apply the rules for courts-martial to Hamdan's military commission.[964] The Court concluded that nothing in the present case demonstrates that applying court-martial rules is impractical.[965] "The absence of any showing of impracticability is particularly disturbing when considered in light of the clear and admitted failure to apply one of the most fundamental protections afforded not just by the Manual for the Courts-Martial but also by the UCMJ itself: the right to be present."[966] Therefore, the Court concluded that court-martial rules must apply and since it was not disputed that Commission Order No. 1 deviates from those rules, they violate Article 36(b).[967]

The Court also held that the procedures established to try Hamdan also violated the Geneva Conventions.[968] The Court of Appeals held that Hamdan could not invoke the Geneva Convention to challenge the government's plan to prosecute him in accordance with Commission

---

[960] *Id.* citing 10 U.S.C. §836(a) (emphasis added).
[961] *Id.* citing 10 U.S.C. §836(b) (emphasis added).
[962] *Id.* at 2791.
[963] *Id.*
[964] *Id.* The Court also noted "even if subsection (b)'s requirement may be satisfied without such an official determination, the requirements of that subsection are not satisfied here." *Id* at 2792.
[965] *Id.* at 2792.
[966] *Id.*
[967] *Id.*
[968] *Id.* at 2793.

Order No. 1 based on a footnote in the Court's decision in *Johnson v. Eisentrager*.[969] The footnote stated:

> "We are not holding that these prisoners have no right which the military authorities are bound to respect…These prisoners claim to be and are entitled to its protection. It is, however, the obvious scheme of the Agreement, that responsibility for observance and enforcement of these rights is upon political and military authorities. Rights of alien enemies are vindicated under it only through protests and intervention of protecting powers as the rights of our citizens against foreign governments are vindicated only by Presidential intervention."[970]

Thus, the Court of Appeals held Hamdan did not have a right to enforce the Geneva Convention in court.[971] However, this Court held that *Eisentrager* does not control the present case. The Court held that, despite the government's claim that the Geneva Convention does not apply to the conflict with al Qaeda, Common Article 3 of the Geneva Convention applies to the conflict with al Qaeda and thus to Hamdan.[972] The government asserted Common Article 3 did not apply to the conflict with al Qaeda because it is "international in scope" and Common Article 3 only applies to "conflict not of an international character."[973] The Court stated the government's argument is an erroneous interpretation and applied their own interpretation. "The term 'conflict not of an international character' is used here in contradistinction to a conflict between nations."[974] The Court interpreted "not of an international character" to mean "Common Article 3…affords some minimal protection, falling short of full protection, falling short of full protection under the Conventions, to individuals associated with neither a signatory nor even a nonsignatory 'Power' who are involved in a conflict 'in the territory of' a

[969] *Id.* citing *Hamdan v. Rumsfeld*, 415 F. 3d at 40.
[970] *Id.* at 1794, citing *Johnson v. Eisentrager*, 339 U.S. 763, 789 n.14 (1950)
[971] *Id.* citing *Hamdan v. Rumsfeld*, 415 F.3d at 40.
[972] *Id.* at 2795.
[973] *Id.* at 2795, citing *Hamdan v. Rumsfeld*, 415 F. 3d at 41.
[974] *Id.* at 2795.

signatory."[975] Thus, the Court stated Common Article 3 differed from Common Article 2[976] because the former does not involve a clash between nations (whether signatories or not).[977]

The Court held the phrase "not of an international character" bears its literal meaning.[978] The Court examined several different authorities concerning Common Article 3 to strengthen their decision that it does apply to the conflict with al Qaeda.[979] Therefore, the Court concluded that Common Article 3 applies to conflict with al Qaeda and therefore, Hamdan must be tried by a "regularly constituted court affording all the judicial guarantees which are recognized as indispensable by civilized peoples."[980] The Court recognized that the Geneva Convention did not articulate the precise meaning of a "regularly constituted court." However, according to the Red Cross "regularly constituted court" means "established and organized in accordance with the laws and procedures already in force in a country."[981] The Court agreed with Justice Kennedy's concurring opinion that "[t]he regular military courts in our system are the courts-martial established by congressional statutes."[982] Justice Kennedy also stated that a military commission may be deemed as 'regularly constituted' by the "standards of our military justice system only if some practical need explains deviations from court-martial practice."[983]

The Court stated "Inextricably intertwined with the question of regular constitution is the evaluation of the procedures governing the

---

975 *Id.* at 2796.

976 *Id.* The Court stated "Common Article 2 provides that 'the present Convention shall apply to all cases of declared war or of any other armed conflict which may arise between two or more of the High Contracting Parties.'" Citing 6 U.S.T., at 3318 (Art. 2, ¶ 1).

977 *Id.*

978 *Id.*

979 *Id.* at 2796. For example, the Court cited from Commentary to the Geneva Conventions and on the Additional Protocols to the Geneva Convention. The Court stated the commentary to the Third Geneva Convention make it clear "that the scope of the Article must be as wide as possible." Commentary on the Third Geneva Convention, *supra* note 288, at 36.

980 *Id.* at 2798 citing 6 U.S.T. at 3320 (Art. 3, ¶1(d)).

981 *Id.* at 2797 citing Int'l Comm. of Red Cross, 1 Customary International Humanitarian Law 355 (2005).

982 *Id.* citing Kennedy J., concurring opinion at 2803.

983 *Id*, citing Kennedy J., concurring opinion at 2804.

tribunal and whether they afford 'all the judicial guarantees which are recognized as indispensable by civilized peoples.'"[984] Thus, they looked to the Geneva Convention for guidance as to what constitutes "all the judicial guarantees which are recognized as indispensable by civilized peoples."[985] The phrase is not defined in the Geneva Convention themselves, however they Court interpreted the phrase to incorporate, at minimum, trial protections that have been recognized by customary international law. The Court noted a majority of such protections are listed in Article 75 of Protocol I.[986]

The Court concluded that Commission Order No. 1 dispensed with the principles recognized in Article 75 as customary international law, more specifically Order No. 1 did not provide "an accused must, absent disruptive conduct or consent, be present for his trial and must be privy to the evidence against him."[987] The Court did not doubt the government's compelling interest to deny Hamdan access to certain sensitive information, however, absent express statutory provision to the contrary, the evidence used to convict a person of a crime must be disclosed to him.[988] While the Court acknowledged the requirements in Common Article 3 are general ones "crafted to accommodate a wide variety of legal systems" they are nonetheless requirements.[989] And the military commission convened by President Bush to try Hamdan fails to meet any of those requirements.

Applying some deference to the President's determinations, the Court assumed the government's charge against Hamdan was true and moreover, that Hamdan is a dangerous individual. However, if the government wished to prosecute Hamdan and subject him to criminal punishment, they must comply with the Rule of Law.[990] Therefore, the

---

[984] *Id.* citing 6 U.S.T., at 3320 (Art. 3, ¶1(d).

[985] *Id.*

[986] *Id.* Additional Protocol to the Geneva Conventions of 1949, (Protocol 1), *supra* note 100, at art. 75. The Court also examined law review articles to look for the definition of the phrase.

[987] *Id.* at 2798.

[988] *Id.* at 2798.

[989] *Id.*

[990] *Id.*

Court reversed the Court of Appeals decision and remanded Hamdan's case for further proceedings.[991]

In response to the Supreme Court's decision in *Hamdan v. Rumsfeld*, President Bush submitted a legislative proposal to Congress which would authorize military commissions for alien enemy combatants detained by the United States. President Bush stated he would like to find a way to ultimately close the Guantanamo Bay facility.[992] He stated "I have told the people that I would like for there to be a way to return people from Guantanamo to their home countries, but some of the people need to be tried in our courts."[993] Additionally, in response to the Supreme Court's decision that Common Article 3 is applicable to the conflict with al Qaeda, on July 7, 2006, US Deputy Defense Secretary England sent a memorandum to several DoD officials ordering them to ensure their personnel comply with Common Article 3.[994]

After several committee hearings and amendments to the President's proposal, Congress enacted and the President signed into law the Military Commission Act of 2006.[995] President Bush signed the MCA on October 17, 2006 and stated "With the bill I'm about to sign, the men our intelligence officials believe orchestrated the murder of nearly 3,000 innocent people will face justice."[996] Some important sections include Section Seven which discusses habeas corpus matters. This section states, in part, "No court, justice, or judge shall have jurisdiction to hear or consider an application for a writ of habeas corpus filed by or on behalf of an alien detained by the United States

---

[991] *Id.* The Court noted that Chief Justice Roberts did not take part in the consideration or decision of this case. *Id.* at 2799.

[992] Donna Miles, *Bush Reacts to Supreme Court Ruling on Military Tribunals*, American Forces Press Service, June 29, 2006.

[993] *Id.*

[994] US Department of Defense, Office of the Secretary of Defense, Memorandum for Secretaries of the Military Departments, from US Deputy Defense Secretary Gordon England, Application of Common Article 3 of the Geneva Convention to the Treatment of Detainees in the Department of Defense, July 7, 2006.

[995] Military Commission Act of 2006, Pub. L. 109-366 [hereinafter MCA]

[996] Whitehouse, President Bush Signs Military Commissions Act of 2006, Oct. 17, 2006, available at: http://www.whitehouse.gov/news/releases/2006/10/print/20061017-1.html.

who has been determined by the United States to have been properly detained as an enemy combatant or is awaiting such determination."[997] This section applies to all cases pending on or after the date of the enactment of this Act.[998]

Section Five addressed the Geneva Conventions and stated that "no person may invoke the Geneva Conventions or any protocols thereto in any habeas corpus or other civil action or proceeding to which the United States, or a current or former officer…as a source of rights in any court of the United States or its States or territories."[999] Moreover, Section 6 provided the President with the authority to interpret the meaning and application of the Geneva Conventions.[1000] The MCA applies only to alien unlawful combatants.[1001]

Attorney General Alberto Gonzales answered questions about the Military Commission Act of 2006 on "Ask the White House" in October. He stated it was a landmark piece of legislation because it accomplishes two goals that are essential to national security.[1002] The first goal the MCA accomplishes is to allow the Central Intelligence Agency (CIA) to continue its program for questioning key terrorist leaders and operatives.[1003] Secondly, the MCA provides a legal framework for prosecuting terrorists captured on the battlefield.[1004]

---

[997] MCA, *supra* note 995, at § 7. As noted above, the MCA defines unlawful enemy combatant as "a person who has engaged in hostilities or who has purposefully and materially supported hostilities against the United States or its co-belligerents who is not a lawful enemy combatant (including a person who is part of the Taliban, al Qaeda, or associated forces); or a person who before, on, or after the date of the enactment of the Military Commission Act of 2006, has been determined to be an unlawful enemy combatant by a Combatant Status Tribunal or another competent tribunal established under the authority of the President or the Secretary of Defense." §948a(1)(i)&(ii).

[998] *Id.*

[999] MCA, *supra* note 995, at § 5(a).

[1000] *Id.* at § 6(a)(3)(A).

[1001] *Id.* at § 3(948c).

[1002] Whitehouse, Ask the White House, Attorney General Alberto Gonzales, Oct. 18, 2006, available at: http://www.whitehouse.gov/ask/20061018.html.

[1003] *Id.* Attorney Gonzales stated the intelligence community has acknowledged that this program has been an invaluable tool in the US' efforts to prevent terrorist attacks and the MCA ensures that the CIA program will continue to operate in the future.

[1004] *Id.*

"The Military Commission's Act guarantees that every terrorist will receive a full and fair trial, consistent with America's obligations under international and domestic law. At the same time, this new law protects the sources and methods used to collect our most sensitive national intelligence."[1005]

Attorney Gonzales repeatedly stated that the MCA does not apply to American citizens.[1006] Additionally, he answered concerns over whether the MCA suspended the writ of habeas corpus. He asserted that while the MCA prevents detained alien enemy combatants from challenging their detention by habeas corpus, enemy combatants captured outside the United States have never had such a right.[1007] Moreover, the United States has taken a virtually unprecedented step by providing alien enemy combatants a chance to challenge their detention. Every detainee held at Guantanamo Bay has had, or will have, a hearing before a Combatant Status Review Tribunal.[1008] He stated "If the tribunal determines that he may be detained (as an enemy combatant), then the individual may appeal that decision to the United States Court of Appeals for the District of Columbia."[1009] Thus, the United States, through the MCA, provides captured al Qaeda and Taliban members the opportunity to challenge their detention in federal court "which is precisely what the right of habeas corpus is."[1010] Therefore, Attorney Gonzales denied that the MCA suspended the writ of habeas corpus.[1011]

A detainee tried by military commission under the MCA will have the right to counsel, be presumed innocent unless proven guilty beyond a reasonable doubt, and he may see and respond to all the evidence

---

1005 *Id.*

1006 *Id.* at 3.

1007 *Id.*

1008 *Id.*

1009 *Id.*

1010 *Id.*

1011 *Id.* In response to a question about suspending the writ, Attorney Gonzales stated the MCA should not be understood as suspending the writ. "Habeas corpus is a civilian remedy, and enemy combatants captured outside the United States have never had the right to file a habeas claim under the United States Constitution in prior armed conflict. Thus, the new law's restrictions on habeas corpus do not, and cannot deprive enemy combatants of any constitutional right that they have ever had under the United States law." *Id.* at 4.

introduced.[1012] Moreover, he may introduce his own evidence and has the opportunity to call witnesses on his behalf. If the accused is found guilty, "he may appeal the commission's decision to a military appeals court, the Court of Military Commission Review, and to the United States Court of Appeals for the District of Columbia Circuit."[1013]

Attorney Gonzales also elaborated on Section Five of the MCA concerning the interpretation of the Geneva Conventions. He noted that Common Article 3's language is "notoriously vague." He stated the MCA provides "clear guidance as to what specific conduct under Common Article 3 constitutes a war crime" and it also authorizes the President to define ambiguous terms so as to provide US personnel with explicit guidelines for their conduct.[1014]

On January 18, 2007, the Department of Defense submitted a report to Congress that contained the military commission procedures.[1015] In a press briefing, two DoD officials provided information on the proposed procedures. Principal Deputy General Counsel Dan Dell'Orto stated, some of the key provisions in the manual consist of:

> "Discretion by and deference to independent military judges, who will serve as presiding officials and who will ensure fairness; an independent defense function to represent defendants zealously and protect against even the appearance of unlawful influence or conflict of interest; the presumption of an accused innocence, and the requirement that the prosecution provide its case beyond a reasonable doubt; a jury system comparable to that used in general courts-martial; a requirement that the accused be provided, in advance, evidence to be introduced against him or her at trial; prohibition against admitting classified evidence and witnesses; a reasonable opportunity for the accused to obtain

[1012] *Id.*
[1013] *Id.*
[1014] *Id.* at 4.
[1015] US Department of Defense, News Transcript, DoD Press Briefing on New Military Commissions Rule, Presenter: Principal Deputy General Counsel Dan Dell'Orto and Legal Adviser Brigadier General Thomas Hemingway, Office of Military Commissions, Jan. 18, 2007.

evidence and witnesses; formal rules of evidence, consistent with federal and courts-martial practice, with those exceptions required to be consistent with the Military Commissions Act of 2006; safeguards to protect the rights of confrontation, protection from self-incrimination, and to protect most common law evidentiary privileges; suppression of statements obtained by torture or in violation of the Detainee Treatment Act of 2005; a requirement that the prosecution provide exculpatory evidence to an accused consistent with the federal and courts-martial practice; and a thorough, comprehensive and independent appellate system."[1016]

The accused will also have access to the Court of Military Commission Review, the Circuit Court for the District of Columbia, and the Supreme Court of the United States.[1017] Legal Advisor Brigadier General Thomas Hemingway, from the Office of Military Commissions reiterated that there is a clear prohibition against evidence that was obtained by torture.[1018] He stated there are three possibilities: if it the evidence was obtained by torture, it stays out. If the evidence is in violation of the Detainee Treatment Act of 2005, it stays out. However, if the evidence was obtained prior to the DTA, "the judge has to make an independent determination as to the reliability of the evidence."[1019] Finally, he stated anything that is admitted to the court, must be shown to the defense team. [1020]

The procedures also clarify how to handle classified information. Deputy Dell'Orto stated the presiding judge will be able to use redacted or summarized versions of the evidence or use substitute material if he deems it necessary.[1021] The Department of Justice, military judge advocates general and representatives from the executive branch agencies all provided input to the manual.[1022] General Hemingway has

---

[1016] *Id.* at 2.
[1017] *Id.*
[1018] *Id.*. at 3.
[1019] *Id.*
[1020] *Id.*
[1021] US Department of Defense, Sgt. Sara Wood, USA, *DoD Releases Military Commissions Manual*, American Forces Information Service, Jan. 18, 2007.
[1022] *Id.* at 2.

stated he expects the military commissions to resume this year at Guantanamo Bay and detainees who were previously charged under military commissions will have to be re-charged under the MCA.[1023]

On January 29, 2007, chief prosecutor USAF Col. Moe Davis stated fewer Guantanamo Bay detainees will be charged with war crimes this week than originally expected.[1024] He stated revised charges were expected to be filed against up to 20 detainees by February, however the "new procedural rules implemented earlier this month will delay the trials for at least have of those detainees."[1025] The new rules mandate that a hearing before a tribunal judge occur within 30 days and the start of trial within 120 days once the charges are filed, or the charges will automatically be dismissed.[1026] Col Davis stated there was only one courtroom at Guantanamo and it is currently undergoing renovations and thus charging more than a few detainees would be "kind of like trying to fit a watermelon through a garden hose."[1027] Col. Davis concluded stating the Pentagon is preparing to request additional funds from Congress to build more courtrooms at Guantanamo but noted it is a time consuming process.[1028]

The US Court of Appeals for the District of Columbia upheld the Military Commission Act in February, 2007.[1029] The court held that alien enemy detainees at Guantanamo Bay may not challenge their detention in US federal courts.[1030] Moreover, the court held it lacked the jurisdiction to entertain whether the military is illegally holding the detainees.[1031] However, in June 2008, the Supreme Court of the United States held that section 7 of the Military Commission Act denies

---

[1023] *Id.*

[1024] Jurist Staff, *Guantanamo Military Trials Face Further Delays*, Jurist, Jan. 29, 2007.

[1025] *Id.*

[1026] Jane Sutton, *New Rules Mean More Delays for Guantanamo Trials*, Reuters, Jan. 29, 2007.

[1027] *Id.* Col Davis noted David Hicks would be among one of the first charged. Australian Prime Minister John Howard gave the United States until-mid February to formally charge Hicks (the only Australian detainee). The Prime Minister did not state what would happen if his deadline was not met.

[1028] *Id.*.at 2.

[1029] *Boumediene v. Bush*, 476 F.3d 981 (DC Cir 2007).

[1030] *Id.*

[1031] *Id.*

federal courts jurisdiction to hear habeas petitions that were pending at the time of its enactment.[1032] The Court stated that petitioners cannot be prevented from seeking habeas relief because they have been designated as enemy combatants or because they are detained at Guantanamo Bay.[1033] In addition, the Court recognized that the great writ may only be suspended when public safety requires it in times of rebellion or invasion.

The Court also stated that the petitioners are entitled to a meaningful opportunity to establish that his detention is unlawful and held that the Combatant Status Review Tribunals did not suffice as an avenue to challenge their detention.[1034] For example, the Court stated during the CSRT process, the petitioner may not have the assistance of counsel and may not be cognizant of the most critical allegations against them. Thus, the Court held there is a great amount of risk in the tribunal's determinations of the combatant's status and as such the petitioners must be entitled to petition federal courts to challenge their detention.[1035]

A chart illustrating the procedures afforded to Guantanamo Bay Detainees is below.

[1032] *Boumediene et al. v. Bush*, No. 16-1195 (U.S. June 12, 2008).
[1033] *Id.* at 22.
[1034] Id. at 63.
[1035] *Id.* at 64.

Table 4: Summary of Processes Granted to Guantanamo Detainees

Process	Definition/Purpose	Applies To	Counsel for Detainee?
Administrative Review Board	Annual review to determine whether the detainee should be released, transferred or should continue to be detained, based on threat or continued intelligence value	All Guantanamo Bay Detainees	No, Assisting Military Officer assigned to assist detainee through the process.
Combatant Status Review Tribunal	One time process to determine whether a detainee meets the criteria to be designated as an enemy combatant	All Guantanamo Bay Detainees	No, (non-attorney personal representative assigned to detainee).
Military Commission	Prosecute enemy combatants who violate the laws of war.	Non-US citizens based upon the individual's participation in al Qaeda and acts of international terrorism.	Yes, military counsel assigned and detainee may hire civilian counsel (subject to certain conditions).

Adapted by: DoD's Guantanamo Processes Chart available at: http://www.defenselink.mil/news/Sep2005/d20050908process.pdf

SECTION FOUR: Public Response

Several legal scholars and academics responded to the proposed Military Commission Act of 2006 and the US policy to detain suspected terrorists at Guantanamo Bay. The American Bar Association stated it will continue to challenge key provisions of the MCA.[1036] Neal Sonnett, who chairs the ABA's Task Force on Treatment of Enemy Combatants, stated "It's a sweeping denial of habeas, so that any alien who is detained by the US can be detained forever without any hope of ever getting to a court. That's just wrong."[1037] He also stated the MCA is "one of the worst pieces of legislation in decades. It sets back the rule of law substantially, especially the court-stripping provisions which the ABA will continue to fight."[1038]

Nancy Pelosi (D-CA), House Minority Leader, stated "Legal challenges to the bill may result in convictions being overturned, punishments being set aside, and justice being further delayed."[1039] She elaborated that "...because the bill allows the president to interpret the Geneva Conventions through executive order, it invites other countries to do the same, thereby weakening the international legal standards that have protected our troops for decades."[1040] Other organizations also criticized the MCA, including the American Civil Liberties Union, which labeled the law as "one of the worst civil liberties measures ever enacted in American history." Senator Chris Dodd (D-CT) introduced legislation which would restore habeas corpus rights to detainees.[1041] Senator Dodd's bill would also prohibit information that was obtained through coercion from being used in trials and mandate military judges to exclude hearsay evidence they deem to be unreliable.[1042]

[1036] Carl Jones, ABA to Continue Fight Over Detainee Rights, Law.Com, Oct. 13, 2006.

[1037] *Id.*

[1038] Molly McDonough, *Battle Over Terror Law Begins*, ABA News, Oct. 23, 2006.

[1039] Tim Starks, *Bush Signs Military Commissions Bill Into Law*, Congressional Quarterly Today, Oct. 17, 2006.

[1040] *Id.* at 2.

[1041] James M. Yoch, Jr. *US Senator Proposes Amendments to Military Commission Act Restoring Habeas*, Jurist, Nov. 17, 2006.

[1042] Roxana Tiron, *Senate Dems Plan Overhaul of Military Tribunals Bills*, The Hill News, Nov. 16, 2006.

Several retired federal judges wrote a letter to Congress explaining their concerns about the lawfulness of the MCA, more specifically Section Six, which they deemed stripped the federal courts of jurisdiction to test the lawfulness those detained at Guantanamo and elsewhere outside the United States.[1043] The judges applauded Congress for creating procedures to try individuals for war crimes and for ensuring that those procedures prevent secret evidence and evidence obtained through coercion from being used.[1044] The letter stated "Revoking habeas corpus, however, creates the perverse incentive of allowing individuals to be detained indefinitely on that very basis by stripping the federal courts of their historic inquiry into the lawfulness of a prisoner's confinement."[1045] Therefore, they urged Congress to remove Section Six before they approved the Act.

Some law professors also disagreed with the MCA and argued "What the Congress did and what the president signed today essentially revokes over 200 years of American principles and values."[1046] Another professor argued "This act gives the president unlimited power. It's designed so that a non-American designated by the president as an unlawful enemy combatant has no remedy; he's closed our of the courts."[1047] "Remedies are at the heart of the respect for law" the professor explained "If you don't have a remedy, you are without human rights."[1048] Finally, others criticized the MCA provision which allows statements obtained by coercion if they were

---

1043 James M. Yoch, Retired Judges Urge Congress to Retain Habeas Jurisdiction for Guantanamo Detainees, Jurist, PaperChase Newsburst, Sept. 15, 2006, available at: http://jurist.law.pitt.edu/paperchase/2006/09/retired-judges-urge-congress-to-retain.php.

1044 Letter to Members of Congress, Sept. 15, 2006, Former Federal judges, available at: http://jurist.law.pitt.edu/pdf/retiredjudgesletter.pdf.

1045 *Id.*

1046 Robert Longley, Bush and Lincoln both Suspended Habeas Corpus, About News, Oct. 17, 2006, *available at*: http://usgovinfo.about.com/od/rightsandfreedoms/a/habeuscorpus.htm?terms=Bush+and%20Lincoln. Quoting Jonathon Turley, professor of constitutional law at George Washington University.

1047 Bob Yates, *From Hamdan to "Unlawful Enemy Combatant:" The Military Commissions Act*, Chicago Lawyer, November 2006. Citing Mary Ellen O'Connell, a professor of international law at Notre Dame Law School.

1048 *Id.* at 3.

obtained before the DTA. The critics noted that all of the prisoners at Guantanamo were captured and presumably interrogated before the DTA was signed (Dec. 2005) and thus coerced statements will be admissible.[1049] The International Committee of the Red Cross expressed concern over the broad definition of "unlawful enemy combatant" and the fact that there is not an absolute ban on the admission of evidence obtained through coercion.[1050] They also were apprehensive that the MCA omitted certain violations from the list of acts that are war crimes under US domestic law.[1051] However, the ICRC supported the MCA provision which broadened the text of Common Article 3 violations, for example "grave breaches" now includes rape, sexual assault, biological experiments and intentionally causing serious bodily injury.[1052]

Others have supported the MCA and criticized the Supreme Court's decision in *Hamdan v. Rumsfeld.* For example, John Yoo stated the Court's decision was an "unprecedented expansion into what had always been considered the ultimate preserve of the political branches" and called for the president and Congress to restore the supremacy of "battlefield decisions."[1053] Moreover, one author noted the Court's decision "ignores the reality of what terrorists are and what they are not based on a series of legal technicalities."[1054] The author also noted the decision replaced military experts' decisions in the field and replaced it with a panel of judges "with little to no experience in the area."[1055] The author concluded that the MCA is thus an essential

---

[1049] *Id.* at 4.

[1050] International Committee of the Red Cross, Interview, Developments in US Policy and Legislation Towards Detainees: the ICRC Position, Interview with Organization President Jakob Kellenberger, Oct. 10, 2006.

[1051] *Id.* Kellenberger explained the MCA omitted the "prohibition of outrages upon personal dignity, in particular humiliating and degrading treatment, and the prohibition of the denial of the right to a fair trial, which is a basic protection provided for in international law."

[1052] *Id.*

[1053] Allan Cruickshanks, *Combating Enemy Combatants*, The Cavalier Daily, Nov. 28, 2006.

[1054] *Id.*

[1055] *Id.*

tool to the long-term security of the United States and restoring the balance of power within the federal system.[1056]

Another supporter of the MCA asserted the Act provides enemy combatants more access to federal courts than they have ever received.[1057] He found it remarkable that "suspected foreign terrorists captured on the global battlefield being" should have access to federal courts at all.[1058] In testimony supporting the Act before the Senate Judiciary Committee, he stated "[N]othing in the Constitution itself, including the Suspension Clause confers rights of access to our courts for alien enemy combatants being held in the ordinary course of an armed conflict."[1059] In an interview with the Chicago Lawyer, he reiterated that there cannot be an issue of suspension of the writ of habeas corpus if the constitutional habeas right does not exist in the first place.[1060] "The failure of the U.S. Constitution in the general suspension clause to cover enemy combatants held abroad in time of war means that alien enemy combatants do not have a constitutional right to habeas corpus remedy."[1061]

James Carafano, a senior fellow at the Heritage Foundation, supported the MCA and asserted "The notion that these military commissions will be used inside the United States is highly unlikely."[1062] He also argued the nature of the conflict against terrorism warrants new kinds of legal measures and the MCA provides enough protections for suspected terrorists to make it a fair piece of

---

[1056] *Id.*

[1057] Yates, *supra* note 1047, at 6. Bradford Berenson is a partner with Sidley Austin in Washington, D.C.

[1058] *Id.*

[1059] *Id.*

[1060] *Id.*

[1061] *Id.* Brenson also noted detainees will use habeas and litigation in general as a weapon. "I think that a lot of the litigation has proven to be an enormous burden and distraction on the U.S. government, and interfered with operations at Guantanamo." Moreover, the Supreme Court decisions in Hamdan and Rasul "dramatically changed existed law and provided enormous propaganda and public relations benefit to our adversaries." *Id.* at 7.

[1062] Samantha Kenry, *Friend or Foe*? Herald News, Nov. 5, 2006, *available at*: http://www.northjersey.com/page.php?qstr=eXJpcnk3ZjcxN2Y3dnFlZUVFeXkyJmZnYmVsN2Y3dnFlZUVFeXk3MDE1NTM3.

legislation.[1063] He stated "We have concerns about leaking classified materials, concerns that the ways you obtain information on the battlefield is different. We wanted a system that put national security first, and then added in the minimum requirements to make sure there was sufficient judicial process and give people their basic humanitarian rights."[1064]

The United States' treatment of enemy combatants at Guantanamo Bay has also drawn criticism and support from legal scholars, academics and the general public. For example, one scholar visited Guantanamo Bay several times and commented that the detainees were treated well.[1065] The scholar noted that the military flew in special fruits from the Mideast "so the detainees could celebrate Muslim feast days like Ramadan and Eid al Fitr in style."[1066] The scholar acknowledged that while there had been unfortunate instances where soldiers acted improperly, the military immediately responded by punishing those soldiers.[1067] Addressing situations where the government released individuals wrongly held, the scholar noted "Given the fact that the terrorists masquerade as civilians, these mistakes are both very unfortunate and unavoidable."[1068]

The scholar also discussed the United States' efforts to respect the detainee's religion and explained one instance where the military provided the detainees with a tent, to be used as a mosque and told the soldiers were no permitted to enter out of respect for the detainees.[1069]

1063 *Id.*

1064 *Id.*

1065 Ronald Rotunda, *Guantanamo, Another Story*, Republican National Lawyers Association, Newsletter, 2006 (Originally published in German: Rotunda, Frische Datteln fur die Haftlinge, Sueddeutsche Zeitung (Germany), January 2, 2006, at p.2).

1066 *Id.*

1067 *Id.*

1068 *Id.* Rotunda noted an example of the government releasing an individual wrongly held. The military stopped a truck in Afghanistan. Several people inside the truck were dressed like local farmers, however there were also many weapons inside the truck. One individual stated he was not connected with the group and was just a farmer getting a ride. All other individuals in the truck refused to speak to US armed forces and all were taken to Guantanamo. Several months later, "some of the people, impressed by their treatment, started talking and confirmed the first person's story." That person was subsequently released.

1069 *Id.*

However, the detainees abused such privilege and built a massive underground escape tunnel.[1070] A detainee reported the expected prison break to the guards and the guards responded. However, the detainees fought back with make-shift weapons they hid in the tunnel.[1071] After several days of the detainee's rioting, the guards called in for additional support and the detainees surrendered.[1072] The scholar concluded that the government will make mistakes "because all human institutions are fallible" but it is important to know both sides of the story.[1073]

Other countries have criticized the United State's decision to detain suspected terrorists at Guantanamo Bay. In January, 2007 Amnesty International organized a five year anniversary protest of Guantanamo detaining suspected terrorists.[1074] About 100 demonstrators wore Guantanamo-style orange inmate uniforms and surgical masks and formed eight long rows outside the US Embassy in London.[1075] They clapped and chanted "Close Guantanamo Bay!"[1076] According to reports, Prime Minister Tony Blair has also called for the closure of Guantanamo Bay.[1077] Additionally, a BBC World Service Poll of 26,000 people in 25 countries revealed that 67 percent disapprove of the way the United States has treated terror suspects detained at Guantanamo Bay.[1078] James J. Carafano testified before the Senate Armed Services Committee and remarked on the international community's response to Guantanamo Bay.[1079] He stated the United States has recently come under fire from European Union (EU) officials and legislators, urging the United States to close

---

[1070] *Id.*
[1071] *Id.*
[1072] *Id.*
[1073] *Id.*
[1074] Thomas Wagner, *Protestors Urge Blair to Free Detainees at Guantanamo*, Findlaw News, Jan. 11, 2007.
[1075] *Id.*
[1076] *Id.*
[1077] *Id.*
[1078] Associated Press, Poll: *Foreign View of US Deteriorated*, FOXNEWS, Jan. 23, 2007.
[1079] Testimony of James J. Carafano, Ph.D., The Detention and Trial of Unlawful Combatants, before Senate Armed Services Committee, July 19, 2006, available at: http://www.heritage.org/Research/HomelandDefense/tst071906a.cfm.

Guantanamo.[1080] "The EU's condemnation of the Guantanamo facility has echoed those of the United Nations Committee Against Torture and the U.N.'s hugely discredited Commission on Human Rights, which condemned the detention facility without even inspecting it."[1081]

SECTION FIVE: Conclusions and Current Status of Guantanamo Bay Detainees

The Department of Defense has repeatedly defended their policy to detain enemy combatants at the naval base. The DoD asserted the law of armed conflict governs the war between the United States and al Qaeda and also establishes the rules for detention of enemy combatants.[1082] Moreover, the laws of armed conflict permit the United States to detain enemy combatants without charge or trial for the duration of hostilities and detaining such combatants prevents them from assisting the enemy.[1083] DoD reported that the detainees at Guantanamo Bay consist of "rank-and-file jihadists who took up arms against the U.S., as well as senior al Qaida operatives and leaders, and Taliban leaders."[1084] The DoD stated the questioning of Guantanamo detainees has improved the security of the United States and coalition partners by increasing our understanding of al Qaida and other similar groups.[1085] The US Government has used this information to plan and execute counter-terrorism missions.[1086]

[1080] *Id.* at 4.
[1081] *Id.*
[1082] US Department of Defense, Special Report, Guantanamo Detainees, April 2004, available at:
http://www.defenselink.mil/news/Apr2004/d20040406gua.pdf.
[1083] *Id.*
[1084] *Id.* The report lists specific detainees and information they have provided. For example, an "al Qaida member who served as an explosives trainer for al Qaida and designed a prototype shoe bomb for destroying airplanes and a magnetic mine for attacking ships." *Id* at 2.
[1085] *Id.* at 3. The report stated detainees have explained al Qaida leadership structures and funding mechanisms. Additionally, Guantanamo detainees have provided the United States with "significant 'actionable' information on al Qaida explosives training, assembly, and distribution throughout Afghanistan" and "detailed information on travel routes potentially used by terrorists to reach the US v. Latin America."
[1086] *Id.* at 4.

The detainees, and their entitlement of rights, have created much discourse since the attacks of September 11, 2001. For example, there have been several reports and articles about government misconduct, allegations of detainees being abused and tortured, and critics urging the government to close the naval base. Due to the extensive volume of reports and news articles, the author chose to address a few of the major recent headlines Guantanamo Bay and the detainees held there have made.

In September, 2006, 14 high value detainees were sent to Guantanamo Bay.[1087] The Department of Defense announced the individuals will be treated appropriately and in accordance with policy and procedures for other detainees at the naval base.[1088] According to news reports, Khalid Sheikh Mohammed was one of the high value detainees sent to Guantanamo.[1089] He is accused of masterminding the September 11 terrorist attacks.[1090] Additionally, in September, the Department of Defense released a new policy directive and field manual which articulated clear guidelines on US military detention and interrogation policies.[1091]

For the first time in the department's history, the directorate provides a minimum standard for how all detainees in DoD custody must be treated.[1092] Deputy assistant secretary of defense for detainee affairs, Cully Stimson stated "It sets our policy guidance for all DoD detention operations that is necessary and appropriate to ensure the safe, secure and humane detention of any combatants, both lawful and

---

[1087] US Department of Defense, News Release, *Defense Department Ordered to Take Custody of High-Value Detainees*, Sept. 6, 2006.

[1088] *Id.*

[1089] Associated Press, *Alleged Mastermind of Sept. 11 Attacks to Face Guantanamo Hearing Within 3 Months*, FOXNEWS, Sept. 20, 2006.

[1090] *Id.* He was arrested three years ago in Pakistan and has been in CIA custody until he was released to DoD custody on Sept. 6, 2006.

[1091] Donna Miles, N*ew Documents Outline Detention, Interrogation Policies*, American Forces Information Service, Sept. 6, 2006. The two documents are: DoD Directive 2310.01E, "which provides overreaching guidance on DoD's detainee operations worldwide, and Army Field Manual 2-22.3, which lays out specific guidelines for those directly involved in detention and interrogation efforts." *Id.*

[1092] *Id.*

unlawful, regardless of the nature of the conflict."[1093] The directive also expressly prohibits activities which are deemed to be cruel, inhumane or degrading.

In December 2006, a 28 year old block guard at Guantanamo Bay stated he wished the world had an accurate picture of the place where he serves.[1094] The guard stated he was frustrated that the world does not have an accurate understanding of his mission and how much attention is provided to the detainees.[1095] "I don't think people realize how hard we try to keep the detainees safe and as well cared for as we do, because 'fair, firm and impartial' is exactly what we do here."[1096]

Navy Rear Admiral Harry Harris Jr., the commander of Joint Task Force Guantanamo (JTF-GTMO), stated "There's always the misconception that we're somehow beating these detainees and doing heinous things to them, and that is simply not the case. We've had many outside, independent investigations (into allegations) of detainee abuse and misconduct, and there has not been a single instance—not one—of torture or inhumane treatment that has ever been substantiated."[1097] Admiral Harris also noted the Manchester Document, which British authorities seized in 2000, is a terrorist training manual.[1098] The Manchester Document provides "guidance for captured terrorists on how to provide misinformation to the public, such as suggesting that they have been tortured."[1099] It appears that some detainees have followed that guidance after being released and Admiral Harris hoped that people would be skeptical when former detainees make such allegations.[1100]

[1093] *Id.*

[1094] Sgt. Jim Greenhill, USA, *Outdated Images of Detention Center, Mission Frustrate Guantanamo Troopers*, American Forces Information Service, Dec. 1, 2006.

[1095] *Id.*

[1096] *Id.*

[1097] *Id.* at 1-2.

[1098] *Id.* at 4. *See also*, Donna Miles, *Al Qaeda Manual Drives Detainee Behavior at Guantanamo Bay*, American Forces Information Service, June 29, 2005. The final chapter "teaches al Qaeda operatives how to operate in prison or detention center. It directs detainees to 'insist on proving that torture was inflicted' and to 'complain of mistreatment while in prison.'"

[1099] *Id.*

[1100] *Id.*

Many individuals serving at the Naval Base share the same frustrations as the 28 year old guard. Most stated they are especially frustrated by "repeatedly seeing television, movie and print images of detainees being held at Camp X-Ray, a considerably more austere temporary facility that was operated for only four months and has been closed for four years."[1101] More than 1,000 members of the media have toured the naval base.[1102] The naval base commander, Navy Captain Mark Leary, explained to the visiting reporters that it was important for them to visit the operation. He also stated "We may not bring you around to believe as we do, but I think it's helpful that you see for yourself and make your own decision on what you see. We're doing an important mission down here. It's important for the United States. It's important for the world. You may disagree, but you'll make an informed decision after coming and actually seeing for yourself. That's the best we can hope for."[1103]

To counter negative images projected about Guantanamo Bay, the government asserts that the detainees receive prayer beads, caps, rugs, backgammon and chess sets, and even soccer balls and basketballs.[1104]

[1101] *Id.* at 2. Sgt Greenhill noted that many international new stories still use old pictures of Camp X-Ray.

[1102] *Id.* at 2.

[1103] *Id.*

[1104] Sgt. Jim Greenhill, USA, *Outdated Images of Detention Center, Mission Frustrate Guantanamo Troopers*, American Forces Information Service, Dec. 1, 2006 at 3. See also, Associated Press, In Guantanamo, *Teens Await their Fate*, New York Times, Nov. 29, 2003, available at: http://www.pegc.us/archive/Press/NY_Times/nyt_digest_2003.txt. (Stating human rights advocates urged the United States military to release the boys ages 13-15. Major General Geoffrey Mill stated their "freedom is being held up at a higher levels." Maj. Gen. Miller stated that the boys always had guards with them, undergo more than an hour of group therapy two times a week and also meet with psychiatrists. The boys study their native language, social studies and geography and they are allowed time for board games and movies. Additionally, the boys exchange mail with their family through the ICRC. One teenager was charged with a military commission and his commission began in the spring of 2006, but was halted after the Supreme Court's decision in *Hamdan v. Rumsfeld.* Omar Ahmed Khadr was taken to Guantanamo when he was 15 and later charged with throwing a grenade that killed a US solider and injured another soldier (who lost one eye). Kathleen T. Rhem, *Canadian Teen*

They stated that the United States taxpayers have spent over $100 million on improvements at the naval base and detainees may order books from a 5,000-volume library which is increasing at a rapid rate.[1105] Additionally, the government states that every day, on average, five attorneys visit with detainees and detainees are provided with recreation time and have access to exercise equipment and sports.[1106] News from numerous other countries is posted in the camps. Admiral Harris concluded that while it is difficult to communicate the reality of life at Guantanamo Bay, it is improving.[1107] "Americans are coming to realize that the troopers here are doing a great job, and it is a hard job."[1108]

A report released by the Department of Defense in July, 2006 stated they have gathered a plethora of intelligence from the detainees at Guantanamo Bay and the information has prevented terrorist attacks and saved lives.[1109] For example, detainees have provided intelligence concerning the organization structure of al Qaeda (and other terrorist groups), al Qaeda's pursuit of weapons of mass destruction and terrorist skill sets, including general and specialized operative training.[1110] The report stated the information provided by the detainees continues to be an essential tool to defeat violate extremist groups like al Qaeda and its supporters.[1111] The report also listed future steps the DoD is planning on taking to make the living environment more suitable for long-term detention. For example, the DoD will expand communal living environments, increase the opportunity for exercise and group activities, enhance the medical facilities, and finally, increase mail privileges and access to foreign language materials.[1112]

In December, 2006, Director of the Joint Intelligence Group at Guantanamo Bay, Paul Rester, stated about one-third of the detainees

---

Accused of Murdering US Solider Appears in Court, American Forces Information Service, Jan. 12, 2006.

[1105] *Id.*

[1106] *Id.*

[1107] *Id.* at 4.

[1108] *Id.*. at 4.

[1109] US Department of Defense, Guantanamo Today, July 2006.

[1110] *Id.*

[1111] *Id.*

[1112] *Id.* at 3.

are still being interrogated.[1113] However, he noted the military allows the detainees to skip scheduled interrogation sessions.[1114] Some detainees participate in the sessions to leave their cells and those who cooperate have been granted special privileges. For example, some have been allowed to eat sandwiches from Subway restaurant on the base and watch movies or sporting events.[1115]

January, 2007 marked the five year anniversary of the first arrival of detainees at Guantanamo Bay. As of May, 2008 there are currently 270 of detainees being held at Guantanamo Bay and more than 520 detainees have been either released or transferred.[1116] The United States' decision to detain enemy combatants at Guantanamo Bay has raised several issues about alien enemy combatant's rights during an armed conflict. New policies and procedures have been implemented to deal with a new type of threat and a new enemy. These policies have been established to ensure that the United States' detention of alien enemy combatants complies with the laws of war and US policy. The executive, legislative and judicial branch have all contributed to the new processes. While some of the new processes have been implemented, such as the Combatant Status Review Tribunal and the Administrative Review Boards, the Military Commission Act of 2006 is still at a preliminary stage and have begun the first trials on prosecuting unlawful combatants who violated the laws of war. As the new commissions begin, new questions of interpretation and implementation are sure to arise and will be debated by all branches of government.

[1113] Michael Melia, *Gitmo Interrogators Seeking Rapport*, FOXNEWS, Dec. 6, 2006.

[1114] *Id.*

[1115] *Id.*

[1116] Navy Lt. Jennifer Cragg, Guantanamo Differs From Pop Culture Perception, Admiral Says, American Forces Press Service News Article, May 21, 2008.

CHAPTER FIVE

Conclusion

> The United States is a nation that has terrorism as part of its past, present and future.
>
> Joseph McCann[1117]

Although terrorism on American soil is not unprecedented,[1118] the horrific attacks on September 11, 2001 unsettled the United States and its citizens in several ways. Many American citizens and people from around the world watched in horror and shock at the collapse of the World Trade Center buildings, the envelopment of the Pentagon, the very symbol of United States defense, in flames, and the charring remains of a plane that crashed in a field Pennsylvania. More importantly, these individuals witnessed an act of war against the United States and the emergence of a battle with Islamic extremists. The President, with the explicit authorization of Congress, launched attacks against the Taliban in Afghanistan, who were harboring al Qaeda members; whose organization claimed responsibility for the attacks. The armed forces subsequently captured and detained thousands of enemy fighters.

The terrorist attacks and the actions initiated by the government to protect future attacks has precipitated multiple discussions concerning the appropriateness of the application of the rules of war on the armed conflict and on captured al Qaeda and Taliban combatants. Particularly contentious have been the debates on unlawful combatants and the role of international law in relation to the war on terror.

The purpose of this book was to examine the issue of the application of customary laws and treaties to the conflict initiated by the attacks on September 11, 2001. Accordingly, central to this matter is the continued detention of al Qaeda and Taliban members, classified as unlawful combatants, and rights and processes accorded to enemy combatants detained at the naval base in Guantanamo Bay.

[1117] Joseph McCann, *Terrorism on American Soil: A Concise History of Plots and Perpetrators from the Famous to the Forgotten* at 290 (2006).

[1118] *Id.*

Additionally, this book studied the Congressional Resolution, Authorization to Use Military Force, and any limits imposed by this doctrine on the President's authority to detain United States citizens, designated as enemy combatants, in the United States without charge. Finally, this book examined how enemy combatants can be prosecuted without jeopardizing the United States' national security. This is a critical question because as stated by one scholar, "Continuing to detain persons who are no longer threats to the United States is undesirable...On the other hand, releasing persons who in fact intend to commit mass violence against the United States or to rejoin the ranks of those fighting our military is also undesirable."[1119]

The issues this book sought to examine are immersed in extensive and detailed judicial decisions, law review articles, and other scholarly literature. Many questions evolving from events beginning with the terrorist attacks on September 11 continue to be hotly debated and contested. United States citizens are active participants in the ongoing debates, voicing their support for US decisions or asserting their discord with these decisions. The active debates and discussions demonstrate the amount of attention these issues have received from the American public and are continuing to receive with discussions and platforms of the current candidates for President. Additionally, the international community has been very vocal declaring either their support or opposition to US decisions concerning military and the legality of decisions concerning the War on Terror. The monumental amount of attention these issues have received clearly demonstrates the importance and caliber of the issues and their resolution.

Understanding the appropriateness of the designation of individuals as unlawful combatants, resides within the broader question of defining the nature of the armed conflicts. Legal doctrines of applying conditions to jus in bello ("law in war" or rules about methods of war and protection of those not engaged in conflict) contrasted with *jus ad bellum* ("law to war" or rules about recourse to war or when it is

[1119] Tung Yin, *Ending the War on Terrorism One Terrorist at a Time: A Noncriminal Detention Model for Holding and Releasing Guantanamo Bay Detainees,* 29 Harv. J. L. & Pub. Pol'y 149, 151.

proper to resort to armed conflict)[1120] were discussed throughout Chapter Two. Traditionally, non-state actors have not been viewed as an international threats or a threat capable of initiating an international armed conflict. Non-state actors, as a significant resistance to occupying powers, were not recognized by the drafters of international treaties as a possible issue requiring adaptations of international laws. Such notions are reflected in early adaptations in the Geneva and Hague Conventions. For example, as one scholar noted, prior to 1949, the laws of war were framed on the assumption that in order for an armed conflict to amount to a war, it must be conducted between states and such internal conflicts were only matters for domestic law enforcement.[1121] Additionally, the author noted non-state actors were rarely recognized as belligerents and therefore not accorded the privileges and rights of international law. The following table illustrates the key differences between criminal law and the law of armed conflict.

Table 5: Criminal Law vs. Laws of Armed Conflict

	Criminal Law	**Law of Armed Conflict**
Focus	Individual culpability	Group status
Purpose of Confinement	Retribution (punishment)	Prevention (incapacitation)
Length of Confinement	Set by judicial sentence	Duration of the armed conflict

Adapted from Tung Yin, *Ending the War on Terrorism One Terrorist at a Time: A Noncriminal Detention Model for Holding and Releasing Guantanamo Bay Detainees*, 29 Harv. J.L. & Pub. Pol'y 149, 162 (2005-2006)

1120 Nathaniel Berman, "*Privileging Conflict? Contemporary Conflict & the Legal Construction of War*," 43 Columbia J. of Transnational Law, 1 (2004) (rethinking the role of international law in relation to war). Emphasis added.

1121 Mark A. Drumbl, *Victimhood in Our Neighborhood: Terrorist Crime, Taliban Guilt, and the Asymmetries of the International Legal Order*, 81 N.C.L. REV. 1 at 30 (2002).

However, non-state actors began initiating violence in a manner exceedingly similar in scope to an international armed conflict, which influenced the drafters of the 1949 Geneva Convention to create Common Article 3. The language in Article 3 articulates that it is only applicable to conflicts "not of an international character."[1122] Furthermore, it elucidates that basic humanitarian standards are required to all parties involved, regardless of the level or intensity of the conflict.[1123] However, the drafter's intent to govern conflicts "not of an international character" is flawed with ambiguity. As one author commented, the language in Common Article 3 produced uncertainties in its application: the language does not specify what constitutes an "armed conflict not of international character."[1124] Due to its vagueness, Common Article 3 has been viewed by many as an unsuccessful attempt to govern conflicts with non-state actors.

Two distinct, but fervent, participants in the present conflict are the Taliban, the former governmental authority over Afghanistan, and the terrorist organization, al Qaeda. Should these individuals associated with their respective groups be considered as one entity, or can distinctions be made between the two forces? Agreement as of yet has not been fully resolved, particularly as to regards international laws.

The United States government determined that the conflict with the Taliban was governed by the Geneva Conventions because the Taliban were in de facto control of Afghanistan and Afghanistan was a signatory to the Conventions.[1125] However, President Bush avowed that Taliban members failed to satisfy the four requirements stated in Article 4 of the Third Geneva Convention and therefore would not be entitled to status as prisoners of war.[1126] Additionally, President Bush determined the conflict with al Qaeda was not governed by the Geneva Conventions due to their category as a terrorist organization, not a state,

---

[1122] Geneva Convention (I) for the Amelioration of the Condition of the Wounded and Sick in Armed Forces in the Field, August 12, 1949, 6 U.S.T. 3115, T.I.A.S. 3362, 75 U.N.T.S. art.3 (1) (hereinafter GWS).

[1123] Major Alex G. Peterson, *Order out of Chaos: Domestic Enforcement of the Law of Internal Armed Conflict*, 171 MIL. L. REV. 1 at 18 (2002).

[1124] Derek Jinks, *September 11 and the Laws of War*, 28 Yale J. Int'l L. 1 at 9 (2003).

[1125] Office of the White House Press Secretary. Fact sheet: Status of Detainees at Guantanamo (Feb. 7, 2002).

[1126] *Id.*

and as a result would also not be recognized as prisoners of war. A majority of legal scholars agree with the status of al Qaeda and that the Geneva Conventions do not apply to captured members and the conflict as a whole. In response to these mandates and edicts, captured al Qaeda and Taliban members were detained as unlawful combatants and not accorded the treatment as prisoners of war.

Included in the detention and capture of members of the Taliban and al Qaeda were United States citizens participating in hostilities against the United States. One individual was apprehended on the battlefield in Afghanistan and another US citizen was taken into custody at Chicago O'Hare airport as he stepped off a plane. Both individuals were designated by President Bush as enemy combatants and both were held within the United States at a military brig in South Carolina. The issue presented in both of their cases encompassed the scope of the AUMF's power to the President. Numerous voices, however, were raised questioning the language in the AUMF and if the intent of it should extend to US citizens.

In *Hamdi v. Rumsfeld*, the United States Supreme Court examined the question whether the AUMF authorized the President to detain a US citizen as an enemy combatant who was captured in the zone of battle. The Court held the Authorization to Use Military Force authorized the President to detain Hamdi as an enemy combatant.[1127] However, the Supreme Court also held that Hamdi had the right to an opportunity to present evidence that he was not an enemy combatant. Hamdi argued his detention was prohibited by 18 U.S.C. § 4001(a).[1128] Section 18 U.S.C. states: No citizen shall be imprisoned or otherwise detained by the United States except pursuant to an Act of Congress.[1129]

The Supreme Court held the AUMF authorized the President to use "all necessary and appropriate force" against "nations, organizations, or persons" connected with the terrorist attacks on September 11, 2001.[1130] The Court stated there can be no doubt that those who fight against the United States in Afghanistan as part of the Taliban are

---

[1127] *Hamdi v. Rumsfeld*, 542 U.S. 507, 124 S. Ct. 2633; 159 L. Ed. 2d 578 (2004).
[1128] *Id.* at 591.
[1129] 18 U.S.C. 4001(a) (2000).
[1130] *Hamdi v. Rumsfeld*, 542 U.S. 507, 592, 124 S. Ct. 2633; 159 L. Ed. 2d 578 (2004), citing 115 Stat 224.

individuals Congress intended to target in enacting the AUMF. The Court concluded "the detention of individuals falling into the limited category we are considering, for the duration of the particular conflict in which they are captured, is so fundamental and accepted an incident to war as to be an exercise of the 'necessary and appropriate' force Congress has authorized the President to use."[1131] Therefore, the Court held Hamdi's detention was not prohibited by 18 U.S.C. 4001(a) because the AUMF provided proper congressional authorization as required in the code.

The Court further discussed whether the fact that Hamdi was a United States citizen prevented the government from detaining him militarily as an enemy combatant. The Court examined their decision in *Ex parte Quirin* which stated "[c]itizens who associate themselves with the military arm of the enemy government, and with its aid, guidance and direction enter this country bent on hostile acts, are enemy belligerents within the meaning of...the law of war."[1132] Furthermore, the Court recognized that even though the US citizen in *Quirin* (Haupt) was not tried for violations of the law of war, nothing in their decision suggests that his citizenship would have prohibited his mere detention for the duration of the relevant hostilities. Finally, the Court stated that both an alien and a US citizen can be "part of or supporting forces hostile to the United States or coalition partners."[1133] Therefore, the Court held the AUMF authorized Hamdi's detention and furthermore his detention was not unlawful because he was a United States citizen.

Another important case relating to limits of the AUMF is *Padilla v. Hanft*. Jose Padilla was seized in Chicago in May, 2002 as he stopped off a plane. The government argued that Padilla trained in al Qaeda camps and intended to detonate a dirty bomb in the United States. In *Padilla v. Hanft*, the United States Court of Appeals for the Fourth Circuit held that the AUMF authorized Padilla's detention as an enemy

---

[1131] *Id.* at 592. Justice Souter, with whom Justice Ginsburg joins argued the government did not establish why the AUMF authorized Hamdi's detention and therefore § 4001(a) prohibits his detention. (at 607). Furthermore, Justice Souter asserted Congress enacted § 4001(a) to prevent repetition of the World War II internment camps and therefore clear congressional authorization is required before any citizen can be placed in a cell. (*Id.* at 608).

[1132] *Id.*. at 592 citing *Ex parte Quirin*, 317 U.S. 1, 37-38 (1942).

[1133] *Id.* at 592-93. citing Brief for Respondents 3.

combatant.[1134] The court of appeals asserted because the AUMF authorized *Hamdi's* detention, it also authorized Padilla's.[1135] Hamdi was captured in a zone of combat in Afghanistan while Padilla was captured at an airport as he stepped off a plane. Padilla argued the Supreme Court's decision in *Hamdi* was limited to the facts in *Hamdi's* case, i.e., that he was captured in the zone of combat, whereas Padilla was captured far from the zone of combat. The Court of Appeals stated both men were associated with forces hostile to the United States and took up arms against the United States. The Court of Appeals also stated "Because, like Hamdi, Padilla is an enemy combatant, and because his detention is no less necessary than was Hamdi's in order to prevent his return to the battlefield, the President is authorized by the AUMF to detain Padilla as a fundamental incident to the conduct of war."[1136] Moreover, the court stated there should not be a distinction between an enemy combatant captured abroad and detained in the United States, such as Hamdi, and an enemy combatant who escaped captured abroad but was ultimately captured and detained in the United States, such as Padilla.[1137] Therefore, the Court of Appeals for the Fourth Circuit also held that the AUMF authorized the President to detain a United States citizen captured in the United States as an enemy combatant.

President Bush also designated a resident alien, Ali-Saleh Kahlah al-Marri, as an enemy combatant in June, 2003.[1138] al-Marri was arrested under a material witness warrant in Illinois and indicted on several crimes and later designated as an enemy combatant by President Bush. The issue presented to the district court for South Carolina was whether or not the President had the authority to detain a resident alien taken into custody in the United States as an enemy combatant? The district court for South Carolina held the AUMF authorized al-Marri's detention.[1139] The Court of Appeals for the Fourth Circuit reversed the district court's holding and remanded the

[1134] *Padilla v. Hanft*, 423 F.3d 386, 389 (4th Cir. 2005).
[1135] *Id.* at 391.
[1136] *Id.* at 392.
[1137] *Id.* at 393.
[1138] *Al-Marri v. Bush*, 274 F. Supp. 2d 1003, 1004 (D.C. Ill., 2003).
[1139] *Al-Marri v. Hanft*, 378 F. Supp. 2d 673 (D.S.C. 2005).

case back to the district court.[1140] The Court of Appeals for the Fourth Circuit heard arguments in this case on October 31, 2007 and has not released their decision at this time.[1141] Al-Marri is currently still detained at the military brig in South Carolina.

The United States' Department of Defense sent hundreds of suspected enemy combatants to the naval base in Guantanamo Bay. President Bush determined captured al Qaeda and Taliban members were not entitled to prisoners of war status but should be designated as unlawful combatants. As mentioned previously, in response to the United States Supreme Court's decision in *Hamdi v. Rumsfeld*[1142] as well as the Court's decision in *Rasul v. Bush*,[1143] the Department of Defense established Combatant Status Review Tribunals.

The tribunals provide the suspected enemy combatant with an opportunity to hear the government's evidence against him and to present evidence his or her own evidence that he or she is not an enemy combatant. The suspected enemy combatant is provided with a military officer to assist him with his hearing. If the tribunal determines the individual is not an enemy combatant, he will be released. However, if the tribunal deems it necessary to detain the individual as enemy combatant, he will remain at Guantanamo Bay.

A detainee at Guantanamo Bay has only one opportunity to go before the Combatant Status Review Tribunals. However, the Administrative Review Boards are an annual review to determine if the enemy combatant still poses a threat to the United States or its allies. The detainee is provided a military officer to assist him with his review. Additionally, the detainee may introduce statements from friends and families as well as statements from the government of his home State. The review board will determine if the detainee should continue to be detained, or should be transferred to his home State, or if the detainee should be released.

Detainees at Guantanamo Bay are also subject to trial by military commission under the Military Commission Act of 2006 (MCA). As Attorney General Gonzales stated, the United States has taken a

---

[1140] Sari Horwitz, *Detainee Rights at Center of Fight*, Washington Post, Feb. 2, 2007.

[1141] *Al-Marri v. Hanft*, 487 F.3d 160 (4th Cir. 2007).

[1142] *Hamdi v. Rumsfeld*, 542 U.S. 507 (2004).

[1143] *Rasul v. Bush*, 542 U.S. 466, 124 S. Ct. 2686, 159 L. Ed. 2d 548 (2004).

virtually unprecedented step by providing alien enemy combatants a chance to challenge their detention.[1144] The MCA provides a detainee an opportunity to challenge the Combatant Status Review Tribunal's decision in federal court. A detainee charged with crimes and trial by military commission has the right to counsel and will be presumed innocent unless proven guilty beyond a reasonable doubt. Additionally, under the MCA the accused detainee may see and respond to all evidence introduced. The accused may also call witnesses on his behalf and introduce his own evidence. Finally, the accused may appeal to a military appeals court, the Court of Military Commission Review, and to the United States Court of Appeals for the District of Columbia.[1145]

Many opponents of prosecuting suspected terrorists through military commissions have criticized President Bush's November 13, 2001 Military Order[1146] because the accused may be excluded from trail if classified information is introduced. However, under the MCA, the accused detainee may see all evidence introduced for his commission. If the government seeks to introduce classified evidence that would jeopardize national security if released to accused, the presiding judge will be able to use a redacted or summarized version of the evidence or use substitute material if he deems it necessary.[1147]

Therefore, military commissions ensure classified information will not be released to the accused or the public while also providing the accused with the opportunity to view and dispute all evidence used against him. Thus, military commissions reduce the risk of classified information from being released and exposing classified sources or resources to the enemy. Protecting classified information is essential to ensuring national security and preventing future attacks and therefore I believe that military commissions are the most appropriate method to prosecute individuals suspected of terrorist activity. As one scholar

---

[1144] Whitehouse, Ask the White House, Attorney General Alberto Gonzales, Oct. 18, 2006, available at: http://www.whitehouse.gov/ask/20061018.html.

[1145] *Id.*

[1146] 10 U.S.C. § 836 (2005). See Detention, Treatment, and Trial of Certain Non-Citizens in the War Against Terrorism, 66 Fed. Reg. 57, 833 (Nov. 16, 2001).

[1147] US Department of Defense, News Transcript, DoD Press Briefing on New Military Commissions Rule, Presenter: Principal Deputy General Counsel Dan Dell'Orto and Legal Adviser Brigadier General Thomas Hemingway, Office of Military Commissions, Jan. 18, 2007.

noted "It is a delicate balance, but the President cannot defend the country if his strategy is subject to discovery requests."[1148]

Balancing the rights of individuals and the security of the United States and other sovereign states is a difficult process especially when "individuals can easily access all the tools of collaboration and superempower themselves, or their small cells, individuals do not need to control a country to threaten large numbers of other people."[1149] The Department of Defense provides detained alien enemy combatants with several processes to ensure the detainee's detention is both appropriate and necessary. The Combatant Status Review Tribunals affords the detainee an opportunity to dispute the evidence supporting his detention as an enemy combatant. It is important to note that a Justice Department official stated nothing like this has been provided for in any previous conflict. Additionally, the Administrative Review Board is an annual process to determine if the detainee still poses a threat or should be released or transferred to his home state. And finally, the detainee may be subject to trial by military commission.

All three processes provide a detainee with an ample opportunity to present evidence he was not involved in hostilities against the United States or it allies and thus should not be detained as an enemy combatant. Additionally, the detainee is provided with a military officer to assist him with the tribunals and the review board process. If the detainee is charged before a military commission, he will be appointed counsel to represent him. Therefore, all processes ensure that the United States is detaining individuals they deem as enemy combatants and pose a threat to the United States and its allies. A large number of detainees the Department of Defense released stated that the process is not biased or one sided. Attorney General Alberto Gonzales stated "This extensive array of procedures and protections are designed to ensure, and will ensure, that we do not detain or prosecute by military commission anyone other than captured terrorists and other alien enemy combatants."[1150]

[1148] Brian Haagensen II, *Federal Courts versus Military Commissions: The Comedy of No Comity*, 32 Ohio N.U.L. Rev 395, 406 (2006).

[1149] Thomas L. Friedman, *The World is Flat: A Brief History of the Twenty-First Century*, 443 (Farrar, Straus & Giroux, 2005).

[1150] Whitehouse, Ask the White House, Attorney General Alberto Gonzales, Oct. 18, 2006, available at: http://www.whitehouse.gov/ask/20061018.html.

While scholars debated whether or not the tragic events on September 11, 2001 constituted an act of war or a criminal act, the American public agreed on one thing, individuals responsible for the appalling events must be brought to justice.[1151] The question became what is the most appropriate method of prosecuting individuals involved with the attacks and associated with al Qaeda.

A variety of opinions were expressed by legal scholars relevant to the matter of prosecuting terrorists. As noted above, some scholars argued the United States should prosecute suspected terrorists in federal court because of previous successfully prosecutions. Other scholars declared those responsible for the attacks should be prosecuted in an international tribunal. Some argued regular courts-martial is the most appropriate method to prosecute responsible individuals. And finally, other scholars agreed with the Bush Administration that military commissions were the most effective means to prosecute suspected terrorists while ensuring national security concerns.

The tragic events on September 11, 2001 invalidated traditional notions that a non-state actor lacked the capability to initiate an armed conflict. In less than one hour, three planes were hijacked and used as missiles crashing into significant US buildings while a fourth hijacked plane never reached its final destination due to the heroism of the passengers onboard. That historic hour thrust the United States into an armed conflict with an extremist organization that sought to enforce their ideology through violence and terror. Three thousands individuals perished as a result of these attacks. It is imperative that the United States not only vigorously act to prevent future attacks on American soil, but the United States must also never forget the three thousand lives lost as a result of the atrocities.

As a scholar noted above "The United States is a nation that has terrorism as part of its past, present and future.[1152] Al Qaeda claimed responsibility for several attacks prior to the September 11, 2001 attacks. Moreover, al Qaeda has launched several attacks against United States armed forces overseas and has unsuccessfully attempted to carry out attacks in the United States. Thus, the author's statement is accurate as al Qaeda and Islamic extremists continue to be a significant

---

[1151] Benedetto, Richard & Patrick O'Driscoll, *Poll finds a United Nation*, USA Today, Sept. 16, 2002.

[1152] McCann, *supra* note 1117, at 290.

threat to the United States and American citizens. Furthermore, al Qaeda's relentless and vigorous hatred of the United States' freedom and values demand that the United States fervently yet effectively respond to their threats. One important aspect to the United States' response and fight with al Qaeda is to properly classify attacks as acts of war that are well organized and financed and so severe in nature that they surpass mere criminal acts.

Additionally, it is equally imperative for the United States to deny prisoner of war status to those individuals who consistently and demonstrably violate the laws of war and purposefully seek to injure and kill innocent civilians. As noted above, the foundations of the Geneva Conventions were based on the fundamental purpose to protect innocent civilians during armed conflicts. If the United States granted prisoner of war status to those who so blatantly and intentionally disregard all laws and customs of war, such action would surely place the thousands on innocent lives lost on September 11, 2001 in vain.

REFERENCES

CASES

Abu Ali vs. Ashcroft, 350 F. Supp. 2d 28, 46 (D.D.C. 2004).
Aherns v. Clark, 335 U. S. 188, 92 L. Ed. (1989), 68 S. Ct. 1443 (1948).
Al-Marri v. Hanft, 378 F. Supp. 2d 673 (D.S.C. 2005).
Al-Marri v. Rumsfeld, 543 U. S. 809, 160 L. Ed. 2d 11, 125 S. Ct. 34 (2004).
Al-Marri v. Wright, 443 F. Supp. 2d 774, 777 (D. S. C. 2006).
Al-Marri v. Wright, 487 F.3d 160 (4th Cir. 2007).
Boumediene v. Bush, 476 F.3d 981 (DC Cir 2007).
Boumediene et al. v. Bush, No. 16-1195 (U.S. June 12, 2008).
Braden v. 30th Judicial Circuit Court, 410 U. S. 484, 35 L. Ed. 2d 443, 92, S. Ct. 1123 (1973).
Campbell v. Clinton, 340 U. S. App. D. C. 149, 203 F. 3d 19, 27 (D. C. Cir. 2000).
Chicago & Southern Air Lines Inc. v. Waterman S. S. Corp., 333 U. S. 103, 111, 68 S. Ct. 431, 92 L. Ed. 568 (1948).
Colepaugh v. Looney, 235 F. 2d (10th Cir. 1956).
Dames & Moore v. Regan, 453 U. S. 654, 660-61, 69 L. Ed. 2d 918, 101 S. Ct. 2972 (1981).
Duncan v. Kahanamoku, 327 U. S. 304, 314 (1946).
Ex parte Bollman, 8 U. S. 76, 127-28 (1807).
Ex parte Kawato, 317 U. S. 69, 75, 87 L. Ed. 58, 63 S. Ct. 115 (1942).
Ex parte Milligan, 71 U. S. 2 (1866).
Ex parte Mitsuye Endo, 323 U. S. 283, 65 S. Ct. 208, 89 L. Ed. 243 (1944).
Ex parte Quirin, 317 U. S. 1 (1942).
Field v. Clark, 143 U. S. 649 (1892).
Fleming v. Page, 50 U. S. (9 How.) 603, 615, 13 L. Ed. 276 (1850).
Gillars v. United States, 182 F. 2d 962, 979 (D.C. Cir. 1950).
Haig v. Agee, 453 U.S. 280, 291 (1981).
Hamdan v. Rumsfeld, 344 F. Supp. 2d 152 (D.C. Cir. 2004).
Hamdan v. Rumsfeld, 415 F. 3d 33 (2005).
Hamdan v Rumsfeld, 548 U.S. 557, 126 S. Ct. 2749, 165 L. Ed. 2d 723 (2006).
Hamdi v. Rumsfeld, 243 F. Supp. 2d 527 (4th Cir. Va., 2002).
Hamdi v. Rumsfeld, 296 F. 3d 278 (4th Cir. 2002).
Hamdi v. Rumsfeld, 316 F. 3d 450 (4th Cir. 2003).

Hamdi v. Rumsfeld, 337 F. 3d 335 (4th Cir. 2003) vacated and remanded by 124 S. Ct. 2633 (2004).

Hamdi v. Rumsfeld, 542 U. S. 507, S. Ct. 2633; 159 L. Ed. 2d 578 (2004).

Hanft v. Padilla, 126 S, Ct, 978 (2006).

Harisiades v. Shaughnessy, 342 U.S. 580, 96 L. Ed. 586, 72 S. Ct. 512 (1952).

Harris v. Nelson, 394 U. S. 286, 291 (1969).

Hirota v. Macarthur, 338 U. S. 197, 69 S. Ct. 197, 93 L. Ed. 1902 (1948).

Home Building & Loan Assn. v. Blaisdell, 290 U.S. 398, 426, 78 L. Ed. 413, 54 S. Ct. 231 (1934).

HUD v. Rucker, 535 U. S. 125, 122 S. Ct. 1230, 1235, 152 L. Ed. 2d 258 (2002).

Huynh Thi Anh V. Levi, 586 F. 2d 625, 629 (6th Cir. 1978).

In re Territo, 156 F. 2d 142 (9th Cir. 1946).

Johnson v. Eisentrager, 339 U. S. 763, 94 L. Ed. 1255, 70 S. Ct. 936 (1950).

Jones v. United States, 529 U. S. 848, 146 L. Ed. 2d 902, 120 S. Ct. (1904).

Kawakita v. United States, 343 U. S. 717 (1952).

Kokkonen v. Guardian Life Ins. Co. of America, 511 U. S. 37, 337, 128 L. Ed. 2d 391, 114 S. Ct. (1994).

Korematswu v. United States, 323 U. S. (1944).

Landgraf v. USI Film Products, 511 U. S. 244 (1994).

Loving v. United States, 517 U.S. 748, 756-758, 760 (1996).

Maisoon Mohammad v. Harvey, 456 F. Supp. 2d 115 (D.D.C. 2006).

Marbury v. Madison, 5 U. S. (1 Cranch) 137, 2 L. Ed. 60 (1803).

Mathews v. Diaz, 42 U. S. 67 (1976).

Mathews v. Eldridge, 424 U. S. 319, 47 L. Ed. 2d 18, 96 S. Ct. 893 (1976).

Military Prosecutor v. Kassem, 41 INT'L L. R. 470 (Israel, Military Court, 1969).

Mistretta v. United States, 488 U.S. 361, 380, 102 L. Ed. 2d 714, 109 S. Ct. 647 (1989)

Mitchell v. Laird, 488 F. 2d 611 (D.C. Cir. 1973).

Mohamed Ali v. Public Prosecutor, [1969] A. C. 430, 449.

Mohammed et al., v. Harvey, 127 S. Ct. 624, 166 L. Ed. 2d 426 (2006).

Moyer v. Peabody, 212 U. S. 78 (1909).

Munaf et al., v. Harvey, No. 06-5324 (D. C. Cir. Oct. 27, 2006).

Munaf et al., v. Geren, No. 06-1666 (U.S. June 12, 2008).

Omar v. Harvey, 416 F. Supp. 2d 19 (2006).

O'Sullivan v. Boerckel, 526 U. S. 828, 844, 845 (1999).

Padilla ex rel. Newman v. Rumsfeld, 243 F. Supp. 2d 42 (S.D.N.Y. 2003)

Padilla v. Rumsfeld, 352 F. 3d 695 (2nd Cir. 2003).

Padilla v. Bush, 233 F. Supp. 2d 564 (S.D.N.Y. 2002).

Padilla v. Hanft, 423 F. 3d 386 (4th Cir. 2005).

Padilla v. Hanft, 126 S. Ct. 978, 163 L. Ed. 2d 721 (2006).

Padilla v. Hanft, 389 F. Supp. 2d 678 (D.S.C. 2005).

Padilla v. Hanft, 432 F. 3d 582, 584 (4th Cir. 2005).

The Prize Cases, 67 U. S. 635 (1862).

Public Prosecutor v. Koi, [1967] A. C. 829.

Quackenbush v. Allstate Ins. Co., 517 U. S. 706, 716 (1996).

Rasul v. Padilla, 542 U. S. 466, 124 S. Ct. 2686, 159 L. Ed. 2d 548 (2004).

Rumsfeld v. Padilla et al, 542 U. S. 426, 124 S. Ct. 2711, 159 L. Ed. 513 (2004).

Schlesinger v. Councilman, 420 U. S. 738 (1974).

Stephan v. United States, 133 F. 2d 87 (6th Cir. 1943).

Swain v. Pressley, 430 U. S. 372, 380 n. 13, 51 L. Ed. 2d 411, 97 S. Ct. 1224 (1977).

United States ex rel. Keefe v. Dulles, 94 U. S. App. D. C. 381, 222 F. 2d 390, 392 (D.C. Cir. 1954).

United States ex rel. Attorney General v. Delaware & Hudson Co., 213 U. S. 366, 53 L. Ed. 836, 29 S. Ct. 527 (1909).

United States v. Brown, 441 F. 3d 1330 (11th Cir. 2006).

United States v. Curtiss-Wright Export Corp., 299 U. S. 304 (1936).

United States v. Faris, 162 Fed. Appx. 199 (4th Cir. 2005).

United States v. Fricke, 259 F. 673 (S.D.N.Y. 1919).

United States v. Gadahn, (C.D. Cal. Oct. 2006) No. SA CR05-254(A).

United States v. Lindh, 212 F. Supp. 2d 541 (2002).

United States v. List (The Hostage Case), reported in Trials of War Criminals Before the Nuremberg Military Tribunal 1228, 1238 (1950).

United States v. Mittelsteadt, 790 F. 2d 39 (7th Cir. 1986).

United States v. Morgan, 36 U. S. 502, 74 S. Ct. 247, 98 L. Ed. 248 (1954).

United States v. Oakland Cannabis Buyers' Cooperative, 532 U. S. 483, 494, 149 L. Ed. 2d 722, 121 S. Ct. 1711 (2001).

United States v. Padilla, No. 04-60001 (S. D. Fla. 2006).

United States v. Padilla et al, 2006 U. S. Dist. LEXIS 84497 (2006).

United States v. Robel, 289 U. S. 258, 264, 19 L. Ed. 2d 508, 88 S. Ct. 419 (1967).

United States v. Salerno, 481 U. S. 739, 748, 95 L. Ed. 2d 697,107 S. Ct. 2095 (1987).

Youngstown Sheet & Tube Co. v. Sawyer, 343 U. S. 579 (1952).

CONSTITUTIONS, STATUTES, LEGISLATIVE, ADMINISTRATIVE, AND EXECUTIVE MATERIALS

18 U. S. C. § 2243 (2000).

18 U. S. C. § 3006A (2)(B) (2000).

18 U. S. C. § 4001 (a) (2000).

18 U. S. C. § 4001 (b) (2000).

Alien Enemy Act of 1798, 1 Stat. 577

Attorney General Ashcroft, Letter to the President, (2002).

Authorization for Use of Military Force, Pub. L. No. 107-40, 115 Stat. 224 (2001). http://www.access.gpo.gov/nara/publaw/107publ.html).

President Bush, "President Discusses Creation of Military Commissions to Try Suspected Terrorists." The East Room, Washington, DC. Sept. 2006, Oct. 21. http://www.whitehouse.gov/news/releases/2006/09/20060906-3-html.

Presidential Order, (June 9, 2002).

http://news.lp.findlaw.com/hdocs/padilla/padillabush60902det.pdf.

Vice President Cheney speech, U. S. Chamber of Commerce, (14 Nov. 2001).

Combatant Status review Tribunals Order of the Deputy Secretary of Defense (July 2004).

http://www.defenselink.mil/news/Jul2004/d20040707review.pdf.

DoD, Chapter 2, Law of War.

Department of Defense News Release, Transfer of Detainee Complete (Oct. 2004).

Department of Justice, Jose Padilla Charged with Conspiracy to Murder Individuals Overseas, Providing Material Support to Terrorists (Nov. 2004). http://www.usdoj.gov/opa/pr/2005/November/05_crm_624.html.

Detainee Treatment Act of 2005, Pub. L. 109-148, §§ 1001-1006, Stat. 2739 (2005). http://jurist.law.pitt.edu/gazette/2005/12/detainee-treatment-act-of-2005-white.php.

Federal Rules of Civil Procedure 12 (h)(3).

International & Operational Law Dep't, The Judge Advocate General's Schl., Operational Law Handbook http://www.jagcnet.arm.mil/JAGGCNETInternet/Homepages/AC/CLAMOPubolic.nsf0/1af4860452f962c085256a4900498561/SFILE/Master%20Document.pdf.

Joint Doctrine for Detainee Operations, Final Coordination (March 2003). http://hrw.org/campaigns/torture/jointdoctrine040705.pdf.

Lieber Code - General Order No. 100 (1863). Available at http://www.yale.edu/lawweb/avalohn/lieber.htm.

Memorandum to the Counsel to the President & The Assistant to the President for National Security Affairs, from: Colin L. Powell, Secretary of State, Subject: Draft Decision Memorandum for the President on the Applicability of the Geneva Convention to the Conflict in Afghanistan (Jan. 26, 2002).

Military Commissions Act of 2006, Pub. L. No. 109-366, Stat. 2600 (2006).

Military Order of November 13, 2001; Detention, Treatment and Trial of Certain Noncitizens in the War Against Terrorism, 66 Fed. Reg. 57, 833 (Military Order). http://www.whitehouse.gov/news/releases/2001/11/20011113-27.html.

Non-Detention Act, Public L. 92-128, 85 Stat. 347 (1971).

Office of the White House Press Secretary, Fact Sheet: Status of Detainees at Guantanamo (Feb. 7 2002). http://www.whitehouse.gov/news/releases/2002/02/20020207-13.html.

Order Establishing Combatant Status Review Tribunal, (July 7, 2004). http://www.defenselink.mil/Releases/Release.aspx?ReleasID=7530.

Secretary of Defense Donald Rumsfeld, Press Conference, (2002). http://www.defenselink.mil/Transcripts/Transcript.aspx?TranscriptID=2624.

Final Report of the National Commission on Terrorist Attacks Upon the United States, Official Government Edition, available at http://www.9-11commission.gov/report/911Report.pdf

Uniform Code of Military Justice, 10 U. S. C. § 801. http://www.au.af.mil/au/awc/awcgate/ucmj.htm.

Uniting and Strengthening America by Providing Appropriate Tools Required to Intercept and Obscure Terrorism Act of 2001, (USA PATRIOT Act), Pub. I 107-56, 115 Stat. 272.

U. S. Const. art. 1 § 8.

U. S. Const. art II, §2, cl. 1.

U. S. Const. art II, § 3

U. S. Const. amend. VI

U. S. Const. amend. IXV § 1.

US Department of Defense, DoD Announces Draft Detainee Review Policy (Mar. 3, 2004).

U. S. Dept. of the Army Field Manual 27-10. *The Law of Land Warfare.* (1956).

Paul Wolfowitz, *Prepared Statement for the House & Senate Services Committee: Building a Military for the 21st Century* (Oct. 3-4, 2001); http://www.defenselink.mil/speeches/speech.asp?SpeechID=466.

INTERNATIONAL MATERIALS

Geneva Conventions: Convention for the Amelioration of a Condition of the Wounded and Sick in Armed Forces in the Field. Geneva, (22 August 1864).

Geneva Conventions: Convention (1) for the Amelioration of a Condition of the Wounded and Sick in Armed Forces in the Field. 6 U.S.T. 3115, T.I.A.S. 3362, 75 U.N.T.S., 3362, 75 U.N.T.S., art 3 (August 12, 1949)

Geneva Conventions: Geneva Convention of 1949 for the Protection of War Victims, 6 U.S.T. 3114, 75 U.N.T.S., 3 art. 3 (Aug. 12, 1949).

Geneva Conventions: Geneva Convention Relate to the Treatment of Prisoners of War, art. 4(A) (4), 6 U.S.T. 3316, 75 U.N.T.S. 135 (GPW) (Aug. 12, 1949).

Geneva Conventions: Protocol Additional to the Geneva Convention of 12 August 1949, and Relating to the Protections of Victims of International Armed Conflict (Protocol I), U. N. Doc. A/32/144, Annex I, II (1977).

Hague Conventions: Conventions Between the United States and Other Powers Respecting the Laws and Customs of War on Land, 36 Stat. 2277 (Oct. 18, 1907).

Hague Conventions: Respecting the Laws and Customs of War on Land, with Annex of Regulations, Annex art. 1, 36 Stat. 22777, T. S. No. a539 (Jan. 26, 1910).

International Committee of the Red Cross, the Geneva Conventions: The Core of International Humanitarian Law, http://www.ircc.org/Web/Eng/siteeng0.nsf/html/genevaconventions (Dec. 29, 2006).

International Committee of the Red Cross Press Release (2001). http://www.icrc.org/web/eng/siteeng0.nsf/htmlall/57irl8?opendocument.

Lease of Lands for Coaling and Naval Stations, U. S. – Cuba, Art. III, T. S. No. 418 (Feb. 23, 1903).

North Atlantic Treaty, art. 5, 63 Stat. 241, 34 U. N. T. S. 243 (Apr. 4, 1947).

Rome Statute of the International Criminal Court, art. 25, U. N. Doc. A/CONF/.183/9 (1998). http://www.un.org/law/iccstatute/romefra.htm.

S. C. Res. 1368, U.N. SCOR, 56th Sess. 4370th mtg., U.N. Doc. S/Res4370 (2001).

Security Treaty Between Australia, New Zealand, and United States, 131, U. N. T. S. 83, 86 (Sept. 1, 1951).

United Nations Charter, art. 2, paras. 3-4.

United Nations Security Council Res. 82,83, S/1501, 1511 (June 25, 1950).

BOOKS, PERIODICAL MATERIALS, AND OTHER SECONDARY SOURCES

J. D. Aberbach & B. A. Rockman, *Conducting and Coding Elite Interviews*, PS: Political Science and Politics, 35, 673-676 (2002).

Amnesty International, United States of America –*Rubber Stamping Violations in the 'War on Terror.' Congress Fails Human Rights*(29 September 2006). http://web.mastery.org/library/Inde/ENGAMR511552006?open&of=ENG-2A.

George H. Aldrich, *The Taliban, al Qaeda and the Determination of Illegal Combatants*. (2002).

Curt Anderson, *US Prosecution of Terror Suspect Padilla No Slam Dunk So Far*, The Ledger Online (Sept. 23 2006). http://www.theledger.com/apps/pbcs.dll/article?AID=20060609230379.

Kenneth Anderson, *What to Do with bin Laden and al Qaeda?: A Qualified Defense of Military Commissions and United States Policy on Detainees at Guantanamo Bay Naval Base*, 25 Harv. J.L. & Pub. Pol'y 592, 610 (2001-2001).

Jay Baird, From *Nuremberg to My Lai*, (Lexington: DC Heath and Company, 1972).

Jay Alan Bauer, *Detainees Under Review: Striking the Right Constitutional Balance Between the Executive's War Powers and Judicial Review*, 57 Ala. L. Rev. 1081, 1084 (2006).

Nathaniel Berman, *Privileging Conflict? Contemporary Conflict & the Legal Construction of War*, 43 Columia J. Trasnational Law, I (2004).

Joseph Bialke, *al Qaeda and Taliban: Unlawful Enemy Detainees, Unlawful Belligerents, in the International Law of Armed Conflict*, 55 A.P.F.L. Rev. 1 (2004).

John M. Bickers, *Military Commissions Are Constitutionally Sound: A Response to Professors Katyal and Tribe*, 34 Tex. Tech. L. Rev. 899, 901,917 (2003).

Denise Bindschedler-Roberts, *A Reconsideration of the Law of Armed Conflict. The Law of Armed Conflicts: Report of the Conference on Contemporary Problems of the*

Law of Armed Conflict (1971).

Vanesa Blum, *Judge Orders Government to Share Medical Records of Terror Suspect Jose Padilla*, Sun-Sentinel (Sept. 15, 2006). http://www.sun-sentinel.com/news/local/southflorida/slfcpadillaa15xsep15.04.4323476.story?coll=slfa-home-headlines.

Fred Borch & Paul S. Wilson, *Article 51*, International Law Studies, Vol. 79 (2003).

Curtis Bradley & Jack L. Goldsmith, *Congressional Authorization and the War on Terrorism*, 118.7 Harv. L. Rev. 2047-2133 (2005).

Rosa E. Brooks, *War Everywhere: Rights, National Security Law, and the Law of Armed Conflict in the Age of Terror*, 153 U. Pa. L. Rev. 677, 696 (2004).

Major Thomas S. Bundt, *An Unconventional War: The Philippine Insurrection, 1899*, Military Rev. (2004).

Nathan A. Canestaro, *"Small Wars" and the Law: Options for Prosecuting the Insurgents in Iraq*, 43 Colum. J. Transnat'l L. (2004).

Lee A. Casey, David B. Rivkin, Jr., & Darren R. Bartram, *Unlawful Belligerents and its Implications Under International Law*, The Federalist Society, National Security White Papers. http://www.fed-soc.org/Publications/Terrorism/unlawful/combatants.htm.

Marc Cogen, *The Impact of International Humanitarian Law on Current Security Policy Trends*, Bruges Colloquium (Oct. 26-27, 2001).

Ellen Collier, *Instances of Use of United States Forces Abroad, 1798-1993.* Washington, DC: Congressional Research Services, (Oct. 7, 1993). http://www.history.navy.mil/wars/foabroad.htm.

Allan Cruickshanks, *Combating Enemy Combatants*, The Cavalier Daily, (Nov. 28, 2006).

Leonard Cutler, *The Rule of Law and the Law of War of a Military Commission and Enemy Combatants Post 9/11* (2002).

Albert De Zayas, *The Status of Guantanamo Bay and the Status of the Detainees*, 37 U. B. C. L. Rev. 277, 289 (2004).

Yoram Dinstein, *Unlawful Combatancy: Combatants and Civilians*, 32 Israel Y. B. H. B. (2002).

Yoram Dinstein, *The Conduct of Hostilities Under the Law of International Armed Conflict*, 82 (2004).

Yoram Dinstein, *War Aggression and Self-Defense*, (2005).

Knut Dormann, *The Legal Situation of Unlawful/Unprivileged Combatants in International Review of the Red Cross*, IRRC Vol. 85 (2003).

Mark A. Drumbl, *Victimhood in Our Neighborhood: Terrorist Crimes: Taliban Guild, and the Asymmetries of the International Legal Order*, 81 N. C. L. REV. 1 (2002).

Helen Duffy, *The War on Terror and the Frameworks of International Law*, (2005).

Lt. Col. (Ret.) US Army H. Wayne Elliot, *Terrorism and the Laws of War: September 11 and its Aftermath*, Crimes of War Project, http://www.crimesofwar.org/expert/attack-elliot.html. (2001).

Christopher M. Evans, *Terrorism on Trial: The President's Constitutional Authority to Order the Prosecution of Suspected Terrorists by Military Commission*, 51 Duke L. J. 1831, 1836 (2002).

Robinson O. Everett & Scott L. Sillman, *Forums for Punishing Offenses Against the Law of Nations*, 29 Wake Forest L. Rev. 509 (1994).

Federal Bureau of Investigation, *Terrorism 2000/2001* (Washington, DC, 2001).

Major William H. Ferrell, III, *No-Shirt, No Shoes, No Status: Uniforms, Distinction, and Special Operations in International Armed Conflict*, 178 MIL L. Rev. 94 (2003).

Joan Fitzpatrick, *Sovereignty, Terroritoriality, and the Rule of Law*, 25 Hastings Int'l & Comp. L. Rev. 303 (2002).

Thomas L. Friedman, *The World is Flat: A Brief History of the Twenty-First Century*, 443 (Farrar, Straus & Giroux, 2005).

Gallup Poll, http://brain.gallup.com/search/results.asp?SearchTypeAll=terrorist%20attacks&SearchConType=1&Place=11.

Charles Garraway, Commentary, 79 International Law Studies, 232 (2003).

Terry Gill & Elies van Sliedregt, *Guantanamo Bay: A Reflection on the Legal Status and Rights of Unlawful Enemy Combatants*, http://www.ulrechlawreview.org. Vol. I, Issue I (September 2005).

Tom Farer, *Humanitarian Law and Armed Conflicts: Toward a Definition of "International Armed Conflict,"* 71 Colum. L. Rev. 37, 43 (1971).

Joan Fitzpatrick *Sovereignty, Territoriality, and the Rule of Law*, 25 Hastings Int'l & Comp L. Rev. 303 a 312 (2002).

David Glazier, *Precedents Lost: The Neglected History of the Military Commission*, 46 Va. J. Int'l L. 5, 40 (2005).

Robert K. Goldman & Brian D. Tittemore, *Unprivileged Combatants and the Hostilities in Afghanistan: Their Status and Rights under International Humanitarian and Human Rights Law*, http://www.asil.org/taskforce/index.htm.

Barry Goldwater, *War without Declaration: A Chronological List of 199 U, S, Military Hostilities Abroad without a Declaration of War*, 1798-1972. Congressional Record, V. 119, (July 20, 1973), pp. 14174-14183.

Leslie Green, *Jus in Bello*, 79 International Law Studies, (2003).

Sgt. Jim Greenhill, *Outdated Images of Detention Center, Mission Frustrate Guantanamo Troopers*, American Forces Information Service, (Dec. 1, 2006).

Brian Haagensen II, *Federal Courts versus Military Commissions: The Comedy of No Comity*, 32 Ohio N.U.L. Rev 395, 406 (2006).

Colleen E. Hardy, *Jose Padilla*, CIP Report, Vol. 4 #8 (2006). http://cipp.gmu.edu/research/Padilla-0602Article.php.

29 Harvard Society for Law & Public Policy, Harvard Journal of Law & Public Policy (Fall, 2005).

William J. Haynes, United States Department of Defense. DoD Responds to ABA Enemy Combatant Report (Oct. 2, 2002). http://www.defenselink.mil/releases/2002/b10022002_bt497-02.html.

Michael J. Hoffman, *Rescuing the Laws of War: A Way Forward in an Era of Global Terrorism, 35 Parameters*, US Army War College Quarterly (2005).

Henry Mark Holzer, *Who's Who Among American Terrorists*, Front Page Magazine (Oct. 27, 2002).

Jamie Jansen, *DOJ Argues Federal Court Cannot Block Transfer of American to Iraqi Jurisdiction*, Jurist (Sept. 11, 2006). http://jurist.law.pitt.edu/paperchase/2006/09/doj-argues-federal-court-cannot-block.php.

Thomas Jewett, *Terrorism in Early America: The US Wages War against the Barbara States to End International Blackmail and Terrorism*, Early America Review, (2002).

Derek Jinks, *September 11 and the Laws of War*, 28 Yale J.Int'l L. 1 (2003).

Carl Jones, *ABA to Continue Fight Over Detainee Rights*, Law. Com. (Oct. 13, 2006).

Harold L. Kaplan, *Constitutional Limitations on Trials by Military Commissions*, 3 (1943).

Harold Koh, *The Spirit of the Laws*, 43 Harv. Int'l L. J. 23, 26 (2002).

Harold Koh, *Civil Liberties and National Security: A conversation with Harold Kohn, Norman Dorsen, and John Deutch*, Cambridge, MA (Feb. 4, 2002).

Harold Hongju Koh, *We Have the Right Courts for bin Laden*, N.Y. Times, Nov. 23, 2001, at A33

H. Lauterpacht, *The Problem of the Revision of the Law of War*, 29 Brit. Y. B. Int'l L. 360, 262 (1952).

Richard Leiby, *Terrorists by Another Name: The Barbary Pirates*, Washington, Post (Oct. 15, 2001).

Benjamin A. Lewis, *An Old Means to a Different End: The War on Terror, American Citizens...And the Treason Clause*, 34 Hofstra L. Rev. 1215 (2006).

Neil A. Lewis, *Try Detainees or Free Them, 3 Senators Urge*, New York Times, (Dec. 13, 2006).

Adam Liptak, *In War of Vague Borders, Detainee Longs for Court*, The New York Times (Jan. 2007).

Dahlia Lithwick, *The Pushover*, Slate (July 16, 2002). http://www.slate.com/id/2068128.

Heather Anne Maddox, *After the Dust Settles: Military Tribunal Justice for Terrorists After September 11, 2001*, 28 N. C. J. Int'l L. & Com. Reg. 421 (2002).

Gregory E. Maggs, *Terrorism and the Law*, (Thomas West, 2005).

Jarol B. Manheim, Richard C. Rich, and Laws Willnat, *Empirical Political Analysis: Research Methods in Political Science, 5th ed.* New York: Longman, (2002).

Catherine Marshall & Gretchen B. Rossman, *Designing Qualitative Research, 4th ed.* Thousand Oaks: SAGE Publications, (2006).

Jane Mayer, *Measuring Betrayal*, The New Yorker Online (March 3, 2003).

Joseph T. McCann, *Terrorism on American Soil: A Concise History of Plots and Perpetrators from the Famous to the Forgotten* (Sentinent Publications, 2006).

Molly McDonough, *Battle Over Terror Law Begins*, ABA News, (Oct. 23, 2006).

Donna Miles, *Bush Reacts to Supreme Court Ruling on Military Tribunals*, American Forces Press Service, (June 29, 2006).

Linsay Moir, *The Law of Internal Conflict*, Cambridge Studies in International and Comparative Law (2002).

Daryl A. Mundis, *The Use of Military Commissions to Prosecute Individuals Accused of Terrorist Acts*, 96 Am. J. Int'l L. 320, 322 (2002).

Sean D. Murphy, *Terrorism and the Concept of "Armed Attack" in Article 51 of the U. N. Charter*, 43 Harv. Int'l L. J. 41 (2002).

Karman Nabulsi, *Traditions of War: Occupation, Resistance, and the Law*, 41 ST 15 (1999).

Mary Ellen O'Connell, *Enhancing the Status of Non-state Actors Through a Global War on Terror*? 43 Colum. J. Transnat'l L. 435 at 437 (2003).

James Orenstein, Editorial, *Rooting out Terrorists Just Became Harder*, N.Y. Times, Dec. 6, 2001, at A29.

NBC News/WSJ, http://www.realclearpolitics.com/polls/archive/?poll_id=19.

Jordan J. Paust, *Use of Armed Forces Against Terrorism in Afghanistan, Iraq, and Beyond*, 35 Cornell Int'l L. J. 533 (2002).

Major Alex G. Peterson, *Order out of Chaos: Domestic Enforcement of the Law of Internal Armed Conflict*, 171 MIL. L. REV. 1 (2002).

Toni Pfanner, *Military Uniforms and the Law of War*, IRRC 86 (March 2003).

Jesselyn Radack, *How the Enemy Combatant Label is Being Used*, Part I, The Future of Freedom Foundation (2005). http://www.fff.org/freedom/fd0501g.asp.

Jesselyn Radack, *United States Citizens Detained as Enemy Combatants: The Right to Counsel as a Matter of Ethics*, 12 Wm. & Mary Bill Rts. J. 221 (2003).

Jeffrey N. Rapp, *Task Force for Combating Terrorism* (April 2006). http://www.washingtonpost.com/wp-srv/nation/documents/jeffreyrapp_document.pdf.

Steven R. Ratner, *Terrorism and the Laws of War: September 11 and its Aftermath*, Crimes of War Project, http://www.crimesofwar.org/expert/attack-ratner.html (Sept. 21, 2001).

Kathleen T. Rhem, *Detainees Living in Varied Conditions at Guantanamo*, American Forces Information Service (Feb. 16, 2005).

Kathleen T. Rhem, *Naval Official Reports Review of Detainee Operations*, American Forces Information Service (May 14, 2004).

David Rivkin & Lee Casey, Jr., "*The Gitmo Decision*," The Washington Times, Op-ed (July 11, 2006).

Adam Roberts, *Can we define Terrorism?* Oxford Today (2002), http://www.oxfordtodoay.ox.ac.uk/archieve/0102/14_2/04.html.

Ronald Rotunda, *Guantanamo, Another Story*, Republican National Lawyers Association Newsletter (2006).

Stephen J. Schulhofter, *Rethinking the Patriot Act: Keeping America Safe and Free* (New York: The Century Foundation Press, 2005).

Captain Christopher M. Schumann, *Bring it On: The Supreme Court Opens the Floodgates with Rasul v. Bush*, 55 A. F. L. Rev. 349 (2004).

Katherine Seelye, *A Nation Challenged: The Military Tribunals; In Letter, 300 Law Professors Oppose Tribunals Plan*, New York Times (Dec. 8, 2001).

Jed Handelsman Shugerman, *A Six-Three Rule: Reviving Consensus and Deference on the Supreme Court*, 37 Ga. L. Rev. 893 (2003).

David L. Sloss, *Availability of US Courts to Detainees at Guantanamo Bay Naval Base – Reach of Habeas Corpus – Executive Power in War on Terror*, 98 Am. J. Int'l L. 788, 790 (2004).

Steven Donald Smith, *Guantanamo Detainees Being Held Legally, Official Says*, American Services (Feb. 15, 2006).

Judge Abraham D. Sofar, *Workshop on Customary International Law and the 1977 Protocols Additional to the 1949 Geneva Conventions*, American Journal of International Law and Policy, Vol. 2 (1987).

Abraham D. Sofaer and Paul R. Williams, *Doing Justice During Wartime: Why Military Tribunals Make Sense*, Policy Review, February 2002 at 6.

Neal R. Sonnett, John S. Cooke, Eugene R. Fidell, Albert J. Krieger, Stephen A. Saltzburg & Suzanne E. Spaulding, *American Bar Association: Task Force on Treatment of Enemy Combatants* (2002). http://www.abanet.org/leadership/enemy_combatants.pdf.

Peter Spiro, *Not War, Crime*, Findlaw Commentary (Sept. 19, 2001).

Tim Starks, *Bush Signs Military Commissions Bill into Law*, Congressional Quarterly Today, (Oct. 27, 2006).

Philip J. Strollo, *League of Nations Timeline*: *The World at War*.

Araslan M. Suleman, *Recent Developments, Detainee Treatment Act of 2005*, 19 Harv. Hum Rts. J. 257, 258 (2006).

Jane Sutton, *New Rules Mean More Delays for Guantanamo Trials*, Reuters, (Jan. 29, 2007).

Phillip Thienel, *The Legal Status of Participants in Unconventional Warfare*, American University (1961).

Roxana Tiron, *Senate Dems Plan Overhaul of Military Tribunal Bills*, The Hill News, (Nov.16, 2006).

J. Torman, *Terrorism and the Regulation of Armed Conflict, International Terrorism and Political Crimes* (1973).

Stephen I. Vladeck, *A Small Problem of Precedent: 18 U.S.C. § 4001 (a) and the Dentention of US Citizen Enemy Combatants*, 112 Y. L. J. 961 (2003).

Thomas Wagner, *Protestors Urge Blair to Free Detainees at Guantanamo*, Findlaw News, (Jan. 11, 2007).

Patricia M. Wald, *The Supreme Court Goes to War, Peter Berkowitz, Terrorism, The Laws of War, and the Constitution: Debating the Enemy Combatant Cases*, at 37 (Hoover Press 2005).

Adam J. Wallach, *Afghanistan, Quirin, & Uchiyuama: Does the sauce suit the gander*? Army Lawyer (Nov. 2003).

Seth P. Waxman, *The Combatant Detention Trilogy Through the Lenses of History, Peter Berkowitz, Terrorism, The Laws of War, and the Constitution: Debating the Enemy Combatant Cases*, at 26 (Hoover Press 2005).

Ruth Wedgwood, *al Qaeda, Terrorism, and Military Commissions*, 96 Am. J. Int'l L. 328, 33 (2002).

Ruth Wedgwood, *The Laws of War: How Osama Slipped Away*, National Interest (2001).

Wikipedia, http://en.wikipedia.org/wiki/Attack_on_Pearl_Harbor.

Major J. L. Whitson, *The Laws of Land Warfare: The Privileged Guerrilla and the Deprived Soldier*, (April 6, 1984).

William Winthrop, *Military Law and Precedents*, 330 (2d ed. 1920).

Francis Wormuth & Edwin Firmage, Edwin, *To Chain the Dog of War – The War Power of Congress in History & Law*, University of Illinois Press (1989).

Bob Yates, *From Hamdan to "Unlawful Enemy Combatant:" The Military Commissions Act*, Chicago Lawyer, (Nov. 2006).

Tung Yin, *Ending the War on Terrorism One Terrorist at a Time: A Noncriminal Detention Model for Holding and Releasing Guantanamo Bay Detainees*, 29 Harv. J.L. & Pub. Pol'y 149, 162 (2005-2006)

James M. Yoch, Jr., *US Senator Proposes Amendments to Military Commission Act Restoring Habeas*, Jurist, (Nov. 17, 2006).

John Yoo, *War by Other Means* (2005).

John Yoo, *Enemy Combatants and the Problem of Judicial Competence, Peter Berkowitz, Terrorism, The Laws of War, and the Constitution: Debating the Enemy Combatant Cases*, at 69 (Hoover Press 2005).

John Yoo, Terrorism, *The Laws of War, and the Constitution: Enemy Combatants and the Problem of Judicial Competence*, Hoover Institution Press (2005).

John Yoo & James C. Ho, *The Status of Terrorists*, 44 Va. J. Int'l L. 207, 213 (2004).

Index

CPSIA information can be obtained at www.ICGtesting.com
Printed in the USA
BVOW071231041112

304221BV00002B/2/P

9 781593 323257